Translational Systems Sciences

Volume 41

In 1956, Kenneth Boulding explained the concept of General Systems Theory as a skeleton of science. He describes that it hopes to develop something like a "spectrum" of theories—a system of systems which may perform the function of a "gestalt" in theoretical construction. Such "gestalts" in special fields have been of great value in directing research towards the gaps which they reveal. There were, at that time, other important conceptual frameworks and theories, such as cybernetics. Additional theories and applications developed later, including synergetics, cognitive science, complex adaptive systems, and many others. Some focused on principles within specific domains of knowledge and others crossed areas of knowledge and practice, along the spectrum described by Boulding. Also in 1956, the Society for General Systems Research (now the International Society for the Systems Sciences) was founded. One of the concerns of the founders, even then, was the state of the human condition, and what science could do about it. The present Translational Systems Sciences book series aims at cultivating a new frontier of systems sciences for contributing to the need for practical applications that benefit people. The concept of translational research originally comes from medical science for enhancing human health and well-being. Translational medical research is often labeled as "Bench to Bedside." It places emphasis on translating the findings in basic research (at bench) more quickly and efficiently into medical practice (at bedside). At the same time, needs and demands from practice drive the development of new and innovative ideas and concepts. In this tightly coupled process it is essential to remove barriers to multi-disciplinary collaboration. The present series attempts to bridge and integrate basic research founded in systems concepts, logic, theories and models with systems practices and methodologies, into a process of systems research. Since both bench and bedside involve diverse stakeholder groups, including researchers, practitioners and users, translational systems science works to create common platforms for language to activate the "bench to bedside" cycle. In order to create a resilient and sustainable society in the twenty-first century, we unquestionably need open social innovation through which we create new social values, and realize them in society by connecting diverse ideas and developing new solutions. We assume three types of social values, namely: (1) values relevant to social infrastructure such as safety, security, and amenity; (2) values created by innovation in business, economics, and management practices; and, (3) values necessary for community sustainability brought about by conflict resolution and consensus building. The series will first approach these social values from a systems science perspective by drawing on a range of disciplines in trans-disciplinary and cross-cultural ways. They may include social systems theory, sociology, business administration, management information science, organization science, computational mathematical organization theory, economics, evolutionary economics, international political science, jurisprudence, policy science, socio-information studies, cognitive science, artificial intelligence, complex adaptive systems theory, philosophy of science, and other related disciplines. In addition, this series will promote translational systems science as a means of scientific research that facilitates the translation of findings from basic science to practical applications, and vice versa. We believe that this book series should advance a new frontier in systems sciences by presenting theoretical and conceptual frameworks, as well as theories for design and application, for twenty-first-century socioeconomic systems in a translational and trans-disciplinary context.

Susu Nousala • Gary Metcalf • David Ing
Editors

Industry 4.0 to Industry 5.0

Explorations in the Transition from a Techno-economic to a Socio-technical Future

Springer

Editors
Susu Nousala
Kaunas University of Technology (KTU)
Kaunas, Lithuania

Gary Metcalf
InterConnections, LLC, Ashland, KY, USA

David Ing
Creative Systemic Research Platform Inst
Toronto, ON, Canada

Editors-in-Chief
Kyoichi Kijima

Hiroshi Deguchi

ISSN 2197-8832 ISSN 2197-8840 (electronic)
Translational Systems Sciences
ISBN 978-981-99-9729-9 ISBN 978-981-99-9730-5 (eBook)
https://doi.org/10.1007/978-981-99-9730-5

This work was supported by Kaunas University of Technology

This Springer imprint is published by the registered company Springer Nature Singapore Pte Ltd.
The registered company address is: 152 Beach Road, #21-01/04 Gateway East, Singapore 189721, Singapore

Paper in this product is recyclable.

Foreword

As with any nonfiction work, especially in technology, three questions arise: Why this topic? Why this book? And, why this particular author or team?

Why Industry 5.0?

This in turn poses multiple questions: What is Industry 5.0? Why does this qualify as a major transition? And how will it differ from previous generations?

Industry 5.0 is a major European Union (EU) designation for both an economic transition and an effort to refocus industry, research, and the economy from an industrial paradigm that almost exclusively prioritizes shareholder value and return on investment over human-centered stakeholder value, respect for individual rights, and sustainability for the environment and ecology, society and the workforce, and for even the enterprise itself. The terminology has been adapted more widely and largely corresponds to the earlier concept of Fifth-Generation Industry, and an online search for Industry 5.0 will reveal that, partially because of that resonance, the concept is being considered seriously across the industrialized world, and interacting with environmental and social initiatives in other nations as well. While one could argue that part of the motivation for the designation is a combination of a fascination with quantization and labeling, and part a bit of present-ism that makes features of our era at least as important as any developments in the past, we argue that there are good reasons for distinguishing this transition.

The definitions of the earlier generations and the major transitions are hardly universal. There is fairly universal agreement that Industry 1.0 begins in the eighteenth century, largely in Britain, with the transition from artisan homecraft and shopcraft to factories, with mechanization, standardization of work patterns and schedules, and early commercial and industrial networks. There is also general agreement that Industry 2.0 begins with steam power, the railroad and the telegraph, and the concomitant networks for transportation and communication. From there, timelines diverge. One approach emphasizes the technological framework for transportation, communication, production, and interaction, in which Industry 3.0 arises between the late nineteenth and early twentieth century with steel and electricity, or with the automobile, oil, and mass production, and Industry 4.0 arises with the Computer Age.

Another looks at the focus of industrialization and the transmission of information, and begins Industry 3.0 only with the widespread use of the computer, around 1965, followed by Industry 4.0 around the start of current century, with the spread of e-commerce, cyberphysical systems, the Internet of Things, and cognitive computing.

Other views exist, and it should be clear that one could easily split or merge eras. For example, why not begin a new era in the middle of Industry 1.0, with the development of standardized and replaceable parts and of the tool chain—the increased manufacture of parts and tools for building the machines themselves? And from this perspective, what makes it important to say this is a transition to Industry 5.0?

In the industrial focus view, and simplifying a great deal, Industry 1.0 aims at producing materials such as textiles and industrial goods and devices such as railroad tracks and boilers, with some production of finished consumer goods; Industry 2.0 expands both industrial and consumer goods production, and later the initial industrialization of financial services, and of agriculture and food processing. Industry 3.0, with the computer, industrializes computation and the management of data, and sees increasing internationalization, and Industry 4.0, the industrialization of service and of knowledge. From a purely industrial and commercial perspective, the current era is distinguished by the "industrialization of the consumer." Throughout these eras, particularly from the middle of the twentieth century on, and especially in the computer era, academic, scientific, and even artistic creations and inventions become adapted for broader purposes, then commercialized and industrialized, and turned into profit centers, placing constraints on their benefits, often to the detriment of workers and society, and frequently with undesirable environmental effects.

Industry 5.0 then arises as a reaction to this, combined with other factors. One is the ethical and social judgment that the economic and philosophical basis of Industry 4.0—the Chicago School and extreme economic libertarianism—has overshot in prioritizing and almost exalting short- or medium-term return on investment, the role and value of senior management, and the importance of shareholder value—not only wealth but preferences and even whims.

The prioritization of shareholder interest is above and almost to the exclusion of the interests of other stakeholders, the health and prosperity of the society in which it is embedded, and the resilience and sustainability of the enterprise itself—as evidenced, for example, by the large number of hostile takeovers and destructive mergers, and the prevalence of short-sighted stock buybacks over maintenance, retooling, and standards implementation, or the health, safety, and well-being of their workers, or in fact their potential for career growth and increased value to the organization. While the overall effect of industrialization and technology has—modulo long-term environmental consequences—improved the life of the average human, allowing medical progress and longer lives and a better standard of living, some would argue that continued improvement is being endangered by economic and political factors, partly brought about by the self-centeredness justified by this prioritization.

A second is the challenges raised by technological developments, particularly artificial intelligence (AI) and business analytics, which can and do compromise privacy and autonomy, and create bias and misinformation. This also combines with ever-increasing computer, network, and algorithm sophistication, together with pervasive social media and the Internet of Things to support government and commercial tracking of individuals, and their preferences, habits, and behaviors. The magnitude and perceived severity of these growing problems is giving rise to initiatives to monitor, regulate, and guide the development of AI, seemingly announced almost weekly by governments and professional organizations across the world in the second half of 2023, although balanced by at least equally frequent announcements of AI success in solving "wicked" problems, such as protein folding, or optimizing the process or the solution of such problems.

A third is the challenges to societal institutions, the environment and ecology, and individuals by climate change, the Sixth Great Extinction, and other human-induced ongoing planetary challenges, as well as additional AI risks, from cyber-physical systems, automation, generative AI such as Chat GPT, and predictive AI applications, alone or integrated in various combinations into "smart applications."

Finally, Industry 5.0 seeks to address, at least in the economic sphere, problems of diversity, which have multiple roots in social mores and practices, in political and economic colonialization, and in situations that were problematic but now can be treated through medical or other interventions. As such, it is connected with corporate and government ESG (environmental, social, and corporate governance) and DEI (diversity, equity, and inclusion) initiatives. While this is not the first social movement protesting working conditions and the gross accumulation of wealth—one can look to the Luddites of the eighteenth century and the Progressive movement in the US in the early twentieth century—the Industry 5.0 and related initiatives arguably have a larger footprint and confront more systemic and not easily resolved problems. Further, it is perhaps the first that (at least as broadly understood) is global, intended for and potentially affecting both the fully industrialized and developing world.

Thus, although from a technical perspective Industry 5.0 might be better labeled as a sub-era of Industry 4.0, the social and economic context and the support of the EU (together with at least partial support from other governments and professional organizations across much of the planet) suggest that this should in fact be identified as a major transition.

Why This Book?

The two main arguments for this book are its interdisciplinary perspective and its long-range if tentative view.

The chapters in this book offer multiple perspectives on the potential benefits, opportunities, challenges, and risks associated with the transition to Industry 5.0. They present, both individually and as a collection, an interdisciplinary view, interweaving ethics, a historical perspective, social factors, environment and ecology, and current threats, including climate change and the impacts of AI, identifying problems and suggesting solutions or at least possible paths forward. Beyond just the (much-needed) human-centric view, there is a focus on the interaction of Industry 5.0 with the world, and possible feedforward and feedback loops. There is a recognition that, while prioritizing human rights and dignity, both the health of the underlying economy and industrial base (and of the well-meaning and well-run enterprises implementing changes), on the one hand, and the health of the planet and the environment have to be respected. Further, it is understood that these factors are interwoven, and that major changes in any one need to be preceded by consideration of the effects on the other two, and subsequent interactions.

Moreover, for all three concerns—human, economic, and environmental, the book takes a long-term view, emphasizing sustainability and resilience. In systems engineering terms, design and implementation have to be preceded by and then accompanied by ongoing requirements and risk analysis, and careful and timely assessment to identify problems and support proper evolution. There is also an acknowledgment of the need to deal with different time scales. Some problems may become critical within a few years' span; others may not get to that point for generations—but may be intractable if not addressed or anticipated immediately.

The long-term view, however, does not mean that the book aims to predict the future of the world, or of Industry 5.0, or of its major components and challenges, or that the authors and editors are foolish enough to think they can do so. Almost certainly, for example, no one can predict with any accuracy what AI will look like even by the end of next year, or what it will be doing, or what new challenges it will bring. Also, while the challenges of climate change are largely understood, predicting the rate of change or the sequence of problematic events is difficult at best. These difficulties are also evident through a gamut of stresses and relief, including political challenges to the world order, epidemics on the one hand and medical developments such as recent vaccines for malaria and cholera on the other, and totally unexpected developments such as cryptocurrency. For that reason, the remedies suggested in the book should be viewed not as long-term prescriptions, but as recommendations to be revisited and revised over time.

Rather, the book intends to present a snapshot of the issues, challenges, and possible paths forward as of late 2023, identifying the challenges and opportunities visible at this date, and steps that may work toward addressing the one and realizing the other. It would be wonderful if surprising if its projections were to prove precise and accurate, but a clear understanding of the present, and its (approximate) current position and velocity in the economic and social problem space, may be useful for those taking the next snapshot and seeking course correction.

Why This Team?

The project that resulted (if hopefully not culminated) in this book began with discussions among the Kaunas University of Technology (KTU) research team, who generously and foresightedly welcomed interaction and contributions from other parts of the world, giving the result an international and fully interdisciplinary flavor and breadth of perspective.

Moreover, the team includes practitioners as well as academics, and has chosen to offer a less theoretical snapshot, closer to the present, although the concepts of Industry 5.0, combined with systems science and a cybernetic view, guide the evolution of the text. It also recognizes that good science (and good economics) takes data, that data takes time to collect or generate—especially when examining long-term trends and concerns. Still, in the meantime, it is useful to provide as clear a picture of the situation as can be created, in part to improve the utility of that data once collected.

Not surprisingly for a deliberately interdisciplinary and multi-perspective volume, the editors and chapter authors have widely diverse backgrounds. Most are highly interdisciplinary themselves, having published on a wide variety of topics. Their collective expertise includes technology and computer science, engineering, ethics, philosophy of science, sustainability studies, interdisciplinary studies, education and pedagogy, social science, linguistics, the arts, and more.

The editors and authors also have a long history of interaction and collaboration, with regular formal and informal meetings, joint workshops and presentations, coauthorship, serving on thesis committees for or otherwise assisting each other's students, and more. Many are members of the Creative Systemics Research Platform Institute (CSRP), as am I. CSRP has served as a virtual meeting space and intellectual clearing house for these discussions and others. From personal experience, while these collaborations have served to make each aware of the others' work, and have in many cases broadened and deepened individual perspectives and background, each of the team retains a highly individual perception and articulation of intellectual issues, and a highly individual style of discourse and communication, as can be seen in the chapters of this book.

About the Author

Thomas J. Marlowe is Professor Emeritus of Mathematics and Computer Science at Seton Hall, where he taught in both fields for over 40 years. He holds a Ph.D. from Rutgers University in each discipline. His research has covered areas including but not limited to coalgebras, programming languages and compiler optimizations, programming language aspects of real-time and embedded systems, software engineering and databases, computer science pedagogy including ethical considerations, and interdisciplinary studies. Email: thomas.marlowe@shu.edu

Department of Mathematics and Computer Science
Seton Hall University, South Orange, NJ, USA

Thomas J. Marlowe

Preface

Overview

At the core of this book is the output of the IN4ACT research project funded by a Horizon 2020 grant from the European Union. The project was centered at Kauno Technologijos Universitetas (KTU), the Kaunas University of Technology School of Economics and Business, in Lithuania. On a four-year timeline from 2020, research was chartered to study the impacts of Industry 4.0, as the industrial sector in Europe was being redefined by the adoption of new digital technologies, new materials, and new processes. As Industry 5.0 became better defined, the researchers shifted to the broader scope of ecological sustainability, human centricity, and resilience to shocks after experiencing the COVID-19 pandemic. Nearing finalization of the study in 2023, the unanticipated rapid rise of Generative Artificial Intelligence raised new questions beyond the original charter of 2020.

In late spring 2023, the IN4ACT researchers convened an in-person symposium, inviting international scholars to broaden perspectives on unfolding events. An ambitious timetable to deliver manuscripts within the calendar year was set. A frame of immediacy compacted the views of (a) what we have learned, (b) what we know today, and (c) what we see on the imminent future. As the collective work began to take shape, the contributors expanded to cover three continents. Online instant messaging and email brought together converging and diverging perspectives.

Industrial and societal trends are being pushed toward concerns about sustainability, and human well-being. As the digitalization of Industry 4.0 has matured, the transitions toward sustainability, human-centricity, and resilience of Industry 5.0 continue to evolve. The meaning of *human-centric* was drawn into sharper focus with concerns on the potential benefits and misuses of Generative AI. The final positioning of this book grapples with the dilemma of the scholarly reporting on findings from four years of research, and well-informed insights into expectations for 2024.

About the Chapters and Their Crossovers

This series of chapters reflects a milestone for a multidisciplinary team of researchers with IN4ACT as the nexus. The knowledge accumulated spans years of interaction, both within the core team and across their extended networks. Those core relationships established a foundation for inviting like-minded contributors into a cohesive team of writers. Each chapter stands on its own, with autonomous author(s) coming from a variety of disciplines, cultures, and experiences. A common thread through the chapters is concern for human-centricity, as an industrial and societal transition unfolds. In the subtle distinctions made by each researcher, the astute reader may intuit entering a dialogue, as ongoing, and unfinished.

Chapter 1, written by a leading systems researcher, provides an historic and theoretical context on the development of technologies, from the first Industrial Revolution in the eighteenth century to the present day. The trail from invention of steam engines to Artificial Intelligence (AI) is not linear, but AI did not develop by accident, nor without precedent. Many of the cultural drivers of industry (efficiency and productivity) and of media (corporate-funded advertising and influence) continue to shape technologies and their applications. Whether the same drivers will continue to shape the technologies of the future is an open question.

Chapter 2 is coauthored by three of the lead researchers on the IN4ACT team. Drawing from findings and publications over four years of study, they offer views of iterations and layers of the transition from Industry 4.0 to 5.0. At varying scales, the benefits and impacts considered should include economic, environmental, technological, and social aspects. Applying a typology of discourses on Circular Economy, risks are surfaced on the possibilities of maintaining stability through socioeconomic and environmental transitions with human-centricity in the complex adaptive system. Two case studies of industry transitions in Europe are reviewed, as test beds of innovation.

Chapter 3 reflects the perspective of two researchers focused on organization development and performance management. The emphasis on human-centricity in Industry 5.0, at minimum, requires the development of hard skills, in applying the new technologies. Beyond this recognition of hard skills, the types of soft skills that would support successful transitions to Industry 5.0 are not yet well-understood. Both workers mature in their careers, and newly trained entrants into an industry face psychological challenges, business and managerial challenges, and structural challenges. Gaining a fuller appreciation of soft skills leads to questions on defining the term *complexity* in human organizations, transferability across contexts, and the evaluation of behaviors. Experiences teaching emotion regulation to lab scientists and economists provide insights into potential soft skills transition challenges with Industry 5.0.

Chapter 4 is contributed by a leader in the service science movement, a former research executive for IBM. While Industry 4.0 and 5.0 agendas have largely emphasized the production side of industry with manufacturers in Europe, the breadth of stakeholders is more widely surfaced. Service system entities, at multiple scales, are challenged to look beyond optimizing locally, toward investing in the global ecology of actors. Aims for AI upskilling to improve the productivity of business and nations raise concerns about the responsibility and awareness of actors in ethical use of the technology. Digital twins, as models that partially synchronize interactive capabilities, are better understood for machines than for people, organizations, and other service system actors. Service science is presented as an emerging transdiscipline in which the ecology of entities can be better appreciated,

Chapter 5 was authored by a sustainable economy researcher on the IN4ACT team, who completed his doctorate during the project. In the technological developments across Industry 4.0 to 5.0, the way in which job posting has changed reflects shifts toward human centricity for employees and businesses. The evolution in abilities of machines is characterized as (a) Artificial Narrow Intelligence, (b) Artificial Semi-General Intelligence (ASGI), and (c) Artificial General Intelligence (AGI). Beyond routine job automation, Industry 5.0 could see ASGI encroaching on fields with creative work. As a bold experiment, the Generative AI ChatGPT technology was applied to create the initial draft of the chapter. Scholarly citation of sources is not with the current capabilities of ChatGPT, so refinement by the author was still required.

Chapter 6 has been contributed by a digital technology executive exploring the combination of Human Intelligence and Artificial Intelligence. The aggregate is considered as a Hyper-Selfish Intelligence, where the drives of biological evolution could lead to Artificial General Intelligence producing a Super Intelligence. An argument is made for strong global regulation of AI to preclude human civilization from the most extreme risks. Industry 5.0 is seen as an opportunity to put social and technological development on a positive path.

Chapter 7 was written by a systems researcher with a prior career in consulting and market development at IBM. The labeling of 4.0 and 5.0 is reflected in a variety of generational shifts, including Schumpeterian innovation, the Japan Science and Technology Basic Plan, the EU Industrial Research and Innovation Commission, and the World Economic Forum. Version numbering is explicated to differentiate between incremental adaptations and generational shifts. The Age of Discovery circa 1492 is portrayed in a transition from Era 0 to Era 1, with two synthetic perspectives of Socio-Technical Systems (STS) and Socio-Ecological Systems (SES). The current era is depicted as changes in SES as service economy alongside changes in STS as a knowledge society. The next era is described with changes in SES as a polycrisis ahead of changes in STS that would constitute a generational shift.

Reflections and Conclusions

While most book projects overlap stages and phases on timelines of years, this particular project faced the constraint of a 2023 funding deadline, compressing development into months. With that shortened horizon came the opportunity to bring the immediacy of the intriguing and influential public responses to the rapid rise of

Generative AI in late 2022. These pressures of news headlines every day drove an accelerated timeline for slipstreaming considerations for AI into the book.

In effect, this writing team reflexively experienced the transition from Industry 4.0 to 5.0, in a microcosm. The mandate to create a book as a static artifact capturing the knowledge and experiences of the team ran counter to the give-and-take style of ongoing dialogue, via synchronous online meetings punctuated by drafts and revisions of collective learning. The team agreed to cast this project as a snapshot in time, as a milestone in 2023, comparable to a photograph in a hurricane. Recording the state of knowledge at a point in time was important, with a mindfulness that our dialogue has not ended. Hopefully, this book will serve as a foundation for many more discussions to come, about the state of societies in the midst of disruptive changes, and the possibilities for the decisions that we can make toward the better.

Kaunas, Lithuania — Susu Nousala
Ashland, KY, USA — Gary S. Metcalf
Toronto, ON, Canada — David Ing

Acknowledgments

The contributors to this book would like to acknowledge and give thanks, posthumously, to our colleague and team leader, Panagiotis (Takis) Damaskopoulos, Professorial Chair at Kaunas University of Technology (KTU). Takis was appointed as the Principal Investigator for IN4ACT in 2019. He guided the research team through the development of ideas for many years, resulting in the content published in this book. He will be missed.

We would also like to acknowledge Professor Emeritus Thomas Marlowe for contributing the Preface, as well as his steadfast support in reviewing the chapter manuscripts and providing insights.

Finally, we acknowledge that this book received funding from the European Union's Horizon 2020 research and innovation program under grant agreement No. 810318.

Contents

About the Editors

Susu Nousala is a Project Researcher with the IN4ACT project at Kauno Technologijos Universitetas (KTU) School of Economics and Business. She is Founder and Research Director of the Creative Systemic Research Platform (CSRP) Institute centered in Ticino, Switzerland. Recent appointments have included: Professor at College of Design and Innovation at Tongji University (Shanghai); Chitian Scholar Professor at Wuhan University of Technology; and Senior Research Fellow at Aalto University (Helsinki). Her time is segmented across offices in Espoo, Finland; Móra d'Ebre, Spain; and Melbourne, Australia. Email: s.nousala@gmail.com

Gary S. Metcalf is a principal of InterConnections LLC, coaching executive leaders and consulting on human resources. He serves as Treasurer of the International Society for the Systems Sciences with prior experience as a past-president, and was previously President of the International Federation for Systems Research. Book series that he has edited include *Translational System Sciences* (Springer Japan) and *IFSR Systems Sciences and Systems Engineering* (Springer USA). Appointments have included Professor of Leadership and Management at Saybrook University and Distinguished Lecturer at Sullivan University. He works in Ashland, Kentucky, and Atlanta, Georgia. Email: gmetcalf@InterConnectionsLLC.com

David Ing is a Research Fellow with Creative Systemic Research Platform (CSRP) Institute, as well as a Research Fellow with Code for Canada. He serves as a Trustee for the International Society for the Systems Sciences, with a prior role as past-president. A previous 28-year career at IBM Canada included assignments in management consulting, headquarters planning, and executive education. Previous book projects include *Open Innovation Learning* and *The Marketing Information Revolution*. He resides in Toronto, Canada. Email: coevolving@gmail.com

Chapter 1
An Introduction to Industry 5.0: History, Foundations, and Futures

Gary S. Metcalf

Abstract The meaning of Industry 5.0 continues to evolve. It originally implied a reaction to the excesses of technologies in Industry 4.0, the era of cyber-physical systems and the Internet-of-Things. In the short time since the term was first used, artificial intelligence has taken over public attention, bringing new questions and new meanings. Many of the influences shaping our technologies, however, date back to the first Industrial Revolution: efficiency, profitability, etc. Will those same influences continue to shape future technological developments, or is this an era in which humans can choose to make new choices?

Keywords Industry 4.0 · Industry 5.0 · Artificial intelligence · Transhumanism · Post humanism

Humans have evolved with tools since the dawn of our species; from sharpened stones and fire to the computer systems of today. Each new tool has been an invention, but it has also been part of a lineage of change, not entirely different from biological evolution. A sharpened stone attached to a sturdy stick, made a much more effective axe. A smaller sharpened stone attached to a longer stick created a spear, and so on.

For millennia, tools enhanced our physical capabilities. The domestication of animals for work, such as oxen and horses, supplemented strength and endurance, as did wheels, levers, and pulleys. Engines provided another leap in magnitude, from tiny electric motors to rocket and jet engines.

The development of language by humans represented a different kind of advancement; a tool for communicating (Rushkoff, 2019). Experiences could be shared and collected into a communal system of knowledge and memory. When memories and ideas could be shared in written form, they were more accurate and lasted longer. Mathematics was arguably a next advancement as a language for description, as well as calculation.

G. S. Metcalf (✉)
InterConnections, LLC, Ashland, KY, USA
e-mail: gmetcalf@InterConnectionsLLC.com

S. Nousala et al. (eds.), *Industry 4.0 to Industry 5.0*, Translational Systems Sciences 41, https://doi.org/10.1007/978-981-99-9730-5_1

Computers used machine language to automate the functions of mathematics, and later incorporated coding for written languages. Programs could then be written to capture and automate any number of processes as algorithms.

Many changes have been steady and gradual, lasting over thousands of years. Some, though, have been dramatic, and are marked as revolutions, notably, the Agricultural Revolution, and the Industrial Revolution. Those were not events; they involved many smaller changes over a great deal of time, but cumulatively, those revolutions created significant changes in the ways that humans have lived.

Prior to the Industrial Revolution, tools were extensions of their human users. Artisans and craftsmen wielded tools in expert ways, to create the goods that they produced. The Industrial Revolution, however, changed that relationship. Machines became the focus of work, and humans became their caretakers. For the first time, humans feared being replaced by tools.

Over time, the Industrial Revolution has been segmented into parts, or phases, to distinguish the kinds of technologies most relevant to each. In the broadest terms, the first Industrial Revolution is associated with the use of the steam engine; the second with electricity and the assembly line; the third with computers and digital technology, and the fourth with mobile Internet, the Internet of Things (IoT), and artificial intelligence (AI) (Schwab, 2015, 2016).

Industry 4.0 is a concept developed in the EU, based on Germany's 2011 Industrie 4.0 vision, to increase its competitiveness in manufacturing (Ghobakhloo et al., 2021), and focused on the creation of cyber-physical systems (Grabowska et al., 2022).

Industry 5.0 is meant to describe the most recent phase, but it is not simply the next technological advancement. Rather, it was meant to rebalance what was becoming an excessive reliance on technologies, with the potential for negative consequences on workers and societies. The three core elements of Industry 5.0, as presented by the European Commission, are human-centricity, sustainability and resilience (European Commission, Directorate-General for Research and Innovation, et al., 2021).

In Japan, a similar evolution is captured as Society 1.0 through 5.0, the latter referring to Super Smart Society, in which "people, things, and systems are all connected in cyberspace and optimal results obtained by AI exceeding the capabilities of humans are fed back to physical space" (Onday, 2019, p. 1). It also, however, includes objectives much like those of the UN Sustainable Development Goals.

It is important to remember that these technological revolutions are quite different from geological epochs. They are not universal changes affecting all parts of the world equally, nor are the terms or ideas used and understood across all regions in the same ways. As explained by Schwab (2016), at the time of his writing, only 17% of the world had experienced even the second industrial revolution.

1.1 Historical Foundations

There are aspects of the latest technologies which are industrial, as implied by Industry 4.0 and 5.0 These affect efficiency and productivity in workplace settings; automation of processes and use of robotics, etc., as well as semi-conductors embedded in most every automobile, household device, and so on.

The original industrial technology might be considered the division of labor. Simply segmenting the tasks and focus of human laborers greatly enhanced their productivity, as witnessed in the assembly of something as trivial as straight pins (for sewing) (Smith, 1776). Breaking processes down into identifiable tasks was also necessary for further automation.

The most manual technologies could be considered a long inheritance from the Luddites; the nineteenth century workers who destroyed some of the first textile machines out of fear that they would lose their jobs. The technologies themselves are not inherently dangerous. They may represent a threat to workers in their implementation.

More advanced technologies, such as cyber-physical systems, integrate the physical and computational elements of a system into a feedback process of observation and implementation. Again, though, the technologies themselves seem to pose no necessary threats, unless they are implemented in ways which fully automate functions that create dangers, such as unmonitored use in weapons or energy systems.

The technologies of concern to Industry 4.0 have been described as cyber-physical systems, hyperconnected production systems, the Internet-of-Things, and others. A report by the European Commission cited six technologies that they believed were relevant to Industry 5.0:

> (i) Individualised Human-machine-interaction; (ii) Bio-inspired technologies and smart materials; (iii) Digital twins and simulation; (iv) Data transmission, storage, and analysis technologies; (v) Artificial Intelligence; (vi) Technologies for energy efficiency, renewables, storage and autonomy (European Commission, Directorate-General for Research and Innovation, et al., 2021, p. 7)

Most of the industrial-based technologies have their origins in what would be familiar as tools. These date back to devices such as the power loom, for weaving cloth, from the late 1700s. They changed and evolved incrementally, as they were updated to include additional steps in manufacturing processes. Similarly, the moveable type and ink from the printing press was incorporated into the first typewriters, which later became electric typewriters, then incorporated memory storage, which made way for word processing in computers. Computer-aided design first gave engineers software versions of technical drawings, then expanded into 3D modeling, which allowed for 3D printing, and the foundations for digital twins (i.e., software versions of physical phenomena).

Tools for measurement and calculations date back thousands of years, such as the abacus. In recent history, IBM was founded in 1911 as the Computing-Tabulating-Recording Company (C-T-R) (IBM, 2019). They built their "first general purpose automatic digital computer" in 1944. ENIAC (Electronic Numerical Integrator and Computer) was completed in 1945. It operated as a serial computer, but was "Turing-complete." Building on that technology, Whirlwind I was developed for the U.S. Navy, to run early flight simulators. It used parallel computing and had a magnetic core memory, and was completed in 1951. These were the foundations for Industry 3.0.

1.1.1 From Digital to Networks to Media

There are industrial aspects to the technological advances of recent decades. Consider, for instance, the many, many devices which now operate through the use of semiconductors, or "computer chips," as well as those which have been converted from analogue to digital formats. Watches and phones transformed from mechanical and analogue devices, to digital, to being small computers. Music moved from analogue on vinyl to digital on magnetic tape, to compact discs, to streaming services. Automobiles started widely incorporating computer chips in the 1970s, as monitoring systems, then moved to digitally-controlled systems. The average internal combustion car now uses about 1000 individual chips. Electric Vehicles, operating almost entirely through software coding, use about twice as many, on average (Ferris, 2021). Banks transformed from local places which stored and exchanged paper currency and coins, to globally interconnected financial institutions relying on electronic exchanges, supporting digital transactions, and in some cases, cryptocurrencies.

Digitizing processes allows for two-way communications. Not only can operations be accomplished, they can be monitored, and the data used for analyzing behavior at industrial levels. All of this might be considered a part of the Internet-of-Things, though it is only one of many large categories of technology (Merchant, 2021). The largest impact of technology, including its potential to affect humans at mass scales, lies in the form of media.

Radio was the first form of electronic mass media. Guglielmo Marconi sent the first radio test message in 1897, across the Bristol Channel in the UK. By 1901, he had extended that range across the Atlantic Ocean. Commercial radio was launched in the U.S. in 1920, the first radio advertisement aired in 1922 (McDonough, 2012). Analogue television began to appear in the early 1900s, and was available to the public in many parts of Europe and North America by the 1930s.

Rushkoff (2019) explained how these new media of communications soon became means of manipulation. "As corporations lobbied to monopolize the spectrum and governments sought to control it, radio devolved from a community space to one dominated by advertising and propaganda" (p. 26). Television followed the same path. It was "also originally envisioned as a great connector and educator. But marketing psychologists saw in it a way to mirror a consumer's mind and to insert within it new fantasies—and specific products" (p. 26).

Neither radio nor television invented advertising. They were just the vehicles for mass distribution. Walter Dill Scott published "The Psychology of Advertising" in 1908. In it, he stated:

> Advertising has as its one function the influencing of human minds... As it is the human mind that advertising is dealing with, its only scientific basis is psychology, which is simply a systematic study of those same minds which the advertiser is seeking to influence (Scott, 1908, p. 2).

Scott would later become one of the founding figures in the field of Industrial/Organizational Psychology.

Scott's work was followed two decades later by Edward Bernays, the nephew of Sigmund Freud, with the book, "Propaganda" (1928). He opens his work with the statement:

> The conscious and intelligent manipulation of the organized habits and opinions of the masses is an important element in democratic society. Those who manipulate this unseen mechanism of society constitute an invisible government which is the true ruling power of our country (p. 9).

Rushkoff (2019) saw television programming and advertising both as means of promoting individualism, and creating a sense of alienation between people. The Internet, by contrast, began as a peer-to-peer (P2P) network, sharing and increasing the processing capacity of the connected computers. This interested the defense industry because it valued the distributed architecture as more secure than a centralized one. As the Internet expanded into the World Wide Web, that interest waned.

1.1.2 From Computers to the Internet

J.C.R. Licklider is credited with first envisioning what would become the Internet, in 1962. He worked at MIT, and headed the computer research program at DARPA (The Defense Advanced Research Projects Agency) (Leiner et al., 1997). The first successful experiment involved connecting a computer in Massachusetts with one in California, in 1965. The first version of this computer networking system become ARPANET.

Early digital computers were all mainframe systems. The first portable microcomputers (i.e., laptops) were not produced until the 1980s. The original Internet, then, was entirely institutional.

It was not until 1991 that Tim Berners-Lee opened the World Wide Web, giving public access to individual users (Leiner et al., 1997). In 1993, only 600 websites existed. By 1995, Compuserve, America Online and Prodigy provided web access. Amazon.com, Craigslist, eBay and Match.com, all appeared online that year. Google was founded in 1998, and by 2010, Facebook had reached 400 million users. In January, 2021, 4.66 billion people were connected to the Internet—more than half of the world's population. As of 2023, nearly 5 billion people worldwide used social media platforms (Wong & Bottoff, 2023). The six largest (at present) are: Facebook, YouTube, WhatsApp, Instagram, WeChat, and TikTok.

Somewhere along the way, the grand vision of an Internet as a means of data-sharing and communications became a giant expanse of commerce and consumption; of posting where people happened to be and what they were eating; of "likes" and celebrities and longing for connections. According to Rushkoff (2019):

> Although inhabited originally by scientists and defense contractors, the net soon became the province of cultural progressives, geeks, and intellectuals. The government didn't want it anymore and tried to sell it to AT&T, but even the communications company couldn't see the commercial possibilities of a free medium driven by the pleasure of communication (p. 29).

1.1.3 The Culture of the Internet, via Silicon Valley

Douglas Rushkoff began documenting the culture of Silicon Valley in the early 1990s. As he introduces what he discovered:

> The people you are about to meet interpret the development of the datasphere as the hard-wiring of a global brain. This is to be the final stage in the development of "Gaia," the living being that is the Earth, for which humans serve as the neurons (Rushkoff, 1994, p. 4).

It was a place rampant in the use of hallucinogens (psilocybin, ayahuasca, LSD, etc.), and a fascination with mathematical fractals, and hacking computer systems. "Data surfing" was not about theft. It was like an online game to explore the catacombs of secret cities, to see if you could find a way in, behind locked doors. It was puzzle-solving. It was juvenile humor, like making prank phone calls, but to a high-level corporate executive, or a government official.

For those who were good at it, their skills became valued by corporations and agencies. Sometimes they would test the vulnerabilities of an organization's systems, and sometimes they would be hired to break into a competitor's system. As Rushkoff (1994) further explains: "in the mid-1970s and early 1980s, psychedelics users were the only qualified, computer-literate people available to rapidly growing companies trying to develop software and hardware before their competitors" (p. 23). This created a significant culture clash for many traditional organizations.

It is not hard to imagine how a counter-culture of talented youth, with the tools to connect with each other, largely unseen, around the world, could create a space with few rules or restrictions. It is important to note, as well, that most of these people were more technically than socially talented. In the early 1990s, online space was free to explore. Once that space became populated, it became more interesting to those with power and money.

1.1.4 The Internet as Commerce

Traditional media companies (e.g., radio and television) initially saw the Internet as competition. In 1992 they determined that families with Internet connections watched, on average, nine less hours of television per week than those without the Internet (Rushkoff, 2019). As the Web quickly evolved into a giant shopping mall, that perspective changed. Too many companies tried to crowd into a new space, leading to the dot.com bust.

It seemed for a time that the original intent of the Internet might return. Social media entered, appearing to create a giant space of community. Everyone could have their own website and their own blog, and be their own creator of content. And it was all free.

A well-known adage states, "There ain't no such thing as a free lunch" (TANSTAAFL). The price for listening to, or watching, radio or television was being subjected to advertising. Online, digital communications work in two directions. The companies which hosted free services on the Internet gathered data about users, and either used or sold that data—or both—for purposes of individually targeted marketing.

In addition to his books, Rushkoff has created a number of documentary films. The two which are most pertinent to the discussions in this chapter are "Merchants of Cool" (Rushkoff, 2001), and "Generation Like" (Rushkoff, 2014).

"Merchants of Cool" describes the efforts taken by the advertising industry to develop marketing strategies aimed at adolescents. In the U.S., they had determined that this target group represented $150 billion in spending power ($100 billion at their own disposal, and an additional $50 billion that parents would spend on them). Overly-simplified, corporations created and pushed images which adolescents felt a need to imitate. In order to be "cool," they had to spend money.

By the time of the second documentary, phone calls, blogs, and email had been replaced with true social media, such as Facebook, Instagram, Snapchat, and others. This world had taken involvement to a new level. Teens, and even pre-teens, could interact with friends from their schools and neighborhoods online, but just as easily find peer groups of similar interests around the world. Every engagement, though, fed into algorithms which "suggested" their next interactions; the next video to watch, or site to visit, or item to buy.

This new world also created a new currency of "likes," or its equivalent. A user's popularity was calculated and constantly on display for other users to see, in a never-ending competition for approval and popularity. Out of this morass arose a small number of "social influencers," who, like icons of the earlier phase, represented those who should be mimicked. In this world, young people were not only the consumers, but also the advertisers, pushing the content which got the most attention in the great race for more approval (Rushkoff, 2019).

A landmark along the way, at least in the U.S., was the addendum to legislation regulating telegraphs and telephones, from the earliest days of electronic communications. It is a tiny section which has become the focus of recent political debates involving the U.S. Congress and the titans of some of the world's largest companies. The section in question states:

> (c) Protection for "Good Samaritan" blocking and screening of offensive material
> (1) Treatment of publisher or speaker
> No provider or user of an interactive computer service shall be treated as the publisher or speaker of any information provided by another information content provider (United States Code Title 47—Telegraphs, Telephones, and Radiotelegraphs, 2011).

The effect of this clause is that social media companies cannot be held to any standard of truth or accuracy for what users post on their platforms. Unlike traditional media companies, which have some accountability for what they display, online social media are considered only to be the platforms in which other parties act. The larger statute is meant to protect minors, particularly with respect to sexual exploitation. There are no requirements, however, for protecting consumers from malicious falsehoods, as long as they can be considered a part of free speech.

All of this has set the stage for the latest developments in artificial intelligence, and now generative artificial intelligence. In many ways, we have come full circle from the origins of free markets, as part of the first industrial revolution. We are now parts of a fully commoditized social system. We are our own individual brands, representing whatever we hope that others will value and help us sell to the world. We are profiles and images, designed both to conform, and to gain attention. Our value is relative to the value we add to others' brands, in an ongoing market of attention and approval.

Our value in workplaces is equally tenuous, as automation creeps quickly into new professions and industries. We bring value as workers until that value can be replaced through a system that needs no motivation, takes no time off, never gets bored or has interpersonal conflicts, and never asks for a raise in pay.

1.1.5 From Manufacturing to Cyberspace

The connections between the early days of Silicon Valley and Industry 5.0 may not be obvious. As noted earlier, Industry 4.0 was largely focused on technology related to manufacturing and product-related industries. Industrial production in general, however, accounts for only 20% of GDP across the E.U., and manufacturing only 14.5% (Müller, 2020). This mirrors global economic data, which has remained consistent since 1991 (Nayyar et al., 2021). Service industries, by contrast, have accounted for a rising share of global GDP, exceeding 60% for many years.

The potential for new technologies to affect the work and livelihoods of most people, then, is not restricted to traditional industries. In fact, separating goods from services is something of a false dichotomy. Tangible goods only have value in relation to what they can accomplish, or how they can be used. Likewise, services have to be "assembled" in ways which make them useful, such as software into programs rather than random lines of computer code, or the agreement with a delivery service that items will be moved from one location to another, within certain times for an agreed price.

New technologies, including AI, are affecting a growing span of work roles and industries, including marketing and sales, software engineering, research and development, and the life sciences (Chui et al., 2023). They are also affecting industries such as entertainment, from writers to actors to musicians, in increasingly significant ways. Concerns about the implications of Industry 5.0 need to reflect those expanding horizons, as well.

The following sections of this chapter will explore some of the topics that may shape our human relationships to the latest technologies. The technologies themselves are changing so rapidly that this can only provide a snapshot in time, but the general trends are somewhat predictable. Predictions about the effects of new technologies on organizations, and on employment, will be explored, as well as the many debates over new regulations. Finally, the larger questions will be addressed: Should we fear what is to come? How much control will humans have in determining the evolution of these new technologies, as well as our own futures, and what role does Industry 5.0 play in these questions?

1.2 Artificial Intelligence

"At its simplest form, artificial intelligence is a field, which combines computer science and robust datasets, to enable problem-solving. It also encompasses sub-fields of machine learning and deep learning, which are frequently mentioned in conjunction with artificial intelligence" (IBM, 2022a, par. 6). Deep learning is considered a sub-field of neural networks, which in turn is a sub-field of machine learning.

The origins of AI were born, in part, from the technologies of WWII, including radar, anti-aircraft systems, and encrypted electronic communications. The most important foundations, however, were laid in the field of cybernetics.

Cybernetics is most often associated with a series of conferences sponsored by the Josiah Macy, Jr. Foundation, held between 1946 and 1953 (ASC: Foundations: History of Cybernetics, 2003). The book based on those conferences was written by Norbert Wiener (1965). A British cybernetics group also formed, but more informally as a supper club, calling themselves The Ratio Club, which met from 1949 to 1955 (Husbands & Holland, 2008). There were many commonalities in ideas, as well as some distinctions (and competition) between the two groups, and a good deal of interaction. Ross Ashby, Donald Mackay, and Grey Walter were members of both groups. Warren McCulloch, who chaired the Macy Conferences, was a frequent guest at the Ratio Club, along with Claude Shannon, Walter Pitts, and occasionally Norbert Wiener.

The Macy Conferences included more than 40 participants, 20 of whom were considered to be core members. It was a widely diverse group in terms of backgrounds (e.g., neuropsychiatry, neurophysiology, physiology, anthropology, electrical engineering, psychology, sociology, ecology, mathematics, etc.) In the way that the meetings were run, however, deference was given to the quantitative approaches. The Ratio Club, by contrast, was kept to about 20 members, with a general prohibition against "professors" (i.e., tenured academics). Most had backgrounds in biology or medicine, but were also widely interdisciplinary, and worked in the "brain sciences." At least one exception was made for the mathematician, Alan Turing.

These groups were followed closely by the first meetings formally associated with the term, artificial intelligence, held at Dartmouth College in the summer of 1956 (A Proposal for the Dartmouth Summer Research Project on Artificial Intelligence, 1955). The term artificial intelligence was coined specifically in order to avoid association with cybernetics, which had fallen into some controversies. One of the key organizers of the Dartmouth project was Claude Shannon, and invited participants included Ross Ashby, Donald Mackay, and Warren McCulloch, along with Julien Bigelow (another member of the Macy Conferences).

Turing's work was particularly important to the foundations of AI (Turing, 1937, 1950). His 1950 paper described "the imitation game," which would become known as the Turing Test. He opened that paper with the question, "can computers think?", and then explained how the game would work in order to help answer the question.

Turing makes an interesting point, just as an aside, about what he considers to be important in the game. As he states, "We do not wish to penalise the machine for its inability to shine in beauty competitions, nor to penalise a man for losing in a race against an aeroplane. The conditions of our game make these disabilities irrelevant" (Turing, 1950). He continues by arguing that a computer need not process information like a human in order to be deemed to "think." So, a computer need not display human qualities beyond the ability to communicate, in order to win the game of acting human.

This perspective aligns closely with Claude Shannon's theory of communication, which was also highly influential in AI foundations. As he states:

> The fundamental problem of communication is that of reproducing at one point either exactly or approximately a message selected at another point. Frequently the messages have meaning; that is they refer to or are correlated according to some system with certain physical or conceptual entities. These semantic aspects of communication are irrelevant to the engineering problem. The significant aspect is that the actual message is one selected from a set of possible messages (Shannon, 1948., p. 1).

This perspective was known and debated during the Macy Conferences, where others argued that communication in the absence of context and meaning were inadequate as human communication. Shannon's theory, however, closely aligned with one by Wiener, and technical theories were considered to be superior to those from the social sciences. Shannon's theory remains highly influential in technical realms today.

The proposal for the Dartmouth AI research project proposed seven problems to be investigated. Those included the following:

1. "If a machine can do a job, then an automatic calculator can be programmed to simulate the machine. The speeds and memory capacities of present computers may be insufficient to simulate many of the higher functions of the human brain,

but the major obstacle is not lack of machine capacity, but our inability to write programs taking full advantage of what we have."
2. "It may be speculated that a large part of human thought consists of manipulating words according to rules of reasoning and rules of conjecture. From this point of view, forming a generalization consists of admitting a new word and some rules whereby sentences containing it imply and are implied by others…"
3. "How can a set of (hypothetical) neurons be arranged so as to form concepts…"
4. "If we are given a well-defined problem (one for which it is possible to test mechanically whether or not a proposed answer is a valid answer) one way of solving it is to try all possible answers in order. This method is inefficient, and to exclude it one must have some criterion for efficiency of calculation…"
5. "Probably a truly intelligent machine will carry out activities which may best be described as self-improvement…"
6. "A number of types of 'abstraction' can be distinctly defined and several others less distinctly…"
7. …the difference between creative thinking and unimaginative competent thinking lies in the injection of a (*sic*) some randomness […] the educated guess or the hunch [should] include controlled randomness in otherwise orderly thinking (A Proposal for the Dartmouth Summer Research Project on Artificial Intelligence, 1955).

It is worth highlighting the fact that all of this work was done, and these foundations set, before 1960. These early theorists and practitioners had envisioned "thinking systems" from the inception of computers. They brought with them a technical and quantitative bias to the work, which is not inherently bad or wrong, but is only one of many possible perspectives which could be included in coded models of processing and cognition.

Neural networks had been proposed by Warren McCulloch and Walter Pitts (1943). Their model of human neurology assumed that: "Because of the 'all-or-none' character of nervous activity, neural events and the relations among them can be treated by means of propositional logic" (p. 115). The all-or-none character fit a binary description in mathematics, the 0 or 1 of machine language, and the "on-or-off" state in semiconductors.

Neural networks, or artificial neural networks, are comprised of node layers, which act like the neural nets of McCulloch and Pitts.

> Each node, or artificial neuron, connects to another and has an associated weight and threshold. If the output of any individual node is above the specified threshold value, that node is activated, sending data to the next layer of the network. Otherwise, no data is passed along to the next layer of the network by that node (IBM, 2022b, par. 9).

Machine learning is a branch of AI and computer science, which relies on data and algorithms to mimic human learning. The term was introduced by Arthur Samuel at IBM, in his building of a computer program to play checkers (and to beat a self-proclaimed checkers champion) (IBM, 2022b).

The most common form of machine learning is known as statistical ML, which focuses on complex pattern learning. A newer version of ML is model-driven.

"Statistical ML operates differently from the human mind… Model-driven methods can explain more observations with less training data, just as human scientists do when they derive models from sparse data" (OECD, 2023, p. 30).

Artificial Intelligence (AI) can be classified as Weak, or Narrow, AI, which is designed to focus on specific tasks. Applications include its use in voice-activated assistants such as Amazon's Alexa, and Apple's Siri. Strong AI refers to Artificial General Intelligence (AGI), which could replicate human intelligence, or to Artificial Super Intelligence (ASI), which could surpass it (IBM, 2022a).

Generative AI relies on foundation models, which are a part of deep learning. ("Deep" refers to the many node layers of neural nets). Deep learning can use labeled data sets, in which items are already identified (i.e. supervised learning). It can also use unstructured, unlabeled data (e.g., text, images, computer code), and organize the data itself. "At a high level, generative models encode a simplified representation of their training data and draw from it to create a new work that's similar, but not identical, to the original data" (IBM, 2022a, par. 14). The introduction of variational autoencoders (VAEs) in 2013 allowed for the generation of more realistic images and text than ever before.

Recent advances in Generative AI include the development of "transformers," which are a type of neural network architecture. Transformer models move beyond analyzing individual words, to analyzing phrases and sentences. They do this through a technique of "self-attention," which gives context to words and sentences for a better understanding of meaning.

The latest development in transformers is called Ring Attention (Barr, 2023; Liu et al., 2023). The content windows (the boxes into which prompts are entered) have thus far been limited to about 100,000 "tokens," which translate to about 75,000 actual words, and that is for Anthropic's latest chatbot, Claude. (GPT-4 was limited to about 32,000 tokens.) Ring Attention promises to increase this to millions of tokens which could be processed from a single entry.

This sets the stage for Large Language Models (LLMs), which are a type of foundation model, or neural net, using vast amounts of data that have been "scraped" from different sources. LLMs include ChatGPT, GPT-4, DALL.E 2, Stable Diffusion, Bard, among a list that is growing daily. LLMs use Natural Language Processing to analyze data and generate outputs. The larger the data sets, the more examples that an LLM has for establishing patterns of information.

For instance, if a user requests that DALL.E 2 create an image including a list of subjects and features, in a particular style, the image is much more likely to be satisfying if the LLM has millions of examples from which to form patterns, rather than a few hundred. Having billions of sentences for reference helps to identify the most probable structure of phrases and sentences ever used about a particular topic. Analyzing all possible moves, and the most successful winning moves from past examples, for any game, also provides exceptional amounts of information for predicting successful strategies.

1.2.1 Processing and Cognition

From the inception of AI, there was a belief that if computers could process enough data—particularly in the form of human languages—they could replicate human cognition and knowledge. That was the essence of the Turing Test. A version of that dream began to appear with LLMs, which could not only interact with humans in reasonably satisfactory ways, but could fulfill requests to create outputs that had previously only been done by humans. They could summarize long documents of text, write poems and stories in specific styles, create artistic visuals, write computer code, etc.

Improvement in the capabilities of AI systems, particularly LLMs, was linked to the amounts of data on which they had been trained, and to which they had access for processing. A chatbot which had real-time access to every online library (text and video), academic journal, news report, and social media exchange available at a given point in time, would certainly exceed any human's ability to contemplate. Would that capacity equate with intelligence? More importantly, is intelligence the standard of measure?

Recent demonstrations of computer intelligence involved computers playing against humans in games of chess, Go, and Jeopardy. Chess and Go are games of strategy, played on backgrounds ("boards") defined by grids. That gives each game a finite, though large, number of possible moves. For chess, that number was calculated by Claude Shannon to be approximately 10^{120} (Shannon, 1950). For Go, using a 19 × 19 playing board, the estimate is 10^{360}.

IBM's Deep Blue was built to evaluate 200 million possible chess moves per second, yet Garry Kasparov, the reigning world chess champion at the time, was able to defeat the computer in 1996. A year later, the computer won.

In 2016, DeepMind's AlphaGo beat the reigning Go champion.

> What is noteworthy is that AlphaGo's algorithms do not contain any genuinely novel insights or breakthroughs. The software combines good old-fashioned neural network algorithms and machine-learning techniques… (Koch, 2016).

AlphaGo was first trained on a database of 30 million board positions, taken from 160,000 games of Go. Then, reinforcement learning was used and the computer played games against itself until it was refined enough to compete.

Earlier, in 2011, IBM's Watson had set a new standard for human-like computing, by beating two standing champions in the television game show, Jeopardy. Unlike board games, this required significant computation of natural languages. IBM developed DeepQA for just that task.

> DeepQA works out what the question is asking, then works out some possible answers based on the information it has to hand, creating a thread for each. Every thread uses hundreds of algorithms to study the evidence, looking at factors including what the information says, what type of information it is, its reliability, and how likely it is to be relevant, then creating an individual weighting based on what Watson has previously learned about how likely they are to be right (Best, 2013, par. 31).

Ultimately, DeepQA relied on 200 million pages of information to compete in the Jeopardy games, obviously far more than either of the other contestants had access to, or could even begin to retain in their memories. Watson's first application beyond Jeopardy was in healthcare, helping to find the best treatments for cancer patients.

As impressive as these demonstrations are, what do they represent? Is this knowledge, intelligence, or any form of consciousness? If not, how might consciousness, or sentience, appear?

A recent study proposed three primary tenets, and 14 indicator properties for assessing consciousness in AI systems (Butlin et al., 2023). The first tenet is computational functionalism: "Implementing computations of a certain kind is necessary and sufficient for consciousness, so it is possible in principle for non-organic artificial systems to be conscious" (p. 11). Second, evidence should be supported by current neuroscientific theories of consciousness. And third, any assessment should involve a theory-heaving approach, meaning "one that focuses on how systems work, rather than on whether they display forms of outward behaviour that might be taken to be characteristic of conscious beings" (p. 12).

While markers such as these can be helpful, and will undoubtedly continue to be refined, broader, and more specific questions, remain. Who, for instance, designed each of the AI systems in question, and for what purposes? When IBM Watson was developed to work on healthcare, much of the general knowledge it contained was retained, but new data focused on medical journals and other relevant resources. Additional training was done by medical specialists. That is significantly different than ChatGPT, where the theory seems to have been, "the more, the better," in terms of data sources. Using data from social media and websites at-large, for instance, is questionable, in a world with very few filters or restrictions on what can be posted, and even the few restrictions which exist have little effect.

Should there, then, be standards to which users and citizens could expect AI systems to rise? As long as the drivers remain commercial success, and those, in turn, depend on algorithms which gravitate to the lowest of human tendencies, in order to maximize user attention, little can be expected. Deep fakes and pornography may continue to drive design and algorithms. But those are not issues of technology. Those are issues of human choice.

1.2.2 The Proliferation of Generative AI

Prior to 2014, the most significant machine learning models were produced in academic settings (Maslej et al., 2023). OpenAI was founded in 2015. It is the developer of now-familiar technologies including GPT-1 through GPT-4, ChatGPT, and others. (GPT stands for Generative Pre-trained Transformer). According to its website, "Introducing OpenAI":

> "Our goal is to advance digital intelligence in the way that is most likely to benefit humanity as a whole, unconstrained by a need to generate financial return. Since our research is free

> from financial obligations, we can better focus on a positive human impact" (Brockman et al., 2015).

OpenAI started with promises of $1 billion in investments. In 2019, it formed a for-profit arm called OpenAI LP. According to their announcement, "We'll need to invest billions of dollars in upcoming years into large-scale cloud compute, attracting and retaining talented people, and building AI supercomputers" (Brockman et al., 2019). That led to a $1 billion investment by Microsoft, followed by an additional $10 billion in 2023, which gave Microsoft a 49% share of ownership. Recently, OpenAI discussed a share sale to investors which would value the company at $80 to $90 billion, triple its value at the beginning of 2023 (Hu & Nishat, 2023).

It would be difficult to miss the parallels with changes in the Internet, noted in previous sections of this chapter.

> Silicon Valley came to dominate the internet economy in part by offering services like online search, email and social media to the world free, losing money initially but eventually turning hefty profits on personalized advertising. And ads are probably coming to AI chatbots. But analysts say ads alone probably won't be enough to make cutting-edge AI tools profitable anytime soon (Oremus, 2023, par. 10).

Organizations need resources in order to operate. If they do not come from charitable or government sources, they will come from investors in some form. Investors expect to see returns on their money, which require profits. Globally, private investment in AI increased by 1800% between 2013 and 2022, when it reached USD $91.9 billion (a 26.7% decrease from 2021) (Maslej et al., 2023).

AI companies incur exceptional expenses, relative to those in other industries, which increase the needs for funding. AI companies reportedly hire star researchers at salaries which rival professional athletes. Their processing needs require the most advanced computer chips, which can cost $300,000 for a set of just eight chips. A single ChatGPT query could cost 1000 times as much as a Google search, and the "free" services that OpenAI was offering to users was costing it about $700,000 per day in computing power alone, based on one estimate (Oremus, 2023). Another report noted that corporations such as Microsoft and Google were finding that AI "assistants" were costing about $30 per user per month, which was the latest target price they have planned to charge (Dotan & Seetharaman, 2023). The problem is that the computing power used in the assistants far exceeds the average task for which they are typically employed. The hope is that, over time, computing costs will drop, making the services profitable. However, "Building and training AI products can take years and hundreds of millions of dollars, more than with other types of software" (Dotan & Seetharaman, 2023, par. 7).

Two additional resources needed by GPTs are data, and training. At present, the data are being treated as if they are free. That is despite the fact that large amounts of the data contain copyrighted material, such as books, academic journals, magazines, and newspaper articles. It also includes images, such as original art and photography, and photos of people which can be used and altered without their knowledge or permission.

An equally problematic aspect is the training of AI systems. As explained in one report, "AI learns by finding patterns in enormous quantities of data, but first that data has to be sorted and tagged by people, a vast workforce mostly hidden behind the machines" (Dzieza, 2023, par. 1). In this example, the employee worked for a subcontractor of Scale AI, a large Silicon Valley corporation, which contracted its work to OpenAI, the U.S. Military, and others. For eight h of work as an annotator, the employee in Kenya was paid USD $10. Annotation, in this case, involved improving the accuracy of image recognition by AI programs, by labeling endless numbers of images of objects.

Other workers in Kenya, employed by a different company, were tasked with tagging toxic content, including "situations in graphic detail like child sexual abuse, bestiality, murder, suicide, torture, self harm, and incest" (Perrigo, 2023, par. 6), for roughly the same pay. Many of them reported lasting emotional trauma as a result, and the contract was ultimately terminated by the subcontractor.

In Finland, prisoners have been used in similar work of AI training, but for very boring rather than toxic content. There was a need for native Finnish speakers, and the prisoners could be paid cheaply (Meaker, 2023).

Amazon.com's Mechanical Turk appears to be a common platform for recruiting labor to train AI, as free-lance gig workers. In another twist, those workers are innovating by using technology such as ChatGPT in their training work. One study found that between 33% and 46% of the selected gig workers had done so (Williams, 2023).

> Using AI-generated data to train AI could introduce further errors into already error-prone models. Large language models regularly present false information as fact. If they generate incorrect output that is itself used to train other AI models, the errors can be absorbed by those models and amplified over time, making it more and more difficult to work out their origins… (par. 6).

What gets presented as brilliance or magic is more like an updated division of labor, similar to the factories making and assembling smart phones and other high-tech devices. In an example of the medical use of AI:

> An AI system might be capable of spotting cancer…but only in a certain type of imagery from a certain type of machine; so now, you need a human to check that the AI is being fed the right type of data and maybe another human who checks its work before passing it to another AI that writes a report, which goes to another human, and so on (Dzieza, 2023, par. 16).

1.2.3 AI in Business

Despite the many questions, and recognized limitations of Generative AI, specifically, it is being promoted heavily, and quickly being adopted by organizations. A McKinsey & Co. study found that one-third of responding organizations were regularly using Generative AI in at least one function of their operations (McKinsey & Company, 2023). The most common areas of application included "marketing and sales, product and service development, and service operations," as well as software engineering (p. 3). Those considered to be "high performers" (the early adopters), were twice as likely to use Generative AI for creating new businesses and sources of revenues, rather than for reducing costs, or in traditional manufacturing applications.

The work activities which could potentially be automated using Generative AI increased from 50%, to 60% or 70%, but those did not necessarily translate into job losses (McKinsey & Company, 2023). High performing organizations anticipated much higher levels of upskilling than organizations with lower AI adoption. A World Economic Forum (WEF) white paper noted that 62% of worktime involves language-based tasks, which could significantly increase the impact of LLMs (World Economic Forum, 2023).

Interestingly, the adoption of AI (not just Generative AI) has peaked at about 50% by businesses overall, and over half of the return value to companies came from AI applications that did not include Generative AI (McKinsey & Company, 2023). The most common AI applications included "robotic process automation (39%), computer vision (34%), NL [natural language] text understanding (33%), and virtual agents (33%)" (Maslej et al., 2023). There were 517,000 new industrial robots installed in 2021, bringing the total number of operational robots to 3.47 million, worldwide. Some McKinsey research indicates that more traditional AI technology could continue to produce greater returns on investment than Generative AI.

Similar findings are reflected, using different language, in the WEF white paper. That analysis suggested that jobs involving the greatest repetition were most likely to be *automated* by new technologies, as compared with those needing the most abstract reasoning, which were likely to be *augmented* (i.e., assisted by LLMs, not replaced).

Technology, media and telecom companies were, not surprising, even more enthusiastic about Generative AI than those in other industries. Over half of the executives in a KMPG survey believed that adoption of Generative AI was an imperative for their businesses (Llp, 2023). The leading applications for these companies included software development (including AI virtual reality games), media content generation, summarization of communications, and cybersecurity protection (p. 2).

1.2.4 AI in Science

The journal *Nature* conducted a survey of 1600 scientists about their use and perceptions of AI (Van Noorden & Perkel, 2023). Within the sample, 48% personally studied or developed AI, 30% were users (not developers) of AI in their work, and 22% did not use AI in their research.

ChatGPT and other LLMs were the AI tools most often noted, along with science-specific tools such as those for creating 3D models of protein folding. Interestingly, the most frequent use of LLMs was for "creative fun" not related to research.

Perceptions of AI were both positive and negative. The majority of respondents believed that AI could increase efficiency, such as processing data and speeding up computations. Overall, it could help save time and money. On the negative side, there was a recognition that AI tools might identify patterns with no interpretation of their understanding; could further entrench bias and discrimination; could make fraud easier, and; might increase the potential for irreproducible research (Van Noorden & Perkel, 2023).

The same perceptions were largely mirrored in a book published by the OECD, about the use of AI in science (OECD, 2023). On the positive side, the authors found that:

> While typical machine-learning models are difficult to interpret…they remain useful for tasks such as hypothesis generation, experiment monitoring and precision measurements. Models that create new data – generative AI – can assist with simulations, removing unwanted features from data and converting low resolution, high-noise images into high-resolution, low-noise images, with many useful applications… Innovations in developing causal models – to disentangle correlation from causation – will provide huge benefits for the medical and social sciences (p. 21)

As noted previously in this chapter, however, the great majority of AI systems have not been developed for science. They are proprietary systems driven by commercial interests. In fact, out of 38 AI machine learning systems considered to be "significant" by Epoch (an AI research institute), released in 2022, 32 were produced by industry, and only two by academic institutions (Maslej et al., 2023). Scientists have called for increased government funding to build the AI systems needed for the extensive research facing humans today (OECD, 2023).

Despite the limitations, AI systems are being incorporated into science. A high-level-goal is to increase the efficiency of research. Total R&D expenditures in Germany, for instance, increased by 3.3% each year, from 1992 to 2017. Research productivity, though, fell by 5.2% per year. The results were similar in the U.S. (OECD, 2023). In the pharmaceutical industry, the problem is known as Eroom's Law, where "drug development becomes slower and more expensive over time" (p. 19).

The pharmaceutical industry is a useful example for AI, in a number of ways. The development of new drugs is extremely resource-intensive. The average R&D costs for a new drug range from $1 billion to $2 billion, and only 12% of drugs which make it to clinical trials end up being approved by the FDA (Congressional Budget Office, 2021). In 2018, the cost of one clinical trial was $19 million (OECD, 2023). AI has been suggested as a useful tool in a number of ways. Disease models (much like a digital twin) map processes for which new drugs might be developed. AI systems could help in screening the many possible alternatives for new remedies, and identifying those with the best chances for passing clinical trials. But there are still inherent limitations.

> AI is less likely to yield solutions where gains in R&D productivity are most needed. A main reason for this is that much of the critical data is of insufficient quality. For example, too much of the published biomedical literature is false, irrelevant or both (OECD, 2023, p. 19).

More broadly, AI, particularly using natural language processing (NLP), could help scientists with the excessive amounts of data being generated. One study found that tens of millions of peer-reviewed articles exist just in biomedicine, but that the average scientist could read about 250 articles per year (OECD, 2023). But again, there are limitations.

> The fundamental problem is that NLP techniques lack rich models of the world to which they can ground language… They have no exposure to the entities, relationships, events, experiences and so forth that a text speaks about. As a result, even the most sophisticated models still often generate fabrications or outright nonsense (OECD, 2023, p. 30).

It is probable that the technologies embedded in AI will continue to improve. Technology, however, will not solve the ways in which humans choose to use it. AI language models could be of significant value in processing large amounts of data, such as millions of articles that need to digested. The larger problem, however, may be the human incentive models which are creating excessive amounts of data. As long as scientists are judged by the number of articles that they get published, there is a strong incentive to use tools such as ChatGPT and its later versions simply to generate more words for new articles. Billions of new words, for their own sake, are not helpful. Better science would be.

1.3 Human-Centric, Resilient, and Sustainable

The European Commission (EC) report focused on three key areas related to Industry 5.0: human-centricity, resilience, and sustainability (European Commission, Directorate-General for Research and Innovation, et al., 2021). As the report stated, "Where the paradigm of Industry 4.0 has been primarily driven by the potential of emerging technologies to improve efficiency and productivity, Industry 5.0 is propelled by emerging societal changes and realities" (p. 25).

For the EU, human-centricity at the individual level included personal data and user protections. In industrial settings, it wanted to ensure that workers benefitted from new technologies, and were involved in the transitions. That should include new training, as well as re-skilling and upskilling. Ultimately, it could require changes in labor and social policies, to accommodate changes in employment patterns.

At the most basic level, a human-centric approach to technology adoption could be interpreted as something like ergonomics, where the simplest goal is the prevention of occupational injuries. The technology should do no harm to workers. A broader approach involves human factors engineering (HFE), which involves both psychological and physiological principles in the design of products, processes, and systems. A more encompassing approach would come from a socio-technical systems perspective, where the focus would be a systemic perspective on the relationships between humans and the technologies in question (Emery, 1993; Pasmore et al., 2019).

Resilience often implies stability in the face of change. The EC report prudently notes that optimization of efficiency (a typical goal for organizations), can result in decreasing resilience (European Commission, Directorate-General for Research and Innovation, et al., 2021). Maximum efficiency leaves no excess capacity for change. As with other issues, there are tradeoffs. "While digital interconnection will enable a host of resilient technologies (including data gathering, automated risk analysis and automated mitigation measures), an increased dependence on digital technologies exposes industry to technical disruptions, due to malfunctions as well as cyberattacks" (p. 24).

The larger question about resilience might be, what kind of socio-technical system, integrating humans with AI and other technologies, would have the greatest potential for surviving the rest of this century? That question is not simply about stability of jobs, or about competitive and profitable industries. At societal levels, what relationships between humans and their technologies might create the greatest goods? This leads directly into questions of sustainability.

Like resilience, sustainability can be interpreted at different extremes. Some companies and industries see sustainability in very operational terms: reducing waste, energy use, and carbon emissions, while engaging in activities such as recycling. The EC report takes a larger perspective, moving towards transitions to a circular economy, and ultimately the UN Sustainable Development Goals (SDGs). More specifically, "The Green Deal announced in December 2019 clearly sets out what Europe must do to transition to a sustainable economy" (European Commission, Directorate-General for Research and Innovation, et al., 2021, p. 27).

The relationship between AI and sustainability, at the highest levels, raises some of the most challenging questions. If humans are to survive the climate changes that we have put into motion, we will need all of the help that we can get. Fifty years of scientific data and evidence have left little doubt about human impacts on the biosphere, from greenhouse gasses to industrial farming to energy use, and so on. (IPCC, 2023). Based solely on the science, we need to stop most of our human activities. Obviously, that is not feasible. Finding middle-ground alternatives, though, is exceptionally complex.

We need non-damaging sources of energy, but we also need to reconsider the total energy that is actually necessary. We need to implement agricultural practices which regenerate healthy soil and clean water, rather than degrading them. We need to produce waste only in types and quantities that can be re-absorbed and re-used through the natural environment.

While we develop new industrial alternatives, we will also have to live with rapidly changes conditions on our planet. Weather patterns are becoming less predictable, and storms more extreme. The impacts on agriculture, and on human habitats, are increasing, and will predictably create climate-related immigration, as floods, fires, and storms make cities and villages unlivable.

All of those challenges are, on some levels, technical. Computer models and data processing can potentially help with analyzing massive amounts of information, which would be impossible simply through human labor. Computer models will not be enough, though, to make decisions about the social, political, and economic compromises necessary for humans to adapt, as needed. At the least, they might help to avoid some of the worst of the potential catastrophes.

1.4 Should We Fear Technology? The Need for Regulations

Bill Joy published an article in 2000, after a meeting with Ray Kurzweil and Bill Searle, warning of his fears about the dangers of runaway technologies (Joy, 2000). The specific technologies of most concern were genetic engineering, robotics, and nanotechnologies. His general concerns, however, continue to resonate equally today.

The concerns split between two scenarios, one in which humans permitted machines to make all of their own decisions, the other in which humans retained control of the machines. In the former case, the fear was not so much about technologies overtaking humans, but rather that, "People won't be able to just turn the machines off, because they will be so dependent on them that turning them off would amount to suicide" (Joy, 2000).

Kurzweil's vision was that humans would one day be able to fuse themselves with, or download their consciousness to, a robot. Joy's concern was more that the technologies themselves would become self-replicating.

Kurzweil's dream is the essence of the philosophy of transhumanism. Joy's fear raises questions about autopoiesis in non-organic beings, and issues of embodiment. All of these questions remain as relevant today as they were in 2000.

Fast-forward to 2023.

> A group of industry leaders warned…that the artificial intelligence technology they were building might one day pose an existential threat to humanity and should be considered a societal risk on a par with pandemics and nuclear wars (Roose, 2023).

The letter was signed by more than 350 professionals in the fields of AI, including top executives from the companies OpenAI, Google DeepMind, and Anthropic. Six months earlier, another open letter had been signed by 1000 technology executives and researchers, including Elon Musk, calling for a moratorium on AI development, while safeguards were considered (Metz & Schmidt, 2023).

In the meantime, new versions of AI systems are being released, and corporate executives are promising to embed AI in every process where they believe that it might prove profitable.

There are legitimate fears about what might happen as a result of AI and even newer technologies. The probability of a computer system becoming a conscious being and taking over the planet is one of the less likely at present. It would be foolish to rule out any possibility, but the probabilities would seem to rise in relation to other developments. If an AI system, for instance, was able to self-replicate (in an autopoietic fashion), and was able to achieve a sense of autonomy such that its first instinct was for its own survival, then the probabilities of threat would increase. At present, though, Bill Joy's concern appears to be more realistic, that humans would become so dependent on the ways in which they chose to use these technologies, the dependence would create the threat—much like we became dependent on fossil fuels.

The more imminent dangers seem to be the ways in which we are already using AI systems, in particular, and allowing them to be used. The latest technologies are quickly creating "fakes" of humans such that they are becoming ever more convincing to a general public, and harder to detect. This is happening with photos and videos, and with voice systems.

A society cannot function without a basic sense of trust. That is not just a moral or ethical issue, it is extremely practical. If you could not trust that the currency in your bank account was worth what you believed it to be, and you could not trust that when you exchanged it, it went to the right recipient (even standing at a retail checkout counter) how could you conduct business? If every electronic communication that you received was suspect, and that even a voice call to verify the message could not be trusted, how could normal social functioning occur? (The simplest answer to both problems would be to fall back to face-to-face bartering in local exchanges, shutting down global commerce.)

Likewise, if even the most trusted media sources could not necessarily verify the stories they needed to report, how could any sense of truth be supported? More likely would be a scenario, in which traditional journalistic sources found themselves reporting mass reactions to false reports, before real information could be verified and reported. Imagine, for instance, a video showing a senior natural leader burning a Qur'an, only to find that the entire production was fake. What would be the chances of stopping mass riots, but instead, having to report the riots rather than the truth of the original story?

1.4.1 Regulating AI

As this book prepares to go to print, significant activity is occurring with respect to AI regulation by governments around the world. The European Commission had begun work on policies to regulate robotics, and (separately) AI, in 2017 (Madiega, 2023). On October 30, 2023, the European Commission issued an International Code of Conduct for Organizations Developing Advanced AI Systems (European Commission, 2023).

Also on October 30, 2023, the President of the United States issued an Executive Order, which "establishes new standards for AI safety and security, protects Americans' privacy, advances equity and civil rights, stands up for consumers and workers, promotes innovation and competition, advances American leadership around the world, and more" (The White House, 2023). One source found the executive order to be comprehensive and intelligent (Jones, 2023). Another cited experts, who believed that it was a good beginning, but not yet adequate (Leffer, 2023).

A two day summit was held in the UK, billed as being "the first Global Summit on AI Safety" (UK Department for Science, Innovation, & Technology, 2023). On the opening day, a first-ever international pledge was signed, committing to cooperation on monitoring the risks of coming AI systems (now referred to as AI models) (Schechner, 2023).

It obviously remains to be seen whether policies or legislation can begin to keep up with the rapid developments in AI, and how governments will attempt to cooperate, while also working to create strategic advantages in their own interests. As noted early in this chapter, both propaganda and commercial interests run deep in media, back to beginning of the twentieth century. Cooperation requires trust, or at the least, mutual vested interests in avoiding harm. Recent warnings from technology leaders and experts have gotten attention, for now, but this new era seems only just to have begun.

1.5 The Future

For people who believe in a deterministic universe, the past predicts the future. What will happen is inevitable. A different view is that history strongly influences future events, through shaping the context in which actors behave and decisions are made.

Every era of the Industrial Revolutions has been shaped by forces, where efficiencies created greater production and profitability. Many of the decisions have been made by a small number of elite and powerful individuals. Many of them controlled the industries and technologies of their times. Others controlled or influenced the policies and regulatory environments in which the industries and technologies developed. Those factors remain true today.

Billions of dollars have been invested in the latest technologies, primarily under the general umbrella of Artificial Intelligence. Those investments have been made, to a great extent, by corporations, investment firms, and other profit-making entities. They have not been made as charitable donations, and the motives for profits shape the ways in which the technologies are designed, as well as how they are used.

To be clear, these are not the only possibilities. Similar technologies could have been—and potentially could still be—designed for other purposes. AI systems could be focused on scientific data for better understanding and anticipating climate change and the many related outcomes. They could be developing novel possibilities for social and political conflicts, identifying those with higher probabilities for success, for consideration by stakeholders. They could be linking young people as citizen scientists around the world, rather than feeding their cravings for attention and desperation for acceptance. Creating those alternatives, however, would require a different set of incentive structures and investments, underpinning different designs.

There are also larger influences at play, in the fundamental philosophies and belief systems which shape decisions. Many of the scientists and engineers behind the technologies of the Industrial Revolutions seem to believe in some version of "salvation through technology." Human biology is frail, and can better be overcome or replaced with better alternatives. Machines are stronger and faster than humans in performing physical tasks (e.g., plowing a field, moving objects weighing tons, welding parts on a factory line). Machines can process data faster than humans, and can store and access amounts of data far beyond human capacities. Humans get old, tired and sick, and need to be cared for. Machines get repaired or replaced. In general, machines are superior to humans, and just need to become more advanced.

The terms transhumanist and post humanist both have many variations in use and interpretation. Nick Bostrom (2005), traces the origins of transhumanism back to rational humanism; the idea that humans could transcend themselves using scientific knowledge. Katherine Hayles traces the history of posthumanism from the cybernetics of the Macy Conferences, through both academic literature and science fiction, to the present day. As she describes it, "In the posthuman, there are no essential differences or absolute demarcations between bodily existence and computer simulation, cybernetic mechanism and biological organism, robot teleology and human goals" (Hayles, 1999, p. 3). These views argue for the continued investments and development which brought us to the current states of our technologies and societies.

A useful distinction was made, though, by Hans Moravec (1988). His work in robotics produced the observation which has become known as the *Moravec Paradox*, essentially, that computers are exceptionally good at doing things which humans find difficult, but exceptionally poor at doing things which come natural to most humans, almost regardless of intelligence levels. This would seem to help account for the immense advances in Generative AI systems, but continuing limitations in applications such as self-driving automobiles.

Moravec (1988) explains the dilemma through a distinction between the approaches taken in cybernetics, and AI:

> The cybernetics researchers, whose self-contained experiments were often animal-like and mobile, began their investigation of nervous systems by attempting to duplicate the sensorimotor abilities of animals. The artificial intelligence community ignored this approach in their early work and instead set their sights directly on the intellectual acme of human thought, in experiments running on large, stationary mainframe computers dedicated to mechanizing pure reasoning. This "top-down" approach to machine intelligence made impressive strides at first but has produced few fundamental gains in over a decade. While cybernetics scratched from the underside of real intelligence, artificial intelligence scratched the topside. The interior bulk of the problems remain inviolate (p. 16)

One of the key questions posed in post humanism is about *embodiment*. In that context, it is less an argument for biology, per se, and more fundamentally a question about intelligence. Is it possible to separate human-like intelligence from the biological bodies which generate and support it? If not, then the current trajectories for AI may be inherently limited to those functions that might be characterized as *information processing*, or a limited form of cognition, without ever achieving a higher level of existence.

Questions about embodiment raise additional issues about experiences, and the role of experiences in human functioning. Mathematically-based models (as found in science and technology) follow rules and logic. Human behavior at macro-levels can be captured in identifiable patterns, but to say that individual humans operate through rules and logically-based decisions at micro-levels across all cultures and regions, is simply not supportable. Humans anticipate, behave, experience, respond, and act again. Sometimes they learn in the process, but as organisms, not as machines.

These questions get to the place of technologies in our human societies, both in terms of what we can expect, and what we can control. At present, high-tech development is controlled by a tiny fraction of the global population. While many improvements in living conditions can be traced to industrial technologies, dating through the Industrial Revolutions, there have obviously been tradeoffs (e.g., the impact of burning fossil fuels on the natural environment). How will decisions about the next phases of technology design be made, by whom, and for whose benefits?

The final, critically important point for this chapter is: *It's not the technology*. The benefits or harms coming out of AI, and other current and future technologies, are choices of design and implementation. Robots have no need to compete for human jobs. AI systems have no more inherent interests in sexuality (as they are being used in *deep fakes*), than they have in recipes or cooking. The technologies are, however, having profound impacts on our societies.

None of this is out of human control—yet. It is possible that humans could create new systems, equally as dangerous as nuclear weapons, in different ways. Those are not technological failures. They are issues of human morality and leadership. The next decisions need to bring our humanity face-to-face with the technologies, in deciding who we want to be as a species.

References

A Proposal for the Dartmouth Summer Research Project on Artificial Intelligence. (1955). Retrieved from http://www-formal.stanford.edu/jmc/history/dartmouth/dartmouth.html

ASC: Foundations: History of Cybernetics. (2003). Retrieved August 4, 2023, from https://asc--cybernetics.org/foundations/history2.htm#MacySum

Barr, A. (2023, October). *Google researcher finds a way for AI models to analyze millions of words at once*. Insider. Retrieved from https://www.businessinsider.com/google-researcher-ai-models-analyze-millions-of-words-at-once-2023-10

Bernays, E. L. (1928). *Propaganda*. Horace Liveright.

Best, J. (2013). *IBM Watson: The inside story of how the Jeopardy-winning supercomputer was born, and what it wants to do next*. TechRepublic. Retrieved from https://www.techrepublic.com/article/ibm-watson-the-inside-story-of-how-the-jeopardy-winning-supercomputer-was-born-and-what-it-wants-to-do-next/

Bostrom, N. (2005). A history of transhumanist thought. Originally Published in *Journal of Evolution and Technology, 14*(1). Retrieved from www.nickbostrom.com

Brockman, G., Sutskever, I., & OpenAI. (2015). *Introducing OpenAI*. Retrieved from https://openai.com/blog/introducing-openai

Brockman, G., Sutskever, I., & OpenAI. (2019, March 11). *OpenAI LP*. Retrieved from https://openai.com/blog/openai-lp/

Butlin, P., Long, R., Elmoznino, E., Bengio, Y., Birch, J., Constant, A., Deane, G., Fleming, S. M., Frith, C., Ji, X., Kanai, R., Klein, C., Lindsay, G., Michel, M., Mudrik, L., Peters, M. A. K.,

Schwitzgebel, E., Simon, J., & VanRullen, R. (2023). *Consciousness in artificial intelligence: Insights from the science of consciousness*. Retrieved from http://arxiv.org/abs/2308.08708

Chui, M., Hazan, E., Roberts, R., Singla, A., Smaje, K., Sukharevsky, A., Yee, L., & Zemmel, R. (2023). *The economic potential of generative AI: The next productivity frontier*.

Congressional Budget Office. (2021). *Research and development in the pharmaceutical industry*. Retrieved from https://www.cbo.gov/publication/57025

Dotan, T., & Seetharaman, D. (2023, October 9). Big Tech struggles to turn AI hype into profits. *The Wall Street Journal*. Retrieved from https://www.wsj.com/tech/ai/ais-costly-buildup-could-make-early-products-a-hard-sell-bdd29b9f

Dzieza, J. (2023, June). *Inside the AI Factory: The humans that make tech seem human*. The Verge. Retrieved from https://www.theverge.com/features/23764584/ai-artificial-intelligence-data-notation-labor-scale-surge-remotasks-openai-chatbots

Emery, F. (1993). Characteristics of socio-technical systems. In E. Trist, H. Murray, & B. Trist (Eds.), *The social engagement of social science, a Tavistock anthology* (Vol. 2, pp. 157–186). University of Pennsylvania Press. https://doi.org/10.9783/9781512819052-009

European Commission. (2023, October 30). *Hiroshima process international code of conduct for advanced AI systems*. Retrieved from https://digital-strategy.ec.europa.eu/en/library/hiroshima-process-international-code-conduct-advanced-ai-systems

European Commission, Directorate-General for Research and Innovation, Breque, M., De Nul, L., & Petridis, A. (2021). *Industry 5.0: Towards a sustainable, human centric and resilient European industry*. Publications Office of the European Union. Retrieved from https://data.europa.eu/doi/10.2777/308407

Ferris, D. (2021, November). *Chip shortage threatens Biden's electric vehicle plans, commerce secretary says*. Scientific American. Retrieved from https://www.scientificamerican.com/article/chip-shortage-threatens-bidens-electric-vehicle-plans-commerce-secretary-says/

Ghobakhloo, M., Iranmanesh, M., Grybauskas, A., Vilkas, M., & Petraitė, M. (2021). Industry 4.0, innovation, and sustainable development: A systematic review and a roadmap to sustainable innovation. *Business Strategy and the Environment, 30*(8), 4237–4257. https://doi.org/10.1002/bse.2867

Grabowska, S., Saniuk, S., & Gajdzik, B. (2022). Industry 5.0: Improving humanization and sustainability of Industry 4.0. *Scientometrics, 127*(6), 3117–3144. https://doi.org/10.1007/s11192-022-04370-1

Hayles, N. K. (1999). *How we became posthuman: Virtual bodies in cybernetics, literature, and informatics*. The University of Chicago Press.

Hu, K., & Nishat, N. (2023). *OpenAI, at boosted valuation, in talks to sell existing shares to investors, sources say*. Reuters. Retrieved from https://www.reuters.com/technology/openai-seeks-valuation-up-90-bln-sale-existing-shares-wsj-2023-09-26/.

Husbands, P., & Holland, O. (2008). The ratio club: A hub of British cybernetics. In P. Husbands, O. Holland, & M. Wheeler (Eds.), *The mechanical mind in history* (pp. 91–148). MIT Press.

IBM. (2019). *Chronological history of IBM—1880*. Retrieved October 3, 2023, from https://www.ibm.com/ibm/history/history/decade_1880.html

IBM. (2022a). *What is artificial intelligence (AI)?* Retrieved October 8, 2023, from https://www.ibm.com/topics/artificial-intelligence

IBM. (2022b). *What is machine learning?* Retrieved October 8, 2023, from https://www.ibm.com/topics/machine-learning

IPCC. (2023). In Core Writing Team, H. Lee, & J. Romero (Eds.), *Climate change 2023 synthesis report*. World Meteorological Organization. Retrieved from https://www.ipcc.ch/report/sixth-assessment-report-cycle/

Jones, R. (2023, October). *Biden's executive order "is actually ahead of things," AI expert says*. Fortune. Retrieved from https://fortune.com/2023/10/30/biden-executive-order-ai-artificial-intelligence-smart-strong-ahead-experts/

Joy, B. (2000, April). *Why the future doesn't need us*. Wired. Retrieved from https://www.wired.com/2000/04/joy-2

Koch, C. (2016, March). *How the computer beat the go master*. Scientific American. Retrieved from https://www.scientificamerican.com/article/how-the-computer-beat-the-go-master/

Leffer, L. (2023, October 31). *Biden's executive order on AI is a good start, experts say, but not enough*. Scientific American. Retrieved from https://www.scientificamerican.com/article/bidens-executive-order-on-ai-is-a-good-start-experts-say-but-not-enough/

Leiner, B. M., Cerf, V. G., Clark, D. D., Kahn, R. E., Kleinrock, L., Lynch, D. C., Postel, J., Roberts, L. G., & Wolff, S. (1997). *Brief history of the Internet 1997*. Retrieved from https://www.internetsociety.org/resources/doc/2017/brief-history-internet/

Liu, H., Zaharia, M., & Abbeel, P. (2023). *Ring attention with blockwise transformers for near-infinite context*. Retrieved October 15, 2023, from https://arxiv.org/abs/2310.01889

Llp, K. (2023). *Technology, media, and telecom lead the charge on generative AI*. Retrieved from https://kpmg.com/kpmg-us/content/dam/kpmg/pdf/2023/technology-media-telecom-gen-ai-survey.pdf

Madiega, T. (2023). *Artificial intelligence act*.

Maslej, N., Fattorini, L., Brynjolfsson, E., Etchemendy, J., Ligett, K., Lyons, T., Manyika, J., Ngo, H., Niebles, J. C., Parli, V., Shoham, Y., Wald, R., Clark, J., & Perrault, R. (2023). *The AI index annual report 2023*. Retrieved from https://aiindex.stanford.edu/report/

McCulloch, W. S., & Pitts, W. (1943). A logical calculus of the ideas immanent in nervous activity. *Bulletin of Mathematical Biophysics, 5*, 115–133.

McDonough, J. (2012). *First radio commercial hit airwaves 90 years ago*. All Things Considered: NPR. Retrieved from https://www.npr.org/2012/08/29/160265990/first-radio-commercial-hit-airwaves-90-years-ago

McKinsey & Company. (2023). *The state of AI in 2023: Generative AI's breakout year*. Retrieved from https://www.mckinsey.com/~/media/mckinsey/business%20functions/quantumblack/our%20insights/the%20state%20of%20ai%20in%202023%20generative%20ais%20breakout%20year/the-state-of-ai-in-2023-generative-ais-breakout-year_vf.pdf?shouldIndex=false

Meaker, M. (2023, September). *These prisoners are training AI*. Wired. Retrieved from https://www.wired.com/story/prisoners-training-ai-finland/

Merchant, N. (2021). *What is the Internet of Things—An explainer*. Retrieved from https://www.weforum.org/agenda/2021/03/what-is-the-internet-of-things/.

Metz, C., & Schmidt, G. (2023, March 29). Elon musk and others call for pause on A.I., citing 'risks to society.' *The New York Times*. Retrieved from https://www.nytimes.com/2023/03/29/technology/ai-artificial-intelligence-musk-risks.html

Moravec, H. P. (1988). *Mind children: The future of robot and human intelligence*. Harvard University Press. Retrieved from https://www.google.com/books/edition/Mind_Children/56mb7XuSx3QC?hl=en&gbpv=0&kptab=overview

Müller, J. (2020). Enabling Technologies for Industry 5.0 Results of a workshop with Europe's technology leaders. https://doi.org/10.2777/082634

Nayyar, G., Hallward-Driemeier, M., & Davies, E. (2021). *At your service? The promise of services-led development*. Retrieved from https://openknowledge.worldbank.org/entities/publication/b5f153be-e867-5746-ad02-e12a0774e2d1

OECD. (2023). Artificial intelligence in science: Challenges, opportunities, and the future of research. https://doi.org/10.1787/a8d820bd-en

Onday, O. (2019). Japan's Society 5.0: Going beyond Industry 4.0. *Business and Economics Journal, 10*(2). https://doi.org/10.4172/2151-6219.1000389

Oremus, W. (2023, June 5). AI chatbots lose money every time you use them. That is a problem. *The Washington Post*. Retrieved from https://www.washingtonpost.com/technology/2023/06/05/chatgpt-hidden-cost-gpu-compute/

Pasmore, W., Winby, S., Mohrman, S. A., & Vanasse, R. (2019). Reflections: Sociotechnical systems design and organization change. *Journal of Change Management, 19*(2), 67–85. https://doi.org/10.1080/14697017.2018.1553761

Perrigo, B. (2023, January). *OpenAI used Kenyan workers on less than $2 per hour*. Time. Retrieved from https://time.com/6247678/openai-chatgpt-kenya-workers/

Roose, K. (2023, May 30). AI poses 'risk of extinction,' industry leaders warn. *The New York Times*. Retrieved from https://www.nytimes.com/2023/05/30/technology/ai-threat-warning.html

Rushkoff, D. (1994). *Cyberia: Life in the trenches of hyperspace*. HarperSan Francisco. Retrieved from https://www.amazon.com/Cyberia-Trenches-Hyperspace-Douglas-Rushkoff/dp/006251010X/ref=sr_1_1?crid=K3VKTA01XYLS&keywords=cyberia+douglas+rushkoff&qid=1696341928&sprefix=cyberia+%2Caps%2C140&sr=8-1

Rushkoff, D. (2001). Merchants of cool. *PBS Frontline*. Retrieved from https://www.pbs.org/video/frontline-merchants-cool/

Rushkoff, D. (2014). Generation like. *PBS Frontline*. Retrieved from https://www.pbs.org/video/frontline-generation/.

Rushkoff, D. (2019). *Team human (Kindle)*. W. W. Norton. Retrieved from https://www.amazon.com/gp/product/B07DP62FZB/ref=kinw_myk_ro_title

Schechner, S. (2023, November 1). 'Take science fiction seriously': World leaders sound alarm on AI. *The Wall Street Journal*. Retrieved from https://www.wsj.com/tech/ai/at-artificial-intelligence-summit-a-u-k-official-warns-take-science-fiction-seriously-b3f31608

Schwab, K. (2015). *The Fourth Industrial Revolution: What it means and how to respond*. Foreign Affairs.

Schwab, K. (2016). *The fourth industrial revolution*. Retrieved from www.weforum.org

Scott, W. D. (1908). *The psychology of advertising*. Small, Maynard & Company.

Shannon, C. E. (1948). A mathematical theory of communication. *The Bell System Technical Journal, 27*, 379–423.

Shannon, C. E. (1950). Programming a computer for playing chess. *Philosophical Magazine, Series, 7*(314). Retrieved from http://archive.computerhistory.org/projects/chess/related_materials/text/2-0%20and%202-1.Programming_a_computer_for_playing_chess.shannon/2-0%20and%202-1.Programming_a_computer_for_playing_chess.shannon.062303002.pdf

Smith, A. (1776). *An inquiry into the nature and causes of the wealth of nations*. Project Gutenberg. Retrieved from https://www.gutenberg.org/files/38194/38194-h/38194-h.htm

The White House. (2023). *FACT SHEET: President Biden issues executive order on safe, secure, and trustworthy artificial intelligence*. Retrieved from https://www.whitehouse.gov/briefing-room/statements-releases/2023/10/30/fact-sheet-president-biden-issues-executive-order-on-safe-secure-and-trustworthy-artificial-intelligence/

Turing, A. M. (1937). On computable numbers, with an application to the Entscheidungsproblem. *Proceedings of the London Mathematical Society, 42*(s2), 230–265. https://doi.org/10.1093/oso/9780198250791.003.0005

Turing, A. M. (1950). Computing machinery and intelligence. *Mind, 49*, 433–460.

UK Department for Science, Innovation & Technology. (2023, October 31). *AI safety summit*. Artificial Intelligence. Retrieved from https://www.gov.uk/government/publications/ai-safety-summit-introduction/ai-safety-summit-introduction-html

United States Code Title 47—Telegraphs, Telephones, and Radiotelegraphs, Pub. L. No. 47 (2011). Retrieved from https://www.govinfo.gov/content/pkg/USCODE-2011-title47/html/USCODE-2011-title47.htm

Van Noorden, R., & Perkel, J. M. (2023). AI and science: What 1,600 researchers think. *Nature, 621*, 672–675. https://doi.org/10.1038/d41586-023-02980-0

Wiener, N. (1965). *Cybernetics: Or control and communication in the animal and the machine (Second)*. MIT Press.

Williams, R. (2023, June). The people paid to train AI are outsourcing their work… to AI. *MIT Technology Review*. Retrieved from https://www.technologyreview.com/2023/06/22/1075405/the-people-paid-to-train-ai-are-outsourcing-their-work-to-ai/

Wong, B., & Bottoff, C. (2023). *Top social media statistics and trends of 2023*. Forbes Advisor. Retrieved from https://www.forbes.com/advisor/business/social-media-statistics/

World Economic Forum. (2023). *Jobs of tomorrow: Large language models and jobs*. Retrieved from https://www3.weforum.org/docs/WEF_Jobs_of_Tomorrow_Generative_AI_2023.pdf

Gary S. Metcalf is a principal of InterConnections LLC, coaching executive leaders and consulting on human resources. He is a Past-President and Trustee of the International Society for the Systems Sciences, and was previously President of the International Federation for Systems Research. Book series that he has edited include Translational System Sciences (Springer Japan), and IFSR Systems Sciences and Systems Engineering (Springer USA). Appointments have included Professor of Leadership and Management at Saybrook University, and Distinguished Lecturer at Sullivan University. He works in Ashland, Kentucky and Atlanta, Georgia.

Chapter 2
The Complexity of Sustainable Innovation, Transitional Impacts of Industry 4.0 to 5.0 for Our Societies: Circular Society Exploring the Systemic Nexus of Socioeconomic Transitions

Manuel Morales, Susu Nousala, and Morteza Ghobakhloo

Abstract In this chapter, we explore and analyze the foundations of our societal relationships, in relation to the concept of industrial transitions. When trying to understand how humans, collectively and prospectively, adapt or react to socioeconomic disruptive changes like the one Industry 5.0 is enacting, two concepts emerge. The first concept is the scope at which humans can handle complex issues. The second is the speed at which they are able to reframe their mental models, based on exposure to high-speed information exchange, that may drive thinking towards unexpected and completely different outcomes. We argue that ecosystems and their innovation capabilities are the only available mechanism we collectively have to build creativity and address the prioritizing of societal values. Innovation ecosystems can supply the testbed pathways on which better societal functions may emerge. In summary, this chapter discusses ways in which socioeconomic transitions could be dynamically applied to relevant functional systems, with a time horizon that allows enough time for evaluation of the effects (positive or negative), so that elements could be changed and/or introduced into or for the system. The circular society described in this chapter would have both intended and unintended consequences, as does any social complex adaptive system. As such, changes to any social contract defining particular interactions and relevant issues, would in turn, contribute to the fabric of preconditions and definitions of the transition between Industry 4.0 and Industry 5.0.

M. Morales (✉)
ESC Clermont Business School, Clermont-Ferrand, France
e-mail: manuel.morales@esc-clermont.fr

S. Nousala
Kaunas University of Technology (KTU), Kaunas, Lithuania

M. Ghobakhloo
Industrial Engineering and Management, Uppsala University, Uppsala, Sweden

S. Nousala et al. (eds.), *Industry 4.0 to Industry 5.0*, Translational Systems Sciences 41, https://doi.org/10.1007/978-981-99-9730-5_2

Keywords Industry 4.0 · Industry 5.0 · Circular society · Social Complex Adaptive System

2.1 Introduction

This chapter discusses some of the less obvious but important elements of the transition from Industry 4.0 to a loosely defined Industry 5.0 (Ghobakhloo et al. 2021, 2022). This particular transition has been and remains problematic because of complex and sometimes contradictory objectives set among different layers of the socioeconomic context. A rarely-acknowledged human-centricity nexus exists within the transition towards Industry 5.0, that needs to be analyzed and can no longer be ignored.

The complexities of any aspect of societal transition demand that integration be informed by a systemic approach. These unseen demands of the industrial transition of 4.0–5.0 must, by their very nature, encompass the notion of human-centricity across a board spectrum of interactions. It could be said that Industry 5.0 aims to simultaneously identify the interconnections and patterns that typify a human-centric approach between socioeconomic and environmental transitions.

The socially-constructed human-centric transition within Industry 5.0 (Ghobakhloo et al. 2021) can be described as Social Complex Adaptive System (SCAS) (Nousala et al., 2005; Nousala and Marlowe 2020). When it comes to emergent societal transitions, not all aspects can be controlled, at least not simultaneously. The many moving parts of the socioeconomic ecosystem, are multilayered complexities that constantly emerge and create new connections. A SCAS lens offers a means by which to better anticipate, adapt, and build resilience in a more participatory and balanced way.

2.2 Value Paradox and the Drive for Industry 5.0

The emergence of Industry 5.0, in the wake of Industry 4.0's rapid progress, is a testament to the sustainability and human centricity gaps of the evolving industrial landscape. Industry 4.0 initially took the industrial world by storm, driven by aggressive technological implementations that drastically improved productivity and waste reduction. However, it soon became apparent that Industry 4.0 had overlooked crucial sustainability and human-centric aspects in its design and technology. This void, marked by a lack of consideration for environmental impact, employment concerns, and ethical dilemmas, necessitated a political patch through the Industry 5.0.

Industry 4.0's primary focus on productivity often led to unintended environmental consequences, as some organizations prioritized output over sustainable practices. Increased automation, while boosting efficiency, could contribute to higher energy consumption and increased waste generation. Furthermore, the human element seemed marginalized, as the rapid automation of processes raised concerns about job displacement and the social implications of reduced human involvement. Scholars argue that Industry 4.0 has not adequately addressed the pressing need for creating new job opportunities or upskilling the workforce. Ethical considerations, particularly regarding data privacy, security, and the ethical use of AI and machine learning, have also been inadequately addressed. In line with these arguments, the controversial impacts of Industry 4.0 on social and environmental issues have indeed been extensively scrutinized and brought to the forefront through the comprehensive research efforts of the European project titled "Industry 4.0 Impact on Management Practices and Economics" (IN4ACT). This research initiative focused on assessing the multifaceted consequences of Industry 4.0 by delving into a substantial sample of 527 academic contributions. This research aimed to elucidate the nuanced interplay between Industry 4.0 and various aspects of environmental and social values across microscopic (firm level), mesoscopic (supply chain level), and macroscopic (regional level) analysis levels. As shown in Table 2.1, examining the effects of Industry 4.0 on multiple dimensions of social values provides critical insights into why the swift introduction of Industry 5.0 has become necessary.

Figure 2.1 illustrates that Industry 4.0 offers distinct societal advantages, such as enhancing workplace safety, facilitating product customization, and fostering digital literacy. However, it is also linked to adverse effects on various social values. At

Table 2.1 Four visions of circular economy, (adapted from Martin Calisto Friant et al. 2020)

		Approach to social, economic, environmental and political considerations	
		Holistic	Segmented
Technological innovation and ecological collapse	Optimistic	**Reformist Society** Capitalism mixed with behavioural and technological change, compatible with sustainability and socio-technical innovation, falls short of achieving absolute eco-economic decoupling to avert ecological collapse	**Technocentric Circular Economy** Capitalism, when aligned with sustainability and enabled by technological innovation, can facilitate eco-economic decoupling to prevent ecological collapse
	Skeptical	**Circular Society** Capitalism, in its current form, is incompatible with sustainability, and socio-technical innovation. Emergence of the Industry 5.0 as a paradigm integrating human centricity and seeking to prevent ecological collapse	**Fortress Circular Economy** While no alternative to capitalism is evident, relying solely on socio-technical innovation cannot achieve absolute eco-economic decoupling, risking ecological collapse

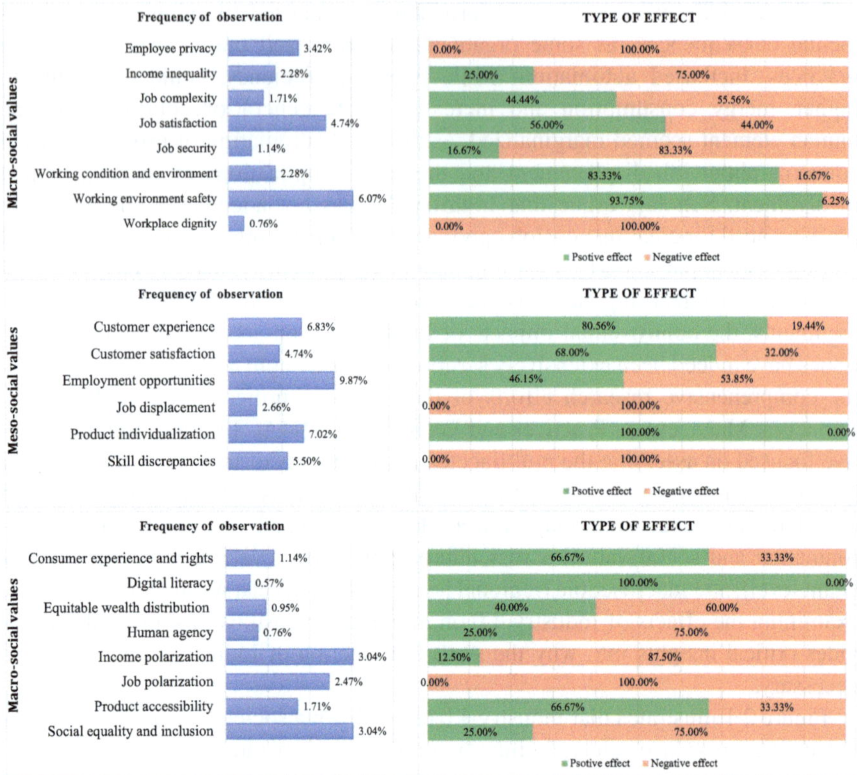

Fig. 2.1 Social implications of Industry 4.0 at various analysis levels (Adapted from Ghobakhloo et al. 2021)

the micro analysis level, the digital transformation associated with Industry 4.0 has been found to compromise employee privacy, exacerbate income inequality among workers, and erode workplace dignity. Moving to the meso analysis level, Industry 4.0 has been connected with substantial job displacement and the emergence of skill disparities within the workforce. These effects are particularly pronounced as companies adopt automation and other disruptive technologies, altering job requirements and workforce dynamics. Zooming out to the macro level, Industry 4.0 has stirred controversy due to its implications for broader societal values. Notably, it has a negative impact on social inclusion, as some groups may face barriers to access and participation in the digital economy. Additionally, there has been a risk of job polarization, where technology-driven job growth occurs primarily in high-skilled and low-skilled sectors, leading to a hollowing out of middle-skilled jobs. This phenomenon can further exacerbate income inequality. Furthermore, Industry 4.0 has posed challenges to human agency, as automated decision-making systems may limit individual control and autonomy in various aspects of life.

In response to these deficiencies, Industry 5.0 emerged as an evolutionary step that builds upon the technological foundation of Industry 4.0 while rectifying some of the problems. It places a renewed emphasis on the human element in the industrial ecosystem, fostering collaboration between humans and machines to create a more inclusive and sustainable working environment. Sustainability takes center stage in Industry 5.0, with a commitment to reducing environmental impact, optimizing resource utilization, and promoting circular economy practices. This includes the incorporation of eco-friendly technologies, energy conservation, and waste minimization. Additionally, Industry 5.0 addresses social issues by actively creating employment opportunities through technological advancements that enhance human skills and promote innovation. It champions ethical Artificial Intelligence (AI) and data usage, ensuring transparency and fairness in decision-making processes. In summary, Industry 5.0 has emerged as a response to Industry 4.0's fast-paced progress, filling the sustainability and human-centric gaps to pave the way for a more balanced and responsible industrial future.

2.3 The Iterations and Layers of Industry 4.0 to 5.0 Transition

The complex spectrum of elements within this industrial transition must also include the complexity of sustainable innovation within the socioeconomic realities. Viewed from a holistic perspective, the current industrial transition reveals a serious lack or missing gap, namely the social dimension (OECD 2013). Large corporations have had an unbalanced view regarding their behavior and have long been considered "net takers." Most firms have lacked an understanding or any real awareness of the industrial ecosystem, as evidenced and witnessed by the imbalance seen in open innovation (H. W. Chesbrough and Appleyard 2007; H. Chesbrough and Brunswicker 2013). Corporations in the USA and Europe have freely used intellectual assets developed by others without any immediate pecuniary compensation. It can also be said that these same USA and European corporations are three times more reluctant to share outbound innovation, referring to the external use of the internal knowledge, preferring to source, find, and develop new ideas from internal projects within the market (H. Chesbrough and Brunswicker 2013).

The transitional pushing actions of Industry 5.0's demand to absorb, must be reconciled with the impact of Industry 4.0 pulling actions at the micro, meso, and macro societal levels. In other words, the technological push should be shifted into a customized transitional pull exerted by the priority of societal needs. With this reconciliation-balancing act in play, the short and recent history of 5.0 emergent changes have been somewhat contradictory. To date, these transitions have grappled with the tensions of man and machine being fully integrated vs. the emergent technological engagement to enhance societal living. These explorations have embraced both ends of the spectrum, with inevitable tensions emerging, providing many more questions asked than answered.

Recent historical pathways have looked at transition from a societal change through the lens of living materials and ecological systems, as specific stages. This approach was reflected in discussions during 2020, suggesting an incremental approach of Industry 4.0 resulting in Industry 4.1, 4.2, etc. This approach and thinking seemed to suggest that the layered transition (the same layers found in systemic approaches and thinking) was not strictly linear and introduced the possibility for simultaneously creating multiple transitional approaches. From 2021, it could be suggested that 5.0 was not necessarily an Industrial Revolution but more of a policy "patch" that had specific goals across the supply chains and human-centric impacts.

Industry 5.0 has, to date, been a concept that describes the latest evolution of industrial ecosystems. It builds upon Industry 4.0, which is characterized by the implementation of advanced technologies like the Internet of Things (IoT), more general AI, machine learning, and robotics to automate innovation and production processes and increase efficiency using a socially constructed human-centric approach. Moreover, Industry 5.0 aims to combine advanced technologies with the unique abilities of human workers, such as creativity, empathy, and problem-solving skills. It emphasizes the importance of human interaction, collaboration, and innovation in the industrial context, aiming to create more sustainable, adaptive, and resilient systems.

It seems that a new theoretical framework is required for a structural transition where a deeper understanding of the drivers is able to define the transition patterns and how they could shape new industry paradigms (Ghisellini et al. 2016). According to the current scientific literature, the most relevant driver of digital transformation in supply chains is innovation, which focuses on a process approach (Marion and Fixson 2021). This process approach highlighted the systemic and dynamic aspect of self-tuning feedback (Del Giudice et al. 2021), even/or emphasizing the management limitations coming from limited resources (De Massis et al. 2018). To date, the scientific community has observed and agreed that innovation should be approached in a systemic manner (Nousala and Marlowe 2020; Iacovidou et al. 2021) because it is the best available way in which society can entail the comprehensive transformation of the entire industrial ecosystem (Kerdlap et al. 2019). These transformations encompass the integration and optimization of processes, products, and services across the value chain (Hofmann 2019; Morales and Lhuillery 2021).

These large integrations can be seen as "systemic innovation" and can comprehensively impact the industrial ecosystem, as they aim to create interconnected and intelligent systems that enable seamless information exchange, real-time data analysis, and adaptive decision-making, which implies continuous technological advancements and iterative improvements.

In turn, the combination of iterative improvements informs the self-tuning model at the macro level. It refers directly to the sectorial ability to rapidly adapt to market changes (organizational agility), learn through experimentation (organizational adaptability), and effectively balance knowledge, technological exploration, and exploitation (organizational ambidexterity). A self-tuning (Del Giudice et al. 2021) model is necessary for a sustainable transition from Industry 4.0 paradigm to 5.0. The transition pathways for a sustainable transition of the Industry 4.0 paradigm have raised the question of agility and adaptability of dynamic innovation approaches in response to rapidly evolving market demands, customer preferences, and competitive landscapes. The agility of these rapidly moving markets has entailed the development of modular methodologies, flexible production systems, and iterative design processes (De Massis et al. 2018) to foster continuous innovation and improvement through IoT devices and sensors that allow machines and systems to communicate and exchange data, facilitating real-time monitoring, predictive maintenance, and optimized resource allocation.

2.4 Adaptability and the Transition: A Deeper Dive into Meso and Macro Level Impacts

Organizational adaptability (Ivanov 2020) has been a worthy competence and outcome of the Industry 4.0 transition patterns, as it has involved the integration of systemic and dynamic innovation with technological changes. This adaptability applied to supply chains has required a holistic approach that considers the interdependencies and synergies (Mancini et al. 2021) among different technological components and innovation strategies. For instance, VINCI Digital has adopted IoT devices that were not sufficient on their own; they needed to be integrated with predictive maintenance and AI capabilities to unlock their full potential. Similarly, dynamic innovation processes should be aligned with systemic changes to ensure compatibility and coherence within the industrial ecosystem (Piezer et al. 2019).

Industry 4.0 has called for a theoretical framework that provides the required means to manage complexity in supply chains. To seek efficiency, profit, environmental sustainability, and social benefits through the interconnection of actors in the value chain, the transition must call for a diverse range of scales of analysis to be simultaneously integrated into the framework. Analyzing the supply chain at a macro level involves considering the overall structure, dynamics, and interconnections of various industries, sectors, and regions. This usually includes an assessment of the flow of goods, services, and information across the entire value chain, identifying dependencies, and understanding the broader economic and geopolitical factors that influence the supply chain.

The meso scale of analysis is crucial in understanding and optimizing value chains in Industry 4.0. The meso scale focuses on the intermediate level, examining the relationships, interactions, and dynamics between different entities within the value chain. Some key aspects of the meso scale analysis have been skill and competency upgrading, internationalization through standards and regulations, circularity added value in business models, inter-organizational relationships, risk management, data integration and interoperability, and performance measurement and metrics. By considering the meso scale of analysis, organizations gain insights into the value chain's interdependencies, collaboration opportunities, and risks. This understanding allows for identifying areas for optimization, fostering more robust partnerships, enhancing data interoperability, and engaging symbiotic relationships to improve overall performance and competitiveness (Bennich et al. 2021; de Oliveira et al. 2018).

Analyzing the industrial supply chains at a micro-level involves examining the operations, processes, and interactions of individual actors within the value chain. This includes assessing the efficiency and effectiveness of production processes, logistics operations, inventory management, and distribution channels. Micro-level analysis enables identifying bottlenecks, optimizing workflows, and improving resource allocation.

Overall, transition patterns in Industry 4.0 encompass the integration of systemic and dynamic innovations among production and organizational processes. These integrations enable industries to effectively leverage advanced technologies, transform operations, and adapt to changing market dynamics. By embracing these transition patterns (Hazen et al. 2021), industries can enhance their production and consumption behavior, leading to increased efficiency, sustainability, and competitiveness.

There has been a lack of research interest in the social dimension of the Industry 5.0 transition (Ghobakhloo et al. 2022). The few existing analyses on social indicators for Industry 4.0 take place at the national level; however, if society aims to build a socially constructed human-centered transition paradigm for Industry 5.0, the social dimension of this transition needs to be strategically prioritized. As the outcome of a preliminary literature review, we have identified three main drivers that influence the social dimension of the Industry 5.0 transition.

The first reason the social dimension of Industry 4.0 lags behind is the complexity of implementing a multidisciplinary approach that combines insights from engineering, computer science, economics, sociology, and other fields (Hannon 2020) needed to address complex social issues.

The second reason is that there is no agreement among the scientific community regarding estimations and measures of social impacts and outcomes (Ghobakhloo et al. 2021; Martinez-Hernandez et al. 2017). Nevertheless, some relevant, although partial, methods for assessing the progress of Industry 4.0 through 5.0 have been constructed, like the Comprehensive Evaluation Frameworks (CEF), systems thinking analysis, long-term integration, and a robust and transparent data analysis monitoring (Morales et al. 2021). Even when those assessing methods could be improved, they provide the first stage for a more comprehensive, sustainable, transparent, and accountable evaluation process, enabling informed decision-making and maximizing the overall positive impact of these technologies. For example, (Huppes et al. 2017) provided a systemic design for long-term climate policy implementation in the European Union using a CEF.

Third and last, the lack of funding and resources available for social research on the Industry 4.0 transition, particularly in comparison to technological or economic research, has been responsible for the lack of interest or awareness among policy-makers, the business sector, and the general public (Abad-Segura et al. 2020). Overall, the lack of political interest in the social dimension of Industry 5.0 has been accentuated because of the reduced funds and resources dedicated to analyzing the social challenges that can make this paradigm transition possible. However, current and newly designed research efforts are underway to address this gap.

It has become clear that Industry 5.0 needs a systemic and comprehensive integration of the economic, technological, environmental, political, and social dimensions of the transition (Saidani et al. 2021). This imbalance in the information generated at different levels and dimensions is one reason that limits the implementation of a systemic and comprehensive framework, which would be capable of depicting the causal effects of the various drivers involved, thus providing access to the bigger picture to understand a broader socioeconomic and environmental transition.

The social transition problems involved in Industry 5.0 have a spin-off effect within the environmental crisis, which are largely attributed to social structural impacts like mass production, unsustainable production and consumption patterns, and an increase in material consumption per capita, particularly in developed countries leading to ecological destruction. While innovation (OECD 2013) is often associated with high-tech advancements, it also encompasses many other technological developments, including low-tech and eco-efficient solutions. To truly understand the influence of social structures in the socio-environmental crisis, we need to move beyond simplistic assumptions that equate economic growth with the creation of well-being (Dzhengiz et al. 2023). Instead, we should adopt a more nuanced and comprehensive approach that considers the broader socio-environmental impacts of technological advancements and embraces alternative models that promote sustainability and justice. The potential negative impacts of technological changes can be overlooked, even when they are meant to address environmental concerns, such as in the Circular Society or the United Nation's Sustainable Development Goals. For instance, eco-design has been recognized for extending the lifetime of materials, thereby reducing their overall environmental impact. However, in certain cases, such as the housing sector, products designed for longevity may become outdated faster due to the rapid pace of technological progress. As a result, eco-design may not always have a purely positive impact and can lead to unforeseen negative consequences.

While innovation (Dooley and Van De Ven 1999) is often viewed as a positive force, it would be a mistake to assume that all types of innovation are beneficial. Unfortunately, the current scientific literature struggles to differentiate between different types of innovation, let alone addressing their complexity. This is particularly problematic in the context of unforeseen disruptions, such as the COVID-19 pandemic or geopolitical conflicts, which can have significant impacts on socioeconomic and environmental transitions.

2.5 Transitions and Impact of Creative Systemic Preconditions Towards Necessary Human-centered Frameworks

Regarding the complexities of Industry 4.0 transitions, society needs to invest in systemic and long-term tools as a means to tackle the impact of the risk of unbalanced calculation and measurement between different scales of analysis. Indeed, some identified strategies to avoid biases in analyzing the transition processes are a comprehensive evaluation, multi-stakeholder engagement, long-term shift, robust data collection and analysis, and transparency and accountability.

The CEF needs to consider multiple dimensions of benefits, including economic, environmental, technological, and social aspects. This framework should incorporate relevant key performance indicators (KPIs) and metrics to assess the impact of disruptive technologies on various stakeholders and the overall value chain. By adopting a holistic approach, it is possible to avoid narrow or biased calculations and ensure more balanced benefits and assessment. Moreover, integrating multi-stakeholder engagement in the evaluation and decision-making processes is required if the assessments seek to gain a more comprehensive understanding of the potential benefits and risks associated with implementing disruptive technologies. The multi-stakeholder analysis needs to include representatives from different departments within the organization, suppliers, customers, industry associations, NGOs, and relevant experts. This engagement also assists in identifying and addressing any potential biases or blind spots in the benefit calculations.

To address the biases and blind spots of complex interconnected systems, models need to account for both short-term and long-term consequences when assessing the benefits. While disruptive technologies may offer significant long-term advantages, we cannot eliminate the short-term challenges because they are essential regarding the impact on implementation costs. The current time frame for economic and strategic decisions in private and public institutions is two years, according to the 2013 global survey of over 1000 board members and C-suite executives, conducted by McKinsey & Co., and the Canada Pension Plan Investment Board (CPPIB) (De Massis et al. 2018). By thoroughly analyzing both time horizons, calculation models can better evaluate the overall balance of benefits and make informed decisions.

To achieve a tangible improvement in the calculation, the data used for analysis and monitoring should be robust and transparent, and well-identified institutions or public actors should be accountable for their performance. The collection and analysis of reliable and relevant data may involve conducting surveys, interviews, and data collection from various sources among public and private actors as well as civil society. Robust data analysis techniques, such as statistical analysis, modeling, and simulation, can help quantify and compare the benefits across different scenarios, enabling a more balanced assessment. The data management process must implement a system for continuous monitoring and review of the benefits derived from the disruptive technologies. This includes regularly tracking the performance metrics, reassessing the benefits, and making necessary adjustments.

Participatory, open decision-making processes should clearly set the assumptions under which they run the analysis, methodologies, and limitations. Additionally, the rigor of the collected data and decisions helps build trust, allowing stakeholders to provide helpful feedback and contribute to refining the calculations. Establishing accountability mechanisms ensures that calculations will be periodically reviewed and validated to minimize unbalanced assessments.

The supply chains must also be analyzed from a social perspective, considering their impacts on workers, communities, and society. The social dimension includes assessing factors such as labor conditions, worker health and safety, diversity and inclusion, ethical sourcing, and community engagement. Supply chain analysis should incorporate social responsibility and strive for fair and ethical practices throughout the value chain. The social dimension in the supply chain also considers the interests of the stakeholders involved in the value chain. This includes collaborating with suppliers, customers, regulators, NGOs, and other relevant parties. Stakeholder engagement enables a comprehensive understanding of the challenges, opportunities, and trade-offs associated with seeking efficiency, profit, and sustainability in the supply chain.

With all the elements involved in the social dimension, it is important to allow the system's interconnection recognition. However, a systemic and creative approach can better support social transitions because it is better equipped to address complex and interconnected problems more systemically and innovatively (de Jesus et al. 2019). Social transitions, such as those caused by Industry 5.0, often involve multiple stakeholders and competing interests. A systemic approach can help to understand these challenges by analyzing the underlying systems and structures that contribute to them. This can help to identify key drivers where interventions can have the greatest expected and emergent impact, and to design interventions that are more effective and sustainable over the long term. Indeed, a systemic and creative approach can also be valuable in social transition studies because it can help to generate new ideas and solutions that may not have been considered. This can be especially important when traditional approaches have failed to produce meaningful change or have led to unintended consequences. A creative approach can help to challenge assumptions, break down silos, and promote collaboration and co-creation among stakeholders (Barreiro-Gen and Lozano 2020). Furthermore, a systemic and creative approach can help promote innovation and experimentation, which is essential for successful social transitions. It can help to put into action the environmental agenda, where public and private stakeholders feel empowered to try new approaches, learn from failures, and adapt strategies as needed. Overall, a systemic and creative approach can better support social transitions by helping to address complex and interconnected problems, generating new ideas and solutions, and promoting innovation.

The unseen systemic processes are by their nature, hidden within the socially constructed human-centric approach of Industry 5.0. Those systemic processes are more easily observed at the level of ecological communities (both non-human and human), serving as an analogy of what is currently happening in the Industry 5.0 socio-environmental structure. With regards to potential and future frameworks,

Complex Adaptive Systems (CAS) (Martín-Gómez et al. 2019) as well as the Social Complex Adaptive Systems (SCAS) (Nousala et al. 2005; Nousala 2009) contribute to the human-centric approach for Industry 5.0. These approaches also impact evolutionary preconditions (Nousala et al. 2021), which underpin the well-being of our societies. It is important to emphasize the potential, acknowledge the preconditions, and explore what is happening before these processes begin, and why this is important. Both adaptive systems refer to the ever-evolving equilibrium that any ecological (biological) community unknowingly strives for, meaning that the balance between sustaining emergent processes and the consequences of its constraints are both positive and negative, internal and external. Herein lies the potential that can lead to the necessary.

From the point of view of sustainability, or the ability to sustain, ecological communities (human societies included), need to be flexible about the idea of reaching a point of sustained equilibrium when approached through complexity and a systemic lens, as socially constructed human-centric paradigms are by nature, dynamic. Therefore, the preposition of preconditions (Nousala et al. 2021) changing according to the time and place they are observed makes this difficult to embrace, yet needs acknowledgment. The *complex connections hidden within the system* should be viewed as a means of translating a representation for mutual understanding across multiple scales (Nousala and Hall 2008). For instance, this mirroring effect could be viewed as the actions between multiple layers, and resembles the motion between chess pieces within a 3D chessboard. These in-between, multilayered actions have unknowable or unintended consequences, with perhaps the exception of the direct actors, and usually neither of them because of an oversimplified understanding of the systems (Carayannis and Campbell 2012).

In the socially constructed human-centric paradigm, the *creative systemic process* (Freire 2020) emerges over the recognition of the system interrelations; therefore, the preconditions offer extended historical views towards descriptors that add multiple layers to the subjective creative process within any ecological (or biological) community. The development of sustainable energy systems is a clear example of an evolutionary societal upgrade relying systemically on the intentions that came before them. Over the past few decades, societies worldwide have recognized the need to shift from fossil fuel-based energy sources to cleaner and more sustainable alternatives. This evolutionary transition is rooted in mitigating climate change, reducing environmental impact, and ensuring long-term energy security. In this instance, the preconditions triggered a transition and increased awareness of the negative consequences of carbon emissions and the importance of preserving natural resources. Therefore, preconditions' role in developing and adopting renewable energy technologies were essential. Moreover, this evolutionary transition has led to the integration of smart grid systems, energy storage technologies, and decentralized energy generation, an example of the potential and the necessary.

By recognizing and acknowledging the role of preconditions (Nousala et al. 2021), societies have been able to transition towards more sustainable, resilient, and human-centered systems, as in the case of Industry 5.0. Societal evolution usually disregards the creative dynamics at play because they are backstage and are not usually a visible part of the current processes, meaning, that what we are focused on usually determines what we miss. That said, focusing on the dynamic processes and their societal preconditioned relationships are not mutually exclusive. Since these processes are cyclical and longitudinal by nature, the concept of never-ending creative cycles continues to emerge.

2.6 Rapid Changes in Industry 5.0 Trigger Even More Complexities Within Systems

In Industry 5.0, workers and machines are expected to be working together in a symbiotic relationship (Shi et al. 2010), through augmented skills, competencies, and performance (Raisch and Krakowski 2021). Machines can handle repetitive and dangerous tasks, while humans focus on tasks that require creativity, critical thinking, and emotional intelligence. Overall, Industry 5.0 represents a shift towards a more human-centric and environmentally-conscious approach to society while still harnessing the power of advanced technologies.

The rapid pace of technological change (Geels and Schot 2007) in Industry 5.0 means that businesses need to adapt and evolve their practices to remain constantly competitive. This can be challenging as new technologies and practices are continually being developed and refined. However, the benefits of Industry 5.0, such as increased efficiency, productivity, and customization, usually make the transitions worth pursuing. Businesses implementing Industry 5.0 technologies and practices can gain a competitive advantage, improve customer satisfaction, and reduce environmental impact. To navigate the transition to Industry 5.0, businesses must adopt a proactive approach, invest in new technologies, and prioritize collaboration and innovation. They also need to develop a clear vision and transition strategies seeking to adapt and change their production and consumption behavior as needed.

The current industrial revolution as a complex adaptive system, embedded in a rapidly evolving field, has some of the available means to deal with its complexity and fast-speed changes, as listed in the following four points:

1. Design thinking and systems thinking have involved a holistic and iterative problem-solving approach, considering the interdependencies between different drivers. By adopting these approaches, stakeholders can better understand the complexity of the socioeconomic and environmental transition and identify opportunities for innovation (Dooley and Van De Ven 1999).
2. Collaboration and partnerships among stakeholders can help build a shared understanding of the challenges and opportunities in Industry 5.0 and facilitate the development of innovative solutions that address these challenges.
3. Policy and regulation (Ayres and Ayres 2002) can be critical for promoting the human-centric and environmentally conscious Industry 5.0 transition, by setting targets and standards, creating incentives for innovative practices, and establishing frameworks for collaboration and coordination among stakeholders.

4. Education and awareness-raising initiatives can help build public support for Industry 5.0 ethical concerns and promote scientific decisions among consumers, businesses, and policymakers.

Overall, dealing with the SCAS exposed rapid changes requires a multidisciplinary and collaborative approach that leverages the four previously mentioned means and strategies. By adopting these means, stakeholders can better understand the challenges and opportunities that Industry 5.0 could deliver to society as it seeks to create a more sustainable and resilient systems transition. The main difference between Industry 5.0 and the previous industrial revolutions lies in their focus and objectives. The first three industrial revolutions (mechanization, mass production, and automation) aimed to increase efficiency and productivity using machines and new production methods (Ghobakhloo et al. 2021). Industry 5.0, as framed by the European Commission, acknowledges the negative impact of previous industrial revolutions on the environment and society, and strives to create more responsible and sustainable practices. It values ethical production methods and waste reduction and supports local communities.

2.7 Exploration of Transition Speed Through Value Chain Interconnections at Circular Economy

In addition to the economic dimension, Industry 5.0 needs to address environmental and social dimensions by developing decision-making frameworks that explicitly consider socio-environmental criteria alongside economic and technological factors. This involves incorporating environmental impact assessments, cost-benefit analyses, and sustainability indicators into decision-making. By integrating environmental considerations into the decision-making framework, organizations can ensure that Industry 5.0 initiatives can handle complexity and align with sustainability goals and environmentally conscious practices. The creativity process and the systemic approach allow organizations to learn from experiences, including the transition patterns to address unintended consequences and optimize sustainability outcomes over time.

The Industry 4.0 transition towards 5.0 has included the circularity principles into a more human-centric socioeconomic model. However, not all the assumptions on which the concept of circular economy has been built fit into the Industry 5.0 theory. A typology of discourses on circular economy presents four visions (Martin Calisto Friant et al. 2020). A matrix categorizes the visions along dimensions of (1) approaches to social, economic, environmental and political considerations, and (2) technological innovation and ecological collapse is shown in Table 2.1.

A holistic-optimistic discourse of *Reformist Society* envisions capitalism mixed with behavioural and technological change, compatible with sustainability and socio-technical innovation, falling short of achieving absolute eco-economic decoupling to avert ecological collapse.

A segmented-optimistic discourse of *Technocentric Circular Economy* envisions a capitalistic approach, aligned with sustainability and enabled by technological innovation, capable of facilitating eco-economic decoupling to prevent ecological collapse.

A segmented-holistic discourse of *Fortress Circular Economy* envisions no alternative to capitalism, then relying solely on socio-technical innovation that cannot achieve absolute eco-economic decoupling, risking ecological collapse.

Finally, a skeptical-wholistic discourse of *Circular Society* envisions capitalism in its current form as incompatible with sustainability, implying that socio-technical innovation alone cannot achieve absolute eco-economic decoupling to prevent ecological collapse.

Only the Circular Society (CS) vision integrates the circular economy principle of slowing, within a human-centric and sustainable paradigm of Industry 5.0. The CS vision aims to extend product lifecycles and reduce overconsumption patterns, thereby reducing the need for continuous growth and resource extraction. It aligns with the notion of prioritizing well-being over endless economic expansion, emphasizing the need for a steady-state economy within ecological limits.

Entailing the CS vision by the Industry 5.0 transition highlights the challenge of achieving stability through socioeconomic and environmental transitions, due to complexity and rapidity of changes. CS is a paradigm shift. It aims to keep resources in the economic system for as long as possible by closing, extending, intensifying, slowing, and making long-lasting products (Blomsma 2018), towards more sustainable, resilient, and human-centric production and consumption. The transition to a CS vision involves significant changes to traditional linear production models, which can be challenging to implement. The complexities of multiple, interconnected layers in the CS vision and Industry 5.0 are only visible through longitudinal data analysis. These interactions critically underpin collaboration and coordination between different stakeholders.

One of the unquestioned risks for coordination among stakeholders is the potential for over-concentration of power and resources in the hands of a few large players. Hindering competition and innovation approaches monopolistic behavior, where a small group of stakeholders controls key resources or technologies, and can set prices or dictate terms to other players in the market. Without transparency in coordination, there is a risk that some stakeholders may seek to gain an unfair advantage over others. For example, if a small group of stakeholders colludes to control a market of recycled materials, they may be able to set prices and terms that are disadvantageous for clients, consumers, and other players in the market.

Organizations can adopt a territorial approach with contextual analysis and comprehensive multidimensional decision-making frameworks. At the scale of local communities, organizational leaders have more credibility to claim effective actions and promote sustainable decisions fostering environmental stewardship through implementing Industry 5.0 principles.

CS and Industry 5.0 share a system of processes and framework with SCAS that continues to evolve. This nexus of creative behavioral patterns can underpin the environmental and socioeconomic dimensions of any human-centric, sustainable, and resilient system. In a practical sense, the design and innovation of the R&D activities, product industrialization, production, and supply chain management (Morana 2013) have usually improved through the lens of a systemic approach. Innovation, when understood as a SCAS, can influence understanding of the preconditions and resulting behavioral patterns (Nousala et al. 2021; Nousala and Marlowe 2020).

The speed of change required to implement a circular economy society can be challenging for businesses to manage. Adopting circular economy practices often involves significant investment in new technologies and infrastructure, as well as organizational changes in processes and supply chains. Rapid changes that might trigger imbalances and increase risks of monopolistic behavior and power concentration in the transition to a circular economy can be deterred through transparency, collaboration, and competition. This can be done by ensuring an open and inclusive coordination process, where all stakeholders have an equal voice and opportunity to participate (Palafox-Alcantar et al. 2020). It is also important to promote a level playing field by ensuring that all stakeholders have access to key resources, such as recycled materials or digital technologies, on fair and equitable terms. Society must play an important role in enforcing social and environmental values to engage in more equitable competition and prevent monopolistic behavior by enforcing anti-trust laws and promoting fair and sustainable competition as in non-profit organizations.

Overall, the complexity and speed of transitions required for Industry 5.0 to be embedded in a Circular Society has emerged as a complex and systemic challenge (Peponi and Morgado 2021). However, the benefits of a circular economy, such as reduced waste, increased resource efficiency, and improved environmental sustainability, propose a worthwhile and necessary transition. Businesses that adopt a transparent, findable, accessible, interoperable, and reusable (FAIR) data management system are able to facilitate collaboration and accelerate the circular economy transition, gaining competitive advantage for a more sustainable future. Circular society emerges as a promising socioeconomic and environmental collective innovation transition due to its potential to reduce resource consumption, waste generation, and environmental impact while also bringing economic benefits and stimulating innovation.

2.8 Two Test Bed Case Study Examples

To illustrate more dynamic approach, two case studies are discussed: (1) a French bio-refinery, and (2) an European digital traceability implementation.

The bio-based French economy case is a human-centric and systemic analysis (Ministry of Agriculture, Agrifood and Forestry 2016). The study is significant, representing 936,000 jobs with a total turnover of 78.4 billion euros (Ministry of Agriculture, Agrifood and Forestry 2016), with a national emphasis, scope and relevance to outcomes. The operation is the French biorefinery ecosystem located in the Pomacle-Bazancourt region. This biorefinery is an exemplar of an industrial symbiosis, with by-products exchanged across innovation ecosystem actors (Morales et al. 2022). Industrial symbiosis deals with the complexity of territorial governance through a more human-centric alternative to collectively making decisions, based on the functions that best respond to the needs of the whole. Industrial symbiosis reveals the impact of a circular society vision on Industry 5.0. The ecosystem is composed of ten actors, including Vivescia/Bletanol, Cristal Union, Cristanol, Chamtor, Givaudan Active Beauty, Wheatoleo, Air Liquide, European de biomasse, the Industrial research center (ARD), and the European Biotechnology and Bioeconomy academic research center (CEBB) (Domenech et al. 2019). Green sugar juice and syrups go across the production chain through crystallization or distillation in the biorefinery, resulting in sugar, alcohol, and bioethanol as the main products.

This agro-industrial innovation ecosystem emerged as a functional testbed of circular society, with SCAS linkages and causal interconnections. It is also an exemplar of a human-centric innovative ecosystem through the collective reappropriating of the social investment in research and innovation decisions. The systems transition was better understood, handling well the complexity of multiple stakeholders' interconnections.

The EU Digital Product Passport initiative implemented by Worldline, Ltd., is a second case for discussion. This initiative sought to exemplify how digital traceability could enable data collection throughout the value chain, and to support and trigger more human-centric and sustainable transitions to boost the circular society. As a testbed for circular society, the digital innovation ecosystems have raised implications of all the stakeholders involved in the value chains. Aims include the deterrence of illicit trades, unethical production practices, fragile supply chains, and environmental impacts, as well as non-human-centric decisions based on fast-track technological changes. The Digital Product Passport shows how traceability can cater to consumer transparency and quality assurance requirements. Innovation ecosystems can build an institutional architecture according to social and political preconditions, and potentially enabling the securing of the skills and competencies required for a systemic human-centric governance of Industry 5.0.

2.9 Innovation Ecosystems Emerging in the Circular Societies as a Testbed for Societal Functions

Current innovation approaches in value chains (VC) are based on linear thinking methodologies that cannot integrate the complexity of the iterative feedback effect, necessary for the circular economy (CE) paradigm to integrate. Therefore, overly-simplistic assumptions claiming that every innovation (OECD 2013) increase will trigger positive circularity is not sufficient to entail circular business models (Huerta Morales 2020; Lewandowski 2016) and industrial ecosystems settled within a circular society framework (Morales et al. 2021). A more integrated and nuanced approach is needed to fully address the challenges and opportunities of circular innovation.

Within the circular society paradigm, innovation (de Jesus et al. 2018) must be approached differently, shedding light on value chains and industrial ecosystems as the mechanisms that support necessary societal functions. This requires analyzing innovation to understand how resources, materials, and knowledge flows occur within a Circular Manufacturing System (CMS). To fully understand and harness the potential of industrial symbiosis, we must take into account the complex interactions and inter-dependencies within the CMS, and develop strategies that promote sustainability, circularity, and resilience (Holling 1973) across the entire value chain. Industrial symbiosis is defined here as a process of multi-stakeholder cooperation that seeks to enhance circularity in a territory (Diemer and Morales 2016). In the service of enhancing the circularity of a territory, most policy agendas are built on a mix of environmental efficiency and resilience to shocks. Efficiency affects the production and distribution of technologies (e.g., zero waste, minimum carbon footprint). Resilience involves the political, economic, and natural environments. Industrial symbiosis principles are: (1) The waste of one firm becomes the input of another; (2) There are economic and environmental benefits; and (3) There is interdependence between different partners.

Through definitions in the theoretical analysis of the circular economy (Kirchherr et al. 2017), the social side of the circular economy has been seen as left behind. Industrial symbiosis, herein considered as an innovation ecosystem example, emphasizes the extending loop principle of circularity, which includes substance cascading, waste to energy conversion, down-cycling, or symbiosis in the same or different value chains and through multiple lifecycles (Roci et al. 2022). The social dimension of circular economy is not only a question of collective organization but offers enormous governance possibilities in terms of skills and competencies upgrading, training of human resources, R&D methodologies and strategies adaptation, job creation, and justice in the consumption of raw materials. Industrial symbiosis appears to be at the heart of the transition to a circular society investing in skills upgrading.

When we talk about Circular Society in the Industry 5.0 transition, industrial symbiosis emerges as the ideal private-public arena to develop innovation ecosystems (Bennich et al. 2021) across the value chain scale where organizations, individuals, and resources come together to foster innovation and create new products, services, and processes. Industrial symbiosis is characterized by a high level of collaboration, knowledge sharing, and experimentation, and plays a critical role in driving sustainability, resilience, and competitiveness. Innovation ecosystems significantly impact the socioeconomic relationships that govern the speed of socioeconomic transitions. By fostering collaboration and knowledge sharing, these ecosystems help to break down silos of knowledge between industries and create new opportunities for cross-sectoral collaboration. This, in turn, helps to drive innovation and accelerate the pace of technological change. However, a fast pace of technological change has some inherent risks related to human adaptation and mismanagement of technologically pushed objectives.

Innovation ecosystems provide a collaborative and supportive environment for creativity (Tsujimoto et al. 2017). These ecosystems help to ensure that the benefits of technological change are widely shared, and that the transitions to new industrial paradigms and circular business models will be as smooth and inclusive as possible. For instance, the digital product passport plays a critical role in shaping socioeconomic relationships that seek to create the mechanisms and tools to respond to the fast-speed traceability needs imposed by industry. Rapid transitions in the industry need to be evaluated through real-time information, open innovation, collaboration, knowledge sharing, and even efficiency and performance information to show evidence of the pervasive effects of non-human-centered fast-speed transitions, which will be able to slow down or even cancel them. Therefore, these innovation ecosystems help to create a more inclusive and sustainable economy that benefits everyone.

The social implications of circularity (M Calisto Friant et al. 2021) on biophysical, monetary, human resources, and information flows are observed and empirically validated using the figure of innovation ecosystems. The social innovations recognized in the circular society are empirically observed in the skills upgrading and training of human resources, stakeholders' participatory decision processes, collaborative strategies like industrial symbiosis, and the R&D adaptation to fast-speed changes. Systemic circular society transitions in the industrial symbiosis face increased high-speed changes, bringing increased complexity to analyzing societal impacts.

Engaging in a participatory decision-making process involving society, the private sector, and the public requires a coherent systemic and dynamic approach. The scientific literature claims that collaborative platforms (Kerdlap et al. 2019; Robert et al. 2020) that bring together representatives from various sectors, including government agencies, businesses, civil society organizations, and academia, are required to provide spaces for dialogue, knowledge sharing, and co-creation of solutions. By fostering collaboration and active participation, diverse perspectives and expertise can be integrated into the decision-making process, claiming for shared vision and goals. Establishing a common understanding of the desired future makes it easier to align regulations, policies, and strategies toward achieving those goals.

Indeed, governance in industrial ecosystems is collectively constructed using systemic approaches to knowledge processes. Value is frequently extracted from innovation ecosystems like industrial symbiosis because the risks of research and innovation activities are socialized, but the rewards thereof are privately appropriated. Therefore, to regulate innovation ecosystems behavior towards achieving more sustainable, circular and resilient governance, the political and social narratives need to be included in the definition of fundamental values. The current scientific literature recognizes regulations, policies, and business strategies as the mechanisms required to shift the production and consumption process (Hosseini-Motlagh et al. 2020; Geldermans 2016). Adaptive governance (supported by SCAS), aims for policy integration and alignment to fulfill human-centric decisions, as evidenced by the environment-water-energy-food nexus described by (Laurens et al.

2017; Chen et al. 2020). Innovation ecosystems with a territorial approach are needed to break down silos and foster coordination among government agencies responsible for regulations and policies relevant to the topic at hand.

Finally, effective communication and transparency throughout the decision-making process must transparently engage stakeholders by providing accessible and understandable information. Innovation ecosystems should clearly communicate the rationale behind decisions, trade-offs, and expected outcomes. Transparency and accountability of the decision-making process and the collected data seek to foster an environment of trust by keeping stakeholders informed and engaged and actively addressing their concerns and feedback. Indeed, the implementation of the Industry 5.0 change should promote education and awareness among stakeholders about the systemic and dynamic nature of the challenges.

2.10 In Summary, the Intended and Unintended Consequences of SCAS Entail the Transitions Between Industry 4.0 and 5.0

It could be argued that sustainable supply at the regional macro level has not been successful. This is precisely where societal issues have failed in Industry 4.0, bringing about the policy patch discussions of 2021. Again, these tensions between levels and layers have brought about broader questions about relationships between various actors and their regions. To date, the less explored areas between Japan's Society 5.0 and the European Union's Industry 5.0 need better definitions that have yet to emerge. This lack of definition speaks directly to the human-centric question of what is really meant by this term, the human-centric definition, between different regions and their actors. This also leads to the next question of disruptive technologies, and 5.0's abilities to tackle and address societal impacts with the necessary awareness. It is simply not possible to know what we do not know, an obvious statement but one that, again, speaks to the human-centric definition question.

The speed at which the technological transitions demand societal structures poses yet another question of the cyclical and necessary feedback loops required for societal development and the emergence of their respective SCAS. Simply put, what are the significant developmental impacts on these systemic feedback loops within our societies? Given that the 5.0-definition boundary has yet to be clarified, the question of 5.0 being merely a policy patch seems have already been superseded by the speed of the technological development and impact of AI. The issue and tensions of how, why, what, and where a SCAS learns, develops, and evolves do not neatly follow linear transitional timelines, but instead evolve systemically, regardless of who, why or what actors may or may not be involved. This line of questioning again loops, follows, and leads back to what human-centric involvement is and what approaches support humans within our societal spheres. How will our governments and all the actors, that make up our societies strive for transparency whilst delivering sustainable governance for the long term? This is indeed a question to be grappled with and one that is complex, so it must be approached via systemic thinking. This said, if AI continues to develop algorithms within algorithms, the question of what is human-centric may become moot since algorithms, for the sake of its algorithms, are not something that is connected to humans any longer and do not necessarily serve or support the particular human-centric approach.

That said, the preconditions on all levels will continue to evolve, and acknowledgment of human creativity remains valid and necessary to analyze the complex circular society, paving the way toward the Industry 5.0 transition. This type of approach would improve the societal understanding of the human-driven condition, to source enhancement rather than remaining a hidden spring of potential without any clear background. Without acknowledging the source of the information, data, and knowledge can easily become fragmented and disconnected from societal values. Thus, even when in certain circles we recognize the prominence of the outcomes regardless of the means and processes that drive us there, this is a point worth mentioning when defining what human-centered foundations are.

For instance, the boundaries of human-centric decisions become fuzzy when data, information, and knowledge are considered interchangeable due to AI's entrance into the playground. It was debatable before, but an argument can be made that this is now the case. Whilst ChatGPT, for example, has the possibility to blur our previous definitions, it is worth considering that this is a precondition in the making. The preconditions set up the fundamental question of why, what, and how ontology and epistemology should remain in the human-centric process. This question is not new. Societies have been creating and supporting ways of maintaining knowledge bases for centuries, mostly paper-based, but other forms of data and records also exist. With the introduction of our machine-readable data and information, public institutions have struggled over many decades to maintain our public records. The loss of working devices meant the loss of data and information. How, for example, can ChatGPT address this? Can it be addressed, or will it not be seen as necessary?

These questions are part of the preconditions evolving now, and with it, there is the question of knowledge provenance and origins. Is it of value from a societal perspective or not? Do we still value or need to validate our threads of knowledge and providence for what is being communicated to each other and our societies as a whole?

Paraphrasing Albert Einstein: "The same level of thinking that created the problem, won't solve the problem." Questioning the validity of previous economic assumptions is crucial if society seeks to counter the production and consumption patterns that have contributed to the current social and environmental crisis. The current crisis highlights the limitations and negative consequences of certain economic paradigms and assumptions. Some of the assumptions that we have found to be important are:

1. Sustainability: The current social and environmental crisis is, to a significant extent, a result of unsustainable production and consumption patterns driven by

economic assumptions that prioritize endless growth, resource exploitation, and short-term profit. By questioning these assumptions, society can challenge the notion that economic growth should always take precedence over environmental sustainability and societal well-being.

2. Externalities and Systemic Issues: Many traditional economic assumptions fail to adequately account for externalities and socialize the rewards resulting from the socialized risks of research and innovation benefiting subventions that are rarely internalized by the market. These externalities include environmental degradation, social inequalities, disruptive innovations, and the depletion of natural resources, among others. By questioning previous economic assumptions, society can seek to address these systemic issues and develop economic models.
3. Alternative Metrics of Success: Conventional economic assumptions often prioritize GDP growth as the primary indicator of success, neglecting other important dimensions of well-being such as social equity, health, and environmental quality. By questioning these assumptions, society can explore alternative metrics of success that incorporate a broader range of factors, including measures of social progress, ecological footprint, and the well-being of future generations.
4. Collaborative and Participatory Decision-making: Society can foster more inclusive and participatory processes by questioning mainstream top-down decision-making methods. Holistic and participatory processes encourage the engagement of diverse stakeholders, including communities, civil society organizations, and marginalized groups, in shaping economic policies and strategies. This ensures that a wider range of perspectives and values are taken into account, leading to more equitable and sustainable outcomes.

Overall, questioning the validity of previous economic assumptions is essential for rethinking and turning into a Circular society that uses Industry 5.0 paradigms to tackle the current social and environmental crisis through human-centered decisions to fulfill fundamental human needs. Circular society aims to pave the way for more sustainable and inclusive economic models that prioritize the well-being of people and the planet.

References

Abad-Segura, E., Morales, M. E., Cortés-García, F. J., & Belmonte-Ureña, L. J. (2020). Industrial processes management for a sustainable society: Global research analysis. *Processes, 8*(5), 631. https://doi.org/10.3390/PR8050631

Ayres, R. U., & Ayres, L. (2002). *A handbook of industrial ecology*. Edward Elgar Pub.

Barreiro-Gen, M., & Lozano, R. (2020). How circular is the circular economy? Analysing the implementation of circular economy in organisations. *Business Strategy and the Environment, 29*(8), 3484–3494. https://doi.org/10.1002/bse.2590

Bennich, T., Belyazid, S., Stjernquist, I., Diemer, A., Seifollahi-Aghmiuni, S., & Kalantari, Z. (2021, February) The bio-based economy, 2030 agenda, and strong sustainability—A regional-scale assessment of sustainability goal interactions. *Journal of Cleaner Production, 283*. https://doi.org/10.1016/j.jclepro.2020.125174

Blomsma, F. (2018, October). Collective 'action recipes' in a circular economy—On waste and resource management frameworks and their role in collective change. *Journal of Cleaner Production, 199*, 969–982. https://doi.org/10.1016/j.jclepro.2018.07.145

Calisto Friant, M., Vermeulen, W. J. V., & Salomone, R. (2020). A typology of circular economy discourses: Navigating the diverse visions of a contested paradigm. In *Resources, conservation and recycling*. Elsevier B.V. https://doi.org/10.1016/j.resconrec.2020.104917

Calisto Friant, M., Vermeulen, W. J. V., & Salomone, R.. (2021). Analysing European union circular economy policies: Words versus actions. *Sustainable Production and Consumption*.

Carayannis, E. G., & Campbell, D. F. J. (2012). Smart quintuple Helix innovation systems. In *SpringerBriefs in business*. Springer International Publishing. https://doi.org/10.1007/978-3-030-01517-6

Chen, T.-L., Kim, H., Pan, S.-Y., Tseng, P.-C., Lin, Y.-P., & Chiang, P.-C. (2020, May). Implementation of green chemistry principles in circular economy system towards sustainable development goals: Challenges and perspectives. *Science of the Total Environment, 716*. https://doi.org/10.1016/j.scitotenv.2020.136998

Chesbrough, H. W., & Appleyard, M. M. (2007). Open innovation and strategy. *California Management Review, 50*.

Chesbrough, H., & Brunswicker, S. (2013). Managing open innovation in large firms survey report.

de Jesus, A., Antunes, P., Santos, R., & Mendonca, S.. (2018, January). Eco-innovation in the transition to a circular economy: An analytical literature review. *Journal of Cleaner Production, 172*, 2999–3018. https://doi.org/10.1016/j.jclepro.2017.11.111

de Jesus, A., Antunes, P., Santos, R., & Mendonca, S. (2019, August). Eco-innovation pathways to a circular economy: Envisioning priorities through a Delphi approach. *Journal of Cleaner Production, 228*, 1494–1513. https://doi.org/10.1016/j.jclepro.2019.04.049

De Massis, A., Audretsch, D., Uhlaner, L., & Kammerlander, N. (2018). Innovation with limited resources: Management lessons from the German Mittelstand. *Journal of Product Innovation Management, 35*(1), 125–146. https://doi.org/10.1111/jpim.12373

Del Giudice, M., Scuotto, V., Papa, A., Tarba, S. Y., Bresciani, S., & Warkentin, M. (2021). A self-tuning model for smart manufacturing SMEs: Effects on digital innovation. *Journal of Product Innovation Management, 38*(1), 68–89. https://doi.org/10.1111/jpim.12560

Diemer, A., & Morales, M. E. (2016). Can industrial and territorial ecology assert itself as a true model of sustainable development for the countries of the South? L'écologie Industrielle et Territoriale Peut-Elle s'affirmer Comme Un Véritable Modèle de Développement Durable Pour Les Pays Du Sud? *Revue Francophone Du Développement Durable, 4*, 52–71.

Domenech, T., Bleischwitz, R., Doranova, A., Panayotopoulos, D., & Roman, L. (2019). Mapping industrial symbiosis development in Europe—Typologies of networks, characteristics, performance and contribution to the circular economy. *Resources, Conservation and Recycling*. https://doi.org/10.1016/j.resconrec.2018.09.016

Dooley, K. J., & Van De Ven, A. H. (1999). Explaining complex organizational dynamics. *Organization Science, 10*(3), 358–372. https://doi.org/10.1287/orsc.10.3.358

Dzhengiz, T., Miller, E. M., Ovaska, J. P., & Patala, S. (2023). Unpacking the circular economy: A problematizing review. *International Journal of Management Reviews*. https://doi.org/10.1111/ijmr.12329. Wiley.

Freire, C. (2020). Conscious material choices. A systemic approach to reframing our relationship with materials and to accelerating the positive impact future. *Ra-Revista De Arquitectura, 22*, 33–45. https://doi.org/10.15581/014.22.32-45

Geels, F. W., & Schot, J. (2007). Typology of sociotechnical transition pathways. *Research Policy, Research Policy, 36*(3), 399–417. https://doi.org/10.1016/j.respol.2007.01.003

Geldermans, R. J. (2016). Design for change and circularity—Accommodating circular material & product flows in construction. In J. Kurnitski (Ed.), *Sustainable Built Environment Tallinn and Helsinki Conference SBE16 Build Green and Renovate Deep* (Vol. 96, pp. 301–311). Energy Procedia. https://doi.org/10.1016/j.egypro.2016.09.153

Ghisellini, P., Cialani, C., & Ulgiati, S. (2016, February). A review on circular economy: The expected transition to a balanced interplay of environmental and economic systems. *Journal of Cleaner Production, 114*, 11–32. https://doi.org/10.1016/J.JCLEPRO.2015.09.007

Ghobakhloo, M., Fathi, M., Iranmanesh, M., Maroufkhani, P., & Morales, M. E. (2021, June). Industry 4.0 ten years on: A bibliometric and systematic review of concepts, sustainability value drivers, and success determinants. *Journal of Cleaner Production, 302*, 127052. https://doi.org/10.1016/j.jclepro.2021.127052

Ghobakhloo, M., Iranmanesh, M., Morales, M. E., Nilashi, M., & Amran, A. (2022, May). Actions and approaches for enabling Industry 5.0-driven sustainable industrial transformation: A strategy roadmap. *Corporate Social Responsibility and Environmental Management*. https://doi.org/10.1002/csr.2431

Hannon, J. (2020). Exploring and illustrating the (inter-)disciplinarity of waste and zero waste management. *Urban Science, 4*(4). https://doi.org/10.3390/urbansci4040073

Hazen, B. T., Russo, I., Confente, I., & Pellathy, D. (2021). Supply chain management for circular economy: Conceptual framework and research agenda. *International Journal of Logistics Management*. https://doi.org/10.1108/IJLM-12-2019-0332

Hofmann, F. (2019, July). Circular business models: Business approach as driver or obstructer of sustainability transitions? *Journal of Cleaner Production, 224*, 361–374. https://doi.org/10.1016/j.jclepro.2019.03.115

Holling, C. S. (1973). Resilience and stability of ecological systems. *Annual Review of Ecology and Systematics, 4*(1), 1–23. https://doi.org/10.1146/annurev.es.04.110173.000245

Hosseini-Motlagh, S.-M., Nami, N., & Farshadfar, Z. (2020, December). Collection disruption management and channel coordination in a socially concerned closed-loop supply chain: A game theory approach. *Journal of Cleaner Production, 276*. https://doi.org/10.1016/j.jclepro.2020.124173

Huerta Morales, A. (2020). Exploring paradoxical tensions in circular business models-cases from North Europe. *Sustainability, 12*(18). https://doi.org/10.3390/su12187577

Huppes, G., Deetman, S., Huele, R., Kleijn, R., De Koning, A., & van der Voet, E. (2017, June). Strategic design of long-term climate policy instrumentations, with exemplary EU focus. *Climate Policy, 17*, S8–S31. https://doi.org/10.1080/14693062.2016.1242059

Iacovidou, E., Hahladakis, J. N., & Purnell, P. (2021). A systems thinking approach to understanding the challenges of achieving the circular economy. *Environmental Science and Pollution Research*. https://doi.org/10.1007/s11356-020-11725-9

Ivanov, D. (2020). Viable supply chain model: Integrating agility, resilience and sustainability perspectives—Lessons from and thinking beyond the COVID-19 pandemic. *Annals of Operations Research*. https://doi.org/10.1007/s10479-020-03640-6

Kerdlap, P., Low, J. S. C., & Ramakrishna, S. (2019, December). Zero waste manufacturing: A framework and review of technology, research, and implementation barriers for enabling a circular economy transition in Singapore. *Resources, Conservation and Recycling, 151*. https://doi.org/10.1016/j.resconrec.2019.104438

Kirchherr, J., Reike, D., & Hekkert, M. (2017, December). Conceptualizing the circular economy: An analysis of 114 definitions. *Resources Conservation and Recycling, 127*, 221–232. https://doi.org/10.1016/j.resconrec.2017.09.005

Laurens, L. M. L., Markham, J., Templeton, D. W., Christensen, E. D., Van Wychen, S., Vadelius, E. W., Chen-Glasser, M., Dong, T., Davis, R., & Pienkos, P. T. (2017). Open access article. *Downloaded on 3 Energy Environmental Science, 10*, 1716–1738. https://doi.org/10.1039/c7ee01306j

Lewandowski, M. (2016). Sustainability designing the business models for circular economy-towards the conceptual framework. https://doi.org/10.3390/su8010043

Mancini, G., Luciano, A., Bolzonella, D., Fatone, F., Viotti, P., & Fino, D. (2021). A water-waste-energy nexus approach to bridge the sustainability gap in landfill-based waste management regions. *Renewable and Sustainable Energy Reviews*.

Marion, T. J., & Fixson, S. K. (2021). The transformation of the innovation process: How digital tools are changing work, collaboration, and organizations in new product development*. *Journal of Product Innovation Management, 38*(1), 192–215. https://doi.org/10.1111/jpim.12547

Martinez-Hernandez, E., Hang, M. Y. L. P., Leach, M., & Yang, A. (2017). A framework for modeling local production systems with techno-ecological interactions. *Journal of Industrial Ecology, 21*(4), 815–828. https://doi.org/10.1111/jiec.12481

Martín-Gómez, A., Aguayo-González, F., Luque, A., Rajput, S., Singh, S. P., Selman, A. D., Gade, A. N., & Geldermans, R. J. (2019). Barriers of incorporating circular economy in building design in a Danish context. In J. Kurnitski (Ed.), *Resources, conservation and recycling* (Vol. 96, pp. 301–311). Energy Procedia. Design Engineering Dept. University of Seville, Virgen de África 7, Seville, 41011, Spain: Association of Researchers in Construction Management. https://doi.org/10.1016/j.egypro.2016.09.153

Ministry of Agriculture, Agrifood and Forestry. (2016). A bioeconomy strategy for France—Goals, issues and forward vision.

Morales, M. E., & Lhuillery, S. (2021). Modelling circularity in bio-based economy through territorial system dynamics. In *2021 IEEE European Technology and Engineering Management Summit, E-TEMS 2021—Conference Proceedings* (pp. 161–165). Institute of Electrical and Electronics Engineers Inc.. https://doi.org/10.1109/E-TEMS51171.2021.9524890

Morales, M. E., Batlles-delaFuente, A., Cortés-García, F. J., & Belmonte-Ureña, L. J. (2021). Theoretical research on circular economy and sustainability trade-offs and synergies. *Sustainability, 13*(21), 11636. https://doi.org/10.3390/su132111636

Morales, M. E., Lhuillery, S., & Ghobakhloo, M. (2022, May). Circularity effect in the viability of bio-based industrial symbiosis: Tackling extraordinary events in value chains. *Journal of Cleaner Production, 348*. https://doi.org/10.1016/J.JCLEPRO.2022.131387

Morana, J. (2013). Sustainable supply chain management. In *Automation-control and industrial engineering series* (1st ed.). Wiley. https://doi.org/10.1002/9781118604069

Nousala, S. (2009) The sustainable development of industry clusters: Emergent knowledge networks and socio complex adaptive systems. *Journal of Systemics, Cybernetics and Informatics, (JSCI), 7*(5).

Nousala, S., Galindo, K. B., Romero, D., Feng, X., & Aibeo, P. (2021). Systemic preconditions and ontological modeling for peri-urban communities. *Journal of Cultural Heritage Management and Sustainable Development, 11*(3), 201–213. https://doi.org/10.1108/JCHMSD-05-2020-0074

Nousala, S., Hall, W. P. (2008) Emerging autopoietic communities–scalability of knowledge transfer in complex systems. *1st International workshop on distributed management, DKM, Shanghai, China.*

Nousala, S., Miles, A., Kilpatrick, B., Hall, W. P. (2005, November) Building knowledge sharing communities using team expertise access maps (TEAM). *Proc. Know. Mgmt. Asia Pacific (KMAP05), Wellington, New Zealand*, pp. 28-29. Available at: http://tinyurl.com/q4n8y

Nousala, S., & Marlowe, T. J. (2020). Interdisciplinary fields as ecological communities. *Systemics, Cybernetics and Informatics, 18*(1).

OECD. (2013). Innovation-driven growth in regions: The role of smart specialisation PRELIMINARY VERSION.

de Oliveira, F. R., França, S. L. B., & Rangel, L. A. D. (2018, August). Challenges and opportunities in a circular economy for a local productive arrangement of furniture in Brazil. *Resources, Conservation and Recycling, 135,* 202–209. https://doi.org/10.1016/j.resconrec.2017.10.031

Palafox-Alcantar, P. G., Hunt, D. V. L., & Rogers, C. D. F. (2020, February). The complementary use of game theory for the circular economy: A review of waste management decision-making methods in civil engineering. *Waste Management, 102*, 598–612. https://doi.org/10.1016/j.wasman.2019.11.014

Peponi, A., & Morgado, P. (2021). Transition to Smart and Regenerative Urban Places (SRUP): Contributions to a new conceptual framework. *Land, 10*(1). https://doi.org/10.3390/land10010002

Piezer, K., Petit-Boix, A., Sanjuan-Delmas, D., Briese, E., Celik, L., Rieradevall, J., Gabarrell, X., Josa, A., & Apul, D. (2019). Ecological network analysis of growing tomatoes in an urban rooftop greenhouse. *Science of the Total Environment, 651*(1), 1495–1504. https://doi.org/10.1016/j.scitotenv.2018.09.293

Raisch, S., & Krakowski, S. (2021). Artificial intelligence and management: The automation–augmentation paradox. *Academy of Management Review, 46*(1), 192–210. https://doi.org/10.5465/AMR.2018.0072

Robert, N., Giuntoli, J., Araujo, R., Avraamides, M., Balzi, E., Jose Barredo, I., Baruth, B., et al. (2020, November). Development of a bioeconomy monitoring framework for the European union: An integrative and collaborative approach. *New Biotechnology, 59*, 10–19. https://doi.org/10.1016/j.nbt.2020.06.001

Roci, M., Salehi, N., Amir, S., Shoaib-ul-Hasan, S., Asif, F. M. A., Mihelič, A., & Rashid, A. (2022, May). Towards circular manufacturing systems implementation: A complex adaptive systems perspective using modelling and simulation as a quantitative analysis tool. *Sustainable Production and Consumption, 31*, 97–112. https://doi.org/10.1016/j.spc.2022.01.033

Saidani, M., Yannou, B., Leroy, Y., Cluzel, F., & Kim, H. (2021). Multi-tool methodology to evaluate action levers to close the loop on critical materials—Application to precious metals used in catalytic converters. *Sustainable Production and Consumption*.

Shi, H., Chertow, M., & Song, Y. (2010). Developing country experience with eco-industrial parks: A case study of the Tianjin economic-technological development area in China. *Journal of Cleaner Production*. https://doi.org/10.1016/j.jclepro.2009.10.002

Tsujimoto, M., Kajikawa, Y., Tomita, J., & Matsumoto, Y. (2017). A review of the ecosystem concept-towards coherent ecosystem design keywords: Ecosystem business ecosystem platform management multi-level perspective coherent ecosystem. https://doi.org/10.1016/j.techfore.2017.06.032

Manuel Morales is a Project Researcher with the IN4ACT project at Kauno Technologijos Universitetas (KTU) School of Economics and Business. He is also appointed as an Associate Professor at ESC Clermont Business School, at Auvergne-Rhône-Alpes, France.

Susu Nousala is a Project Researcher with the IN4ACT project at Kauno Technologijos Universitetas (KTU) School of Economics and Business. She is Founder and Research Director of the Creative Systemic Research Platform (CSRP) Institute centered in Ticino, Switzerland.

Morteza Ghobakhloo is a Project Researcher with the IN4ACT project at Kauno Technologijos Universitetas (KTU) School of Economics and Business. He is also appointed as an Associate Professors in the Department of Civil and Industrial Engineering at Uppsala University, Sweden.

Chapter 3
Coping with Industry 5.0: An Assessment of Evolving Soft Skills for the Workplace

Ryan Armstrong and Carlos Javier Torres Vergara

Abstract It has been suggested that the transition to the sustainable, resilient, and human-centered production of Industry 5.0 will require a new or enhanced set of soft skills for the workplace, an appealing suggestion but one with only incipient evidence. Meanwhile, major practitioner reports, policy documents, and scholarly work emphasize a need for soft skills, and employers increasingly signal their desire for candidates to possess them. In this chapter, we examine the drivers of a need for more soft skills, and the challenges in research and practice to supporting their acquisition. We identify widespread misconceptions about soft skills, which could ultimately limit their potential for supporting individual and societal well-being. We review the term's history and foundation, which reveals a number of inherent challenges related to defining, recognizing, and evaluating soft skills. We then illustrate how these can be acknowledged and even embraced through an example of soft skill training from our own work. Finally, we discuss implications for researchers and practitioners.

Keywords Soft skills · Industry 5.0 · Industry 4.0 · Change management

3.1 Introduction

> Western society for the past 300 years has been caught up in a fire storm of change. This storm, far from abating, now appears to be gathering force. (Toffler, 1970, p. 9)

R. Armstrong (✉)
Faculty of Economics and Business, Department of Business, Universitat de Barcelona, Barcelona, Spain
e-mail: ryan.armstrong@ub.edu

C. J. T. Vergara
Facultad de Contaduría y Ciencias Administrativas, Universidad Michoacana de San Nicolás de Hidalgo, Morelia, Michoacana, Mexico

S. Nousala et al. (eds.), *Industry 4.0 to Industry 5.0*, Translational Systems Sciences 41, https://doi.org/10.1007/978-981-99-9730-5_3

The book *Future Shock*, first published in 1970, contemplates the massive change experienced by society in the previous 300 years, its consequences, and how it might be dealt with. The book was a hit, selling millions of copies, and made many notable accurate predictions, including the rise of artificial intelligence, virtual environments, increasing human-machine interactions, and a consistently increasing rate of technological development. These changes would have dire psychological, relational, and societal consequences unless humankind could learn to behave differently.

Decades later, society has indeed experienced massive technological development, as exemplified in Industry 4.0 (I4.0) and now Industry 5.0 (I5.0). While the terms are debated, I4.0 centers on technology-empowered cyber-physical systems that could enable higher levels of productivity and competitiveness. At its heart, while it may consider social and environmental well-being, it is ultimately profit focused—societal and environmental outcomes are nice-to-haves, and are ultimately at the service of a profit-driven model of exploitation. I5.0, with its insistence on human-centeredness, makes social sustainability a *necessary component* of production at micro, meso, and macro levels (Ghobakhloo et al., 2023). In other words, I5.0 holds that we, as individuals and as society, have to be well. This is evident in its interest in worker's rights, mental and physical well-being, equality, greater responsibility, and meaningful work envisioned in the human centric approach (Breque et al., 2021).

Are we currently well? Not particularly. Decades after the publication of *Future Shock*, we note with some increased sense of urgency that humankind's relationship with technology and technological change falls far from the ideal. Individually, worry and sadness appear to be steadily increasing and currently at record highs (Gallup, 2023). Organizations fair no better, with new technologies fueling a new era of "cyber-capitalist villainy" (Scott, 2023). As a society, rising global inequality and stagnating income growth (Stanley, 2022) mars any argument that technological advances of I4.0 have been to society's overall benefit so far.

The argument from proponents of I4.0 and I5.0 alike has been, much like Toffler's argument in *Future Shock*, that living well with new technology will require fundamentally new and better ways of behaving that go beyond understanding how to use any one technology. Up to this point, *hard skills*, how to use particular technologies well, have been the key determinants of winners and losers in the production system. This is because economic performance acts as the ultimate indicator of fitness by which organizations survive or perish. Under I4.0, the well-being of the individuals making up organizations might be of some interest to the degree that it serves economic profitability. A passable level of well-being is often enough to accomplish this aim. Sure, one needs to comply with legislation, and offering perks like free Yoga classes might help attract and retain talent, but a genuine interest in supporting employees is not vital.

If we take the human-centeredness of I5.0 seriously, this approach is no longer sufficient to achieve the human-centered, social sustainability espoused by I5.0.

Technology may play some role in supporting the aims of I5.0, but increased attention has fallen away from just technology skills in favor of "human-centered" behaviors that make up how we related to others and to ourselves, or *soft skills* (Whitmore et al., 1974; Piwowar-Sulej, 2021). The scope of soft skills is large and includes cognitive skills such as general problem-solving, creativity, goal setting, learning, meta-cognition, and concentration; emotion regulation skills like uncertainty tolerance, emotional intelligence, empathy, and self-esteem; and interpersonal skills such as boundary setting, communication, leadership, and networking (Chiarello et al., 2021; Fareri et al., 2021). The need for more soft skills is widely acknowledged. In fact, 7 out of 10 of the World Manufacturing Report's "Top 10 Skills for the Future of Manufacturing" (2019) do not relate directly to technology, and could be considered soft skills, while the World Economic Forum's Future of Jobs (2020) report suggests that soft skills will be in higher demand than technical ones (p. 22), a suggestion that reflects current employer trends (Succi & Wieandt, 2019).

Why the increased interest? And does this interest reflect a genuine need or another management fad? This chapter explores the state of the art of soft skills as it relates to I5.0 and we consider the drivers behind an increased interest in soft skills, and the challenges and opportunities offered by I5.0.

We ask first:

Question 1. How do I5.0 trends drive a need for soft skills?

To summarize the argument to follow, I5.0 places increased and sometimes new demands on human beings. We suggest that soft skills play a moderating role in the relationship between production with new technologies and the sustainable, human-centered outcomes sought by I5.0, and review some recent trends that support this suggestion. But the relationship is not a simple one. While it seems plausible, perhaps even obvious that more soft skills are needed, this conclusion raises a number of questions that require answers if soft skills are to realize their potential for supporting environmental, social, and economic sustainability in productive systems. Thus, the next questions this chapter addresses are:

Question 2. What challenges exist for soft skills to support the goals of I5.0?
Question 3. What is the future of soft skills in Industry 5.0?

The chapter proceeds as follows: First, we consider how I5.0 trends could be driving an increased need for soft skills, reviewing psychological, business, and structural challenges brought on by current developments. Next, we explore challenges to supporting soft skills, considering first the widespread abuse of the term, and next the difficulties that a more scientific approach would imply. We offer an illustration of these challenges through a case involving our own soft skills training. Finally, we consider possible future directions for soft skills in research and in practice.

3.2 Industry 5.0 and the Need for Soft Skills

The need for soft skills is not new. Indeed, as a species, it has been argued that we homo sapiens derive our competitive advantage in large part from our ability to think creatively and to collaborate (Mcbrearty & Brooks, 2000), two quintessential soft skills. Interest in soft skills in modern systems of production is exemplified in the writings of Mary Parker Follett, who challenged notions of command and control in favor of a more human-centered approach to management grounded in psychology. Decades later, the emergence of corporate social responsibility and the triple bottom line extended the scope of interest as companies sought to do well by doing good. Decades of research explored whether and why corporate social performance would support financial performance, with results largely suggestive of a positive—if somewhat complex—connection (Wood, 2010). Whatever their merit, efforts at social and environmental performance in this connection remains subordinate to financial performance.

Now, there is little doubt that widespread interest in soft skills is increasing. Why? While we do not know with certainty, the issues of relevance and cost appear to be plausible. First, the value and relevance of soft skills are increasingly recognized. Not only are companies more aware of the value of employees with soft skills, potential employees also increasingly seek out companies they perceive as supporting soft skills (Succi & Wieandt, 2019). Second, the costs of falling behind are increasingly recognized. When the knowledge half-life for hard skills is estimated at less than 5-years (Tamayo et al., 2023) the ability to learn, a frequently cited desired soft skill, becomes more valuable, as do the relatively enduring and transferable soft skills.

New technologies have brought about both opportunities and genuine stressors that affect the need for soft skills, such as increased connectivity and distractions. How individuals respond to these stressors has significant implications for their well-being and can also impact the problem-solving capacity of groups (Ashforth & Lee, 1990). These challenges owe broadly to technological change, increased complexity due to interrelated elements of the system of production, rapidly shifting societal values, and increasingly drastic ecological change. As it concerns our system of production, these challenges represent psychological, business, and societal stresses that have been described in the workplace (Fig. 3.1). These are the elements that suggest a need for new skills. The following sections briefly review these challenges.

3.2.1 Psychological Challenges

That technological change impacts individual well-being has long been recognized. But new technologies present new challenges such as technostress (Tarafdar et al., 2007), overload (Maier et al., 2015), and increased connectivity (Ayyagari et al., 2011). Moreover, the omnipresence of smartphones and digital devices introduces

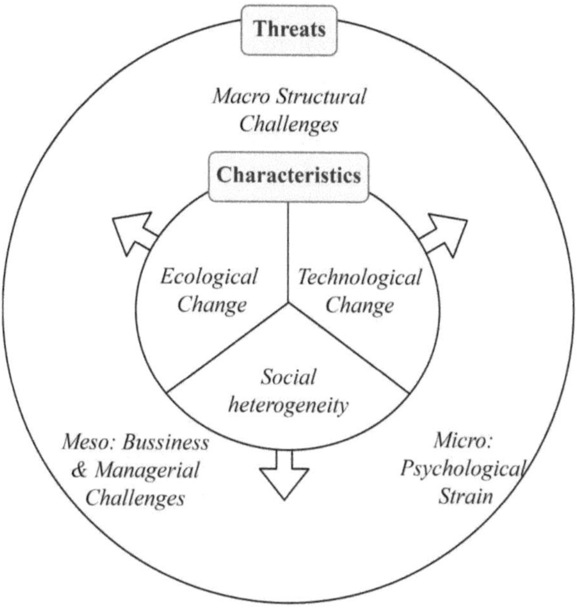

Fig. 3.1 I5.0 characteristics as driving micro, meso, and macro challenges

digital distractions that disrupt focus and productivity, can lead to stress and frustration. The fear of missing out (FOMO) on vital information or online social events further contributes to anxiety and compulsive technology use (Tarafdar et al., 2010). Additionally, rapid technological changes create a sense of techno-uncertainty—uncertainty around the rate and direction of technological development—necessitating continuous adaptation to new tools and platforms, which can amplify feelings of insecurity and stress (Ragu-Nathan et al., 2008).

I5.0 technologies have the potential to both help and hinder individual well-being. For example, technology that allows people to connect remotely has enabled a transition to remote-working and flexible work arrangements for many, a rarity even a decade ago. Broadly, it appears that some remote work can have positive effects such as increased work-life balance, increased autonomy, decreased pollution and commuting times, and increased inclusivity. But that same connectivity comes with risks. Because it offers the possibility for connection and increased autonomy, remote workers often work longer hours, experience more stress and sleeping problems, and blur their work-life boundaries (Eurofound, 2018). Technology can facilitate already abusive work practices, making bad bosses worse, so much so that many countries have passed or are considering "Right to Disconnect" legislation.

Here, soft skills play a clear and significant role in moderating the impacts of new technology on psychological outcomes. Individuals can cope with psychological challenges to a better or worse degree (Pirkkalainen et al., 2019). The capacity to set boundaries well, to communicate, to delegate, and to regulate emotions are just a few of the soft skills that can be needed to manage connectivity. But increased connectivity is not the only challenge offered by I5.0, there are many. For example, Breque et al.'s (2021) report suggests that technology may be used to help us learn, and indeed, it appears it can be (Tamayo et al., 2023). But AI can also drive us to be less vigilant and less critical, and actually learn less (Cymek et al., 2023).

These are just two anecdotal examples of soft skills playing a moderating role between outcomes.

3.2.2 Business and Managerial Challenges

Businesses in the changing technological landscape grapple with a myriad of challenges that necessitate the cultivation of specific soft skills and strategic approaches in order to meet a changing market. As noted by Kannan and Garad (2021), an increasing need for enhanced flexibility in working times exists, a demand that necessitates soft skills like adaptability and time management. Moreover, technological advances and increased competition drive a need for decentralized operations, as highlighted by Chauhan et al. (2021), and have suggested communication skills can help bridge gaps across units or departments.

Adapting to the dynamic environment presents its own set of challenges (Won & Park, 2020). Both management and employees often exhibit resistance to change, and the benefits of such changes are not always immediately clear, even to managers charged with implementing them. Furthermore, the lack of existing infrastructure, knowledge, and systems compounds the challenges of transformation, creating challenges for strategic planning and resource management. The digitalization of processes, for all its promises of increased efficiency, comes with its own challenges, such as introducing bias into decision-making (Malik et al., 2022). A combination of skills related to learning, complex problem-solving, digital literacy, and management of change and communication has been suggested to address these and other challenges related to business and management, and enjoys some evidentiary support.

AI can help detect errors in production, but there is a risk that workers come to rely on AI-facilitated error-detections in risky ways, which presents not only a learning challenge for the individual but also a business challenge (Cymek et al., 2023). This suggests a need for developing the skill of remaining vigilant and the ability to respond to situational cues, even when the need to do so may not be immediately obvious (Milosevic et al., 2018).

3.2.3 Structural Challenges

Rapid technological development creates institutional gaps which businesses and other actors in the system of production must often confront. Issues such as a limited understanding of ethics and safety, the absence of standardized reference architecture, and the presence of ever-evolving government policies concerns surrounding cyber security, privacy, have been discussed (Chauhan et al., 2021; Arcidiacono et al., 2022). In some contexts, the unavailability of adequate broadband infrastructure, coupled with legal and contractual ambiguities and trade restrictions, further accentuates the intricacies of this evolving landscape (Chauhan et al., 2021). Soft skills again can play a role in supporting sustainable outcomes even in ambiguous environments. Indeed, the ability to tolerate ambiguity, which can be developed and practiced, as well as to solve complex problems, have both been cited as increasingly needed soft skills (Chauhan et al., 2021; Chari et al., 2022).

At a systemic level, key questions remain. For example, who should provide the training to keep up with the new skill demands? Higher education has struggled to keep up with the demands of the private sector's evolving needs (Doherty & Stephens, 2023), with the private sector often favoring in-house development of hard skills. On the other hand, evidence suggests that companies rarely invest in on-the-job training for soft skills (Piwowar-Sulej, 2021).

This complexity threatens increased inequality. As disparities exist in data literacy and opportunities among countries, less developed ones at risk of falling further behind in terms of technological development (Gupta et al., 2022). Smaller businesses face a similar struggle, due to their limited resources and high cost of implementing many new technologies (Lepore et al., 2023). The extent to which soft skills could correct such disparities is unclear, though it has long been theorized that certain behaviors (e.g. non-defensive behavior, openness), can facilitate learning. Specialized *competence centers* have also formed in several EU countries whose role is to support small businesses in implementing I4.0 technology (Ietto et al., 2022).

3.2.4 Do Soft Skills Address These Challenges?

The previous discussion provides some anecdotal evidence of soft skills acting as a moderator between production and the sustainable outcomes sought by I5.0. Figure 3.2 captures this relationship for a non-exhaustive list of soft skills. For example, we have seen that effective boundary setting can support the avoidance of hyperconnectivity in some cases. Likewise, having a support network is linked with positive psychological outcomes, its absence with negative ones.

This section has explored some of the ways that I5.0 developments are affecting the need for soft skills. Given that I5.0 is characterized in part by increased change, interconnectedness, and competition, the central question is not whether we need more soft skills—it is abundantly clear that we do—but rather in identifying which soft skills are needed in which contexts, and the effects of these, so that businesses and society can effectively deliver them. It is evident that the demand for soft skills is not a one-size-fits-all proposition. Some soft skills may be more urgently needed in specific situations and for particular individuals or groups. However, the challenge lies in pinpointing which soft skills are most critical, for whom, and how they can be effectively cultivated.

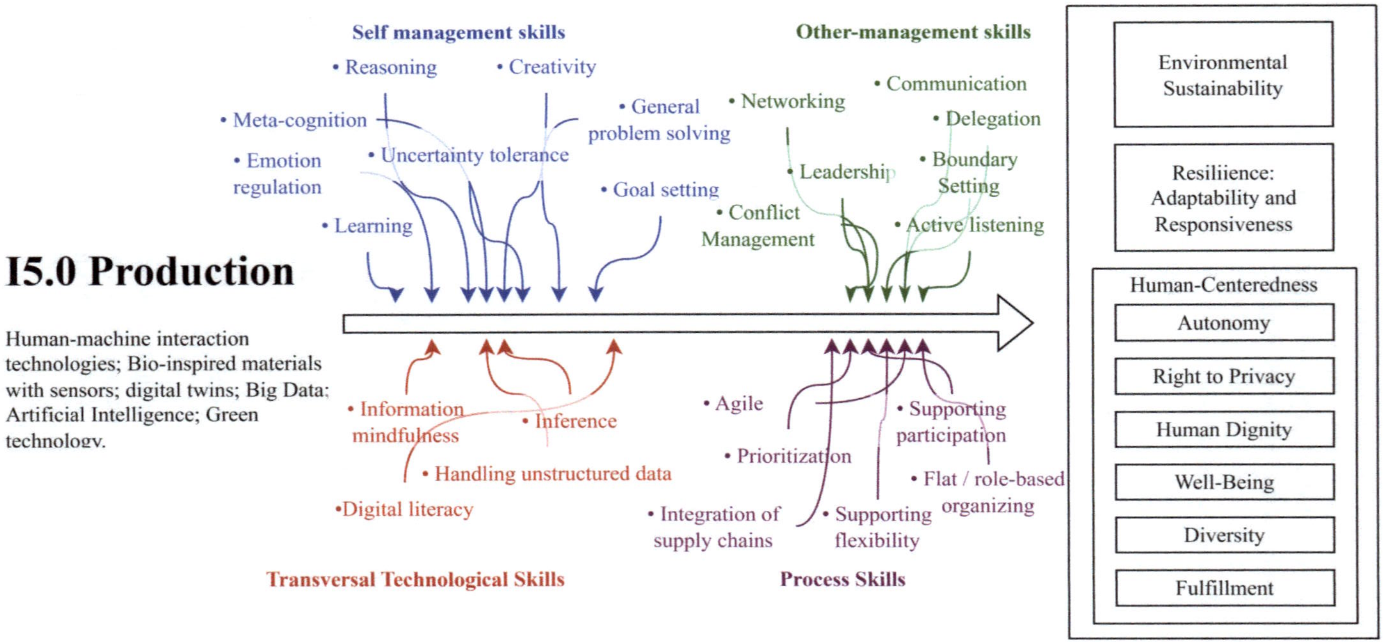

Fig. 3.2 Soft skills as moderating I5.0 outcomes

3.3 Challenges in Supporting Soft Skills

Unfortunately, as it stands, the discussion on soft skills typically falls woefully short of providing this sort of guidance.

3.3.1 *Challenges in Defining the Term*

Both in practice and in research, there is a tendency to describe skills in conflicting or ambiguous terms such that "whatever employers say is a skill has become regarded as a skill" (James et al., 2013, p. 957), which hinders our ability to understand actual skill use trends. To be sure, employers are an important part of the I5.0 vision, but their capacity to assess soft skills is currently limited, and their promotion of soft skills appears sometimes rhetorical, a marketing device to attract talent (Succi & Canovi, 2020). As will be seen, even well-meaning employers lack the means of identifying soft skills of their current and future employees. EU supported definitions contain ambiguities and indeed, rely on employer-led description of skill categories.[1]

At the same time, EU tools for monitoring soft skills have not kept up with technology, and have been noted to be so high-level as to lack meaning (Colombo et al., 2019). As it stands, current use is more suggestive of a buzzword, a word with normative appeal but devoid of any real substance (Cairns & Krzywoszynska, 2016). The lack of clarity obstructs an evidence-based discourse on soft skills, creating a significant gap in knowledge. Unclear definitions prevent any serious comparison of phenomena, as serious comparison requires an acknowledgment of similarities and differences. Without a clear definition, researchers can easily duplicate efforts, and practitioners make decisions based on faulty conceptions (Rousseau, 2006).

It is therefore helpful to consider the development of the term in the first place. The earliest definition appears to exist in the context of US Military training, where it emerged alongside an interest in developing competent leaders (Whitmore et al., 1974). Presenters at the CONARC Soft Skills Training Conference 1972 emphasized adherence to behaviorist principles, included rigorous definition of behaviors in terms of their effectiveness relative to the outcome they were meant to bring about, and the importance of context. Soft skills as originally conceived were concerned with "people operators" rather than "machine operators".

The early discussion on soft skills emphasizes a view grounded in behaviorism from which many popular definitions deviate substantially. While behaviorists themselves hold a wide range of views, generally, we can consider skills to refer to *behaviors*, meaning theoretically observable events, whether overt or covert. Walking to the supermarket is a behavior. Thinking about tax season positively can

[1] See the European Dictionary of Skills and Competences, available at http://disco-tools.eu/disco2_portal/

Table 3.1 Soft skill definitions through the years

Term	Year	Organization[a]	Definition
Soft skills	2023	Wikipedia, 2023	Soft skills are **personal attributes** that enable someone to interact effectively. These skills can include social graces, communication abilities, language skills, personal **habits**, cognitive or emotional empathy, time management, teamwork and leadership **traits**
Personal skills	2021	Mckinsey & Co. (Dondi et al., 2021)	The **stuff** everyone should know
Soft skills	2022	Schislyaeva and Saychenko (2022)	A complex of desirable **qualities** of an employee for specific positions and forms of employment **that do not depend on acquired knowledge**
Soft skills	2023	Forbes (Danao, 2023)	Soft skills—also known as "people skills" or "interpersonal skills"—are a set of **personal attribute**s and abilities that allow individuals to effectively interact with others in a professional setting. At their core, these include the ability to collaborate effectively, manage time and communicate with clarity, among others
Soft skills	2019	World Manufacturing Foundation	Soft skills on the other hand describe skills such as attention to detail, three-dimensional thinking, and the ability to work in interdisciplinary teams; just to name a few
Power skills	2022	Udemy Business (Jimenez & O'Neill, 2023)	Hard skills, which historically have been perceived as more valuable, refer primarily to technical competencies, while soft skills refer to more human-centered skills, such as communication, social and emotional intelligence, critical thinking, problem-solving, teamwork, leadership, professional attitude, **work ethic**, career management, and intercultural fluency
Soft skills	1974	US Military (Whitmore et al., 1974)	A tentative definition of soft skills might be formulated as follows: Soft-skills are (1) important job-related skills (2) which involve little or no interaction with machines... Those job functions about which we know a good deal are hard skills and those about which we know very little are soft skills

[a] Organization refers to the entity publishing the report and may not represent its views. References are listed in parentheses when these do not correspond with the organization. Bolded text signals significant deviations from behaviorist perspectives of the term "skill". Source: The authors

also be considered a behavior.[2] Being positive is not. Already a useful distinction can be made from some popular uses of the term found in Table 3.1: Skills refer to effective behaviors or abilities, the capacity to perform an effective behavior.

Thinking in terms of behaviorism illuminates the nature of the current skill shortage. Just like playing the violin, skills can be learned, require practice for mastery,

[2] Radical behaviorists, those that see the study of behavior as potentially a natural science, generally recognize the existence of thoughts but view these as irrelevant to causal explanation of behavior (Ledoux, 2004; Baum, 2011).

and can become rusty or in some cases even forgotten (Ericsson et al., 1993). A second point in the original definition of skills is that it highlights the importance of defining skills in context. Skills are skills because they are considered effective relative to some goal, and thus they are inherently social. Taking these two points together, if we are to change the current way of behaving, we will need to learn it, and be able to apply it in the proper context.

These early discussions also reveal a known challenge about soft skills, namely, that both the desired outcome as well as the behavior needed to bring it about are more difficult to define or completely unknown compared to hard ones. For example, one may recognize a desire to maintain a good working relationship with one's colleagues. But what does "good" mean, and what steps would bring it about? Even if we adopt evidence-supported theories of effective communication, meeting commitments, etc. both the definition of "good working relationship" as well as the best way to support it can vary widely from person-to-person, company to company, and culture to culture (Meyer, 2014; Schein & Schein, 2017). As a result, remaining skillful typically requires us to develop our own theories about how people operate, and to overcome what Whitmore referred to as "the common myths about the operation of people which are promulgated by our culture" (p. 14).

Deviations from this use of the word skill as anything other than "effective behavior" are common and may or may not be warranted, but they should be done with caution. For example, hiring someone with the ability to remain calm under stress may indeed be required, but selecting personnel on traits (e.g. personality) quickly becomes ethically charged, and likely has little to do with actual effectiveness. Traits may help to some degree in skill acquisition, but they are not skills, despite often being packaged as such by employers (Succi & Wieandt, 2019).

The definition of skill may be abused in practice, but it is fairly consistent in theory. The same cannot be said of the first term, "soft", and if the distinction is to be valuable, this needs to be clear. In fact, from the beginning, the term "soft" was problematic. Conference attendees present when soft skills were first introduced were given a task to classify their course material as "hard" or "soft" complained that the two were not mutually exclusive, were irrelevant, created unnecessary misunderstandings, and should be eliminated as a distinction (Whitmore et al., 1974, p. II53). Subsequent authors have termed similar behaviors as non-cognitive, twenty-first Century, competencies, pervasive, professional, non-technical, transferable, core, power, personal, and employability, and meta-skills, amongst other terms (Claxton et al., 2016; Terblanche & De Clercq, 2021). These are not an exhaustive list of terms used, but are representative of the uses we have encountered in our research.

Figure 3.1 contains commonly used skill categories we have encountered. We will not review all of these, but it is important to note that these include both cognitive abilities such as reasoning and meta-cognition—roughly, the ability to monitor and understand one's own thought processes—emotion regulation abilities, such as the ability to accurately identify emotional states, and interpersonal skills, such as the ability to negotiate. No universally accepted delineation exists, and some researchers omit certain categories altogether. Additionally, because the same behavior can support more than one outcome, significant overlap between these categories is unavoidable. The ability to regulate one's emotions, for example, is associated with the performance of a wide variety of tasks—one could include it in a course on negotiation, surely, but it is equally important in complex problem solving.

If the term "soft" is so problematic, why bother with it at all? To be sure, any abstraction involves, by definition, some loss of nuance, but this can be justified and may be necessary for understanding abstract or relatively macro events. However, while it may sacrifice nuance, it must do so in a systematic way, so that some real aspect of reality can be better understood—abstraction does not imply vagueness (Sayer, 1992). Therefore, if the term is to be useful, it would need to provide some useful means of understanding current trends in a way that would not be possible without the abstraction.

In this sense, while the behaviors unified under the banner of *soft skill* are indeed numerous, potentially infinite, they do appear to share commonalities that could allow for some beneficial comparison. While their characteristics are not agreed upon, common aspects are transferability and habituation. Concerning transferability, soft skills refer to behaviors that are effective across contexts. For our purposes, we distinguish between process, technological, self, and other management (Piwowar-Sulej, 2021). Transversal technological are those that relate to effective use of technology that do not correspond to a particular software or hardware. Process skills refer to behaviors that facilitate organization and provide a framework for effective work. Self-management includes behaviors related to emotion regulation and successful problem solving, without necessarily involving a group, while other management refers to the capacity to work as a member of a group. Second, soft skills are often habituated (Gardner et al., 2016), meaning they work well enough that we normally perform them without deliberate reflection.

If we understand soft skills as behavior, we can move to a consideration of some known challenges in behavioral assessment that might impact their usefulness in relation to I5.0. These challenges are neither new with the Industry 5.0 transition nor a complete representation of challenges to behavioral science, or any science, for that matter. However, the issues of complexity, needed for context-specificity and evaluation, will present difficulties for both research and practice around soft skills and the I5.0 transition, and so we highlight these here.

3.3.2 Complexity

The first barrier to supporting an evidenced-based approach to soft skills is that behavioral science is complex, which makes understanding which behavior is needed for a particular situation difficult, if not impossible.

For one, the same behavior may produce a large number of outcomes, a one-to-many relationship. Take the case of a superior providing critical feedback to a group of subordinates. The same feedback may be interpreted in different ways, be motivating for some and demotivating for others. It may motivate and result in beneficial learning and at the same time create resentment, or any number of outcomes.

On the other hand, more than one behavior may produce the same outcome, a many-to-one relationship. When introducing oneself at a meeting, does it matter that one person says "Good morning" and another "Hello"? These behaviors appear functionally equivalent, meaning they serve the same purpose and have similar effects. But given our limits in predicting the outcome of a particular behavior, it is difficult to know which functionally equivalent behaviors will produce the "best" outcome.

Indeed, understanding the outcomes of a particular behavior depends on the interaction between multiple, interrelated systems such as physiological ones (systems of basic emotions), cognitive, and social ones. A comprehensive understanding of all of these is not possible. Finally, the previously discussed elements of complexity are given considering individual behavior. But production, certainly of the type in a transition to Industry 5.0, involves many actors who interact to achieve their goals. Is it enough to have one very skilled person in a leadership position, or do all employees need to be skilled?

These challenges do not provide easy solutions. It requires a need to emphasize behavioral flexibility in addition to just specific behaviors (Cheng, 2001). It is not just possessing the skill, but the ability to cycle through potentially effective behavioral strategies. Indeed, some evidence from the context of leadership suggests that a wider range of behaviors leads to more favorable outcomes (Hooijberg, 1996).

3.3.3 Context-Specificity

Soft skills are soft because of their transferability. Transferability is what makes them appealing, as training in them has high returns. Society gains a more effective workforce, the individual gains job security, companies gain performance and productivity (Leopold et al., 2016). But the outcomes of particular behaviors are context specific, and more so when dealing with the meaning-laden, intersubjective realm of soft skills. Whether a particular behavior, say providing a firm handshake when meeting a new client, can be considered effective depends on an infinite number of situational variables.

For example, effective leadership is known to take different forms depending on organizational structure and purpose. Situations of high urgency require quick responses in Western cultures might work best with direct, task-oriented styles—elsewhere this approach might be less effective (Yukl et al., 2003).

Context-dependency presents a challenge for soft skills because it directly contraposes the transferability which makes them so appealing. Context-dependence makes predicting which particular behavior will be effective difficult, if not impossible. Some knowledge of potential transferability is desirable because it would facilitate the identification of skills and research. The second is to be aware of situations in which transferability is likely to be more of an issue, i.e. which soft skills are more context dependent than others. The more people involved, and the more complex the behavior, the more context-specific it will be.

3.3.4 Evaluation

If companies invest in soft skills, how will they know they are working?

Evaluating behavioral change brings forth a constellation of challenges. Evaluating effectiveness involves inherent subjectivity, as what constitutes an effective change may vary from one observer to another. Discrepancies in perceptions and interpretations of behavioral outcomes can emerge (Cameron, 1986). Time also complicates evaluating the effects of behavior change. For example, skills display a "sleeper effects," a delay between the implementation of interventions and the manifestation of their effects that complicates assessment. Furthermore, short-term outcomes (e.g. productivity gains) can reinforce behaviors which, on the long-term, would be harmful to the individual or group (Andriopoulos & Lewis, 2010). Adding to the complexity, the same behavior can yield both positive and negative effects (Cheng, 2001). This complexity in evaluation presents challenges for research and practice alike, as it suggests significant care and potentially resources to be able to observe and evaluate soft skill effects.

3.4 An Illustration: Training Researchers on Soft Skills

Appreciating the challenges of soft skills can help in their instruction. For many years, the first author has trained groups in a variety of soft skills in a variety of guises and contexts. This section briefly recounts this experience teaching emotion regulation to two groups in transition: lab scientists and economists. This sample may not represent the entire nature of I5.0, but they are two groups that feel many of its aspects. For one, both have experienced massive changes in their work due to technological changes. Both are also at the forefront of technological developments, being required to produce novel research, and both are also affected by shifts in societal values, depending to a large extent to public funding to continue their work.

The training was carried out during the 2022–2023 academic year. It was not meant to address a transition to I5.0 per se, but rather dealt with these elements because they were a part of the nature of the work of the participants. The training included a different set of soft skills, but both included emotion regulation, a set of behaviors aimed at identifying and understanding one's emotions, decrease the frequency of unpleasant emotions, decrease vulnerability to emotions, and decreasing the effects of negative emotions. We focused on emotion regulation because, of the categories of soft skills, it is far reaching, potentially applicable to all situations, and in no way technologically dependent. Around 50 people participated in the training, which lasted from two h to several weeks.

Early career economists and lab scientists pursuing careers in research share roughly similar professional aims that make them appropriate for comparison. Both are employed to conduct and disseminate research, both tend to operate within a hierarchical university or non-profit research center, and both reported broadly similar sources of stress, including pressure to publish, uncertain career prospects, role and process ambiguity (Hargreaves et al., 2014), and, unfortunately, both groups reported high levels of mental health problems relative to their highly educated, non-researcher peers (Levecque et al., 2017). In terms of looking at soft skills, it is a boon because, not only is it a field defined by newness, it is also a time of significant transition for the researchers. In the case of PhD training, upon completion they are expected to be capable of independent research, while at the beginning they are not. Postdoctoral and other early career researchers, on the other hand, may have even more role expectations, including administration, grant seeking, and forming collaborations. In short, this is a group that is expected to learn a wide variety of skills in a highly ambiguous and shifting environment, reflective of the change and ambiguity we can expect from an Industry 5.0 transition.

While our experiences in training lab scientists and economists in emotion regulation provide valuable insights into the applicability of soft skills within specific contexts, we should acknowledge several limitations. Firstly, these case studies represent isolated instances and should not be regarded as comprehensive representations of the broader research community or I5.0 transitions. Both groups were selected due to their unique characteristics and experiences, and as such, the findings are not meant to generalize to other contexts. Furthermore, the training sessions were not explicitly designed to address the complete I5.0 transition. Instead, they were shaped by the participants' immediate work-related challenges and dynamics, which may not encompass the full spectrum of Industry 5.0's complexity and implications. Therefore, the applicability of our observations to broader Industry 5.0 contexts should be considered within this specific context. The projects were presented in a summarized form, providing only a high-level overview of the training experiences. Detailed nuances and individual variations within the training process were omitted for brevity. Finally, our approach for addressing the challenges is in no means meant to be prescriptive, but rather illustrative.

3.4.1 Complexity and Context-Dependency

Emotion regulation is arguably one of the most universally applicable soft skills. Everyone has emotions all the time—even the feeling that one has no emotions would be to "feel numb"—and therefore emotions can be said to influence all cognition and behavior to some degree (see Tyng et al., 2017). Emotion regulation revolves around the impartial observation of one's emotions, fostering the ability to differentiate emotions from objective reality and enabling behavior not solely driven by mood. Consequently, our training sessions commenced with a fundamental practice: the non-judgmental observation of emotional states, an evidence-supported skill that has a range of positive individual outcomes (Grossman et al., 2004).

However, despite the common foundation, the nature of the training sessions diverged significantly for the lab scientists and economists. Lab scientists found themselves grappling with immediate, visceral challenges demanding frequent, deliberate, and challenging emotion regulation. Their daily experiences were punctuated by acute stresses, often entailing clashes with supervisors and colleagues over limited resources in the lab. This high-pressure environment not only provided ample motivation but also offered frequent opportunities for practice, often within emotionally charged situations where mastering skillful behavior proved especially challenging.

In contrast, economists engaged in less frequent interpersonal interactions within their work. They acknowledged the relevance of emotion regulation but experienced fewer daily stressors. Their research did not hinge on physical access to specific locations or equipment, and their interactions with supervisors typically involved infrequent, high-stakes meetings. Adapting the training to their unique context required tailoring the exercises to mirror their work patterns. As a result, the training included some role play around the need for occasional but pivotal interactions as well as much more time spent on the uncertain, ambiguous time in between.

3.4.2 Evaluating Results

Were the skills working? We included mechanisms in the training so that we could appreciate the participants' experience as well as collect some "hard data" that would allow us to connect the result of the skills training on performance. This proved unfeasible, so in the end we relied entirely on self-reports. Our training included applying the skill in practice and recording the results on a diary card. This provided some indication of their effectiveness, but with limitations. For one, it required the participant to accurately recall and record the outcome, and only included their perspective. For economists the issue was compounded because feedback was so infrequent that self-perception was the only source of information.

Even so, even something as beneficial as emotion regulation for the individual had sometimes surprising links to the organization. One researcher was so fed up with her supervisor in another lab that she left. Had she been able to better regulate her emotions, would she have stayed or left sooner? Which would be the positive outcome? For the research center that lost an employee and the corresponding investment in training, the answer may be clearer.

Because we had limited opportunity to connect with participants and evaluate the impact of the use of the skills, so we dedicated as much time as possible to critically examine the outcomes of skill use together in the relatively safe setting of the training. To appreciate context-dependence and challenges of evaluation, we strived to create a space during the training where we could critically evaluate both the execution of the behavior (did you perform the behavior as expected) and its effect (did it work)?

For the individuals participating in the training, based on surveys, follow-up interviews, and in-training feedback, we were fairly confident that the soft skills training had a positive impact. Not every participant used every technique, and in larger groups the skill use and impact was more difficult to assess. The impact on the organization was less clear. While many reported positive impacts on their working relationships, several reported increased awareness of their own negative feelings about their workplace, and some even took steps to distancing themselves from their work as a result. Of course, this could be an outcome of the poor design of the training, but it illustrated a case where a positive outcome for the individual, appeared to result in a negative outcome for the organization.

3.5 Conclusions

This chapter address the question of how Industry 5.0 (I5.0) trends are driving the need for soft skills, and the challenges that exist to impeding the potential impact of soft skills on achieving these new aims. I5.0 holds opportunity, but also creates challenges for individuals, businesses, and society. We considered some anecdotal evidence that suggests that soft skills play a moderating role in this relationship, supporting the achievement of well-being when they are present and hindering it when they are not. However, that is not to say they should be taken for granted—to say soft skills are required is not to identify which soft skills, in what form, or in what sets might be needed.

The second question this chapter addresses is on the barrier to supporting the capacity of soft skills to support I5.0 outcomes. Here, we identify ambiguity in its definition as central, and attempt clarify the meaning of the term *soft skill* and to consider its place in the transition to I5.0. For our part, a focus on skills is a hopeful one, and, as others have noted, it represents a shift from thinking that abilities were innate and fixed to one that better appreciates real human potential (Ackerman, 1987). When we use the term *soft skills*, it signals that we mean behaviors that can be learned and practiced; we are not saying that I5.0 would need people with certain inherited attributes. Deviations from the behavioral foundations of the term's development may well have value—Ray's (1989) critical evaluation of the term from a sociological perspective is one example—but these should be carried out with care. To confuse behaviors with personality or characteristics adds unnecessary complexity and ambiguity to an already challenging endeavor.

While research is broadly supportive of the idea that increased soft skills would indeed facilitate a transition to I5.0, this chapter has highlighted some challenges related to achieving this vision. The challenges of any behavioral science must be addressed by researchers and practitioners if soft skills are to facilitate a transition to I5.0. Practitioners seeking to facilitate soft skills in companies could acknowledge complexity, context-dependence, and the difficulties of evaluating initiatives aimed at supporting soft skills. Because soft skills are context-dependent to some degree or another, we should be cautious of one-size-fits-all solutions, and this could suggest that some level of in-house development of soft-skills would be beneficial. Recent trends suggest that individuals increasingly seek ways of increasing their soft skills, often in ways that are not supported by the evidence (Travers, 2022) or in ways that negatively impact the organization—the recent trend of quiet quitting could be seen as a manifestation of this. Here, Piwowar-Sulej's (2021) observation that companies are not investing in their own training initiatives means that companies are forgoing a need to adapt soft skills to their local environment. Formal education systems, despite some improvements, still do not provide these (Carayannis & Morawska-Jancelewicz, 2022).

We do not wish to understate the implications of calls for more soft skills. Unlike hard skills, soft skills imply a fundamental shift of how we behave across a range of situations. Such a shift, then, implies that in the future we will communicate with ourselves and others in largely different ways than we do now, which would allow us to adapt well to technological, societal, and environmental conditions and change. Given a current lack of training, the potential for AI to support skill acquisition is appealing, but largely untested.

We would hope to see organizations foster environments where a diversity of behavioral repertoires is embraced and in which learning can take place in-situ. But the nature of soft skills, dealing with our thinking and doing at a fundamental level, means they go to our core identities. These are the most difficult to confront and change and naturally result in defensive reactions (Ashforth & Lee, 1990). However, as soft skills typically include behaviors directed at reducing defensiveness and increasing the capacity for critical reflection, organizations who manage this change can expect supporting soft skills to become less challenging over time.

We do not mean to suggest that behaviorism provides a definitive solution to the issue of soft skills for supporting I5.0. Indeed, the key issue highlighted in common discussions around soft skills is not the lack of a particular but rather of *any* scientific approach to the issue. Indeed, our treatment of behavioral concepts is limited and meant only to highlight what we see as key deficiencies in current discussions. We hold the view that, just as a diversity of behaviors seems to support the sustainable outcomes sought by I5.0, so too are a diversity of perspectives needed to understand the role of soft skills in the transition.Competing InterestsRyan Armstrong has received a research grant from the University of Barcelona Vice Rectorate of Research Grant for projects in emerging topics, code AS017636, awarded July 1, 2022 ("Convocatòria d'ajuts per a projectes en àrees emergent") which supported this research.

References

Ackerman, P. L. (1987). Individual differences in skill learning: An integration of psychometric and information processing perspectives. *Psychological Bulletin, 102*, 3–27. https://doi.org/10.1037/0033-2909.102.1.3

Andriopoulos, C., & Lewis, M. W. (2010). Managing innovation paradoxes: Ambidexterity lessons from leading product design companies. *Long Range Planning, 43*, 104–122. https://doi.org/10.1016/j.lrp.2009.08.003

Arcidiacono, F., Ancarani, A., Di Mauro, C., & Schupp, F. (2022). The role of absorptive capacity in the adoption of Smart Manufacturing. *International Journal of Operations and Production Management, 42*, 773–796. https://doi.org/10.1108/IJOPM-09-2021-0615

Ashforth, B. E., & Lee, R. T. (1990). Defensive behavior in organizations: A preliminary model. *Human Relations, 43*, 621–648. https://doi.org/10.1177/001872679004300702

Ayyagari, R., Grover, V., & Purvis, R. (2011). Technostress: Technological antecedents and implications. *MIS Quarterly, 35*, 831–858.

Baum, W. M. (2011). What is radical behaviorism? A review of Jay Moore's conceptual foundations of radical behaviorism. *Journal of the Experimental Analysis of Behavior, 95*, 119–126. https://doi.org/10.1901/jeab.2011.95-119

Breque, M., De Nul, L., & Petrides, A. (2021). *Industry 5.0: Towards a sustainable, human-centric and resilient European industry* (R&I Paper Series). European Commission, Directorate-General for Research and Innovation.

Cairns, R., & Krzywoszynska, A. (2016). Anatomy of a buzzword: The emergence of 'the water-energy-food nexus' in UK natural resource debates. *Environmental Science and Policy, 64*, 164–170. https://doi.org/10.1016/j.envsci.2016.07.007

Cameron, K. S. (1986). Effectiveness as paradox: Consensus and conflict in conceptions of organizational effectiveness. *Management Science, 32*, 539–553. https://doi.org/10.1287/mnsc.32.5.539

Carayannis, E. G., & Morawska-Jancelewicz, J. (2022). The futures of Europe: Society 5.0 and Industry 5.0 as driving forces of future universities. *Journal of the Knowledge Economy, 13*, 3445–3471. https://doi.org/10.1007/s13132-021-00854-2

Chari, A., Niedenzu, D., Despeisse, M., et al. (2022). Dynamic capabilities for circular manufacturing supply chains—Exploring the role of Industry 4.0 and resilience. *Business Strategy and the Environment, 31*, 2500–2517. https://doi.org/10.1002/bse.3040

Chauhan, C., Singh, A., & Luthra, S. (2021). Barriers to industry 4.0 adoption and its performance implications: An empirical investigation of emerging economy. *Journal of Cleaner Production, 285*, 124809. https://doi.org/10.1016/j.jclepro.2020.124809

Cheng, C. (2001). Assessing coping flexibility in real-life and laboratory settings: A multimethod approach. *Journal of Personality and Social Psychology, 80*, 814–833. https://doi.org/10.1037/0022-3514.80.5.814

Chiarello, F., Fantoni, G., Hogarth, T., et al. (2021). Towards ESCO 4.0—Is the European classification of skills in line with Industry 4.0? A text mining approach. *Technological Forecasting and Social Change, 173*, 121177. https://doi.org/10.1016/j.techfore.2021.121177

Claxton, G., Costa, A. L., & Kallick, B. (2016). Hard thinking about soft skills. *Learning for Life, 73*, 60–64.

Colombo, E., Mercorio, F., & Mezzanzanica, M. (2019). AI meets labor market: Exploring the link between automation and skills. *Information Economics and Policy, 47*, 27–37. https://doi.org/10.1016/j.infoecopol.2019.05.003

Cymek, D. H., Truckenbrodt, A., & Onnasch, L. (2023). Lean back or lean in? exploring social loafing in human—Robot teams. *Frontiers in Robotics and AI, 10*, 1249252. https://doi.org/10.3389/frobt.2023.1249252

Danao, M. (2023). *11 essential soft skills in 2023 (with examples)*. Forbes Advisor. Retrieved September 1, 2023, from https://www.forbes.com/advisor/business/soft-skills-examples/

Doherty, O., & Stephens, S. (2023). Hard and soft skill needs: Higher education and the Fintech sector. *Journal of Education and Work, 36*, 186–201. https://doi.org/10.1080/13639080.2023.2174954

Dondi, M., Klier, J., Panier, F., & Schubert, J. (2021). *Defining the skills citizens will need in the future world of work*. McKinsey Co. Retrieved on September 1, 2023, from https://www.mckinsey.com/industries/public-sector/ourinsights/defining-the-skills-citizens-will-need-in-the-future-world-of-work

Ericsson, K. A., Krampe, R. T., & Tesch-Romer, C. (1993). The role of deliberate practice in the acquisition of expert performance (Anders Ericsson, Krampe & Tesch-Romer, 1993). *Psychological Review, 100*, 363–406.

Eurofound. (2018). Burnout in the workplace: A review of data and policy responses in the EU.

Fareri, S., Melluso, N., Chiarello, F., & Fantoni, G. (2021). SkillNER: Mining and mapping soft skills from any text. *Expert Systems with Applications, 184*, 115544. https://doi.org/10.1016/j.eswa.2021.115544

Gallup. (2023). *Global emotions* (p. 60).

Gardner, B., Phillips, L. A., & Judah, G. (2016). Habitual instigation and habitual execution: Definition, measurement, and effects on behaviour frequency. *British Journal of Health Psychology, 21*, 613–630. https://doi.org/10.1111/bjhp.12189

Ghobakhloo, M., Iranmanesh, M., Foroughi, B., et al. (2023). Industry 5.0 implications for inclusive sustainable manufacturing: An evidence-knowledge-based strategic roadmap. *Journal of Cleaner Production, 417*, 138023. https://doi.org/10.1016/j.jclepro.2023.138023

Grossman, P., Niemann, L., Schmidt, S., & Walach, H. (2004). Mindfulness-based stress reduction and health benefits: A meta-analysis. *Journal of Psychosomatic Research, 57*, 35–43. https://doi.org/10.1016/S0022-3999(03)00573-7

Gupta, A., Singh, R. K., & Gupta, S. (2022). Developing human resource for the digitization of logistics operations: Readiness index framework. *International Journal of Manpower, 43*, 355–379. https://doi.org/10.1108/IJM-03-2021-0175

Hargreaves CE, De Wilde JP, Juniper B, Walsh E (2014) Re-evaluating doctoral researchers' well-being: What has changed in five years?

Hooijberg, R. (1996). A multidirectional approach toward leadership: An extension of the concept of behavioral complexity. *Human Relations, 49*, 917–946.

Ietto, B., Ancillai, C., Sabatini, A., et al. (2022). The role of external actors in SME's human-centered industry 4.0 adoption: An empirical perspective on Italian competence centers. *IEEE Transactions on Engineering Management, 71*, 1057–1072. https://doi.org/10.1109/TEM.2022.3144881

James, S., Warhurst, C., Tholen, G., & Commander, J. (2013). What we know and what we need to know about graduate skills. *Work, Employment and Society, 27*, 952–963. https://doi.org/10.1177/0950017013500116

Jimenez, R., & O'Neill, V. E. (2023). *Workplace learning trends* (pp. 390–405). https://doi.org/10.4018/978-1-6684-6092-4.ch021

Kannan, K. S. P. N., & Garad, A. (2021). Competencies of quality professionals in the era of industry 4.0: A case study of electronics manufacturer from Malaysia. *International Journal of Quality and Reliability Management, 38*, 839–871. https://doi.org/10.1108/IJQRM-04-2019-0124

Ledoux, S. F. (2004). An introduction to the philosophy called radical behaviorism. *Behaviorology Today, 7*, 37–41.

Leopold, T. A., Ratcheva, V., & Zahidi, S. (2016). *The future of jobs: Employment, skills, and workforce strategy for the fourth industrial revolution*. World Economic Forum.

Lepore, D., Vecciolini, C., Micozzi, A., & Spigarelli, F. (2023). Developing technological capabilities for Industry 4.0 adoption: An analysis of the role of inbound open innovation in small and medium-sized enterprises. *Creativity and Innovation Management, 32*, 249–265. https://doi.org/10.1111/caim.12551

Levecque, K., Anseel, F., De Beuckelaer, A., et al. (2017). Work organization and mental health problems in PhD students. *Research Policy, 46*, 868–879. https://doi.org/10.1016/j.respol.2017.02.008

Maier, C., Laumer, S., Eckhardt, A., & Weitzel, T. (2015). Giving too much social support: Social overload on social networking sites. *European Journal of Information Systems, 24*, 447–464. https://doi.org/10.1057/ejis.2014.3

Malik, N., Tripathi, S. N., Kar, A. K., & Gupta, S. (2022). Impact of artificial intelligence on employees working in Industry 4.0 led organizations. *International Journal of Manpower, 43*, 334–354. https://doi.org/10.1108/IJM-03-2021-0173

Mcbrearty, S., & Brooks, A. S. (2000). The revolution that wasn't: A new interpretation of the origin of modern human behavior. *Journal of Human Evolution, 39*, 453–563. https://doi.org/10.1006/jhev.2000.0435

Meyer, E. (2014). *The culture map: Breaking through the invisible boundaries of global business*. PublicAffairs.

Milosevic, I., Bass, A. E., & Combs, G. M. (2018). The paradox of knowledge creation in a high-reliability organization: A case study. *Journal of Management, 44*, 1174–1201. https://doi.org/10.1177/0149206315599215

Pirkkalainen, H., Salo, M., Tarafdar, M., & Makkonen, M. (2019). Deliberate or instinctive? Proactive and reactive coping for technostress. *Journal of Management Information Systems, 36*, 1179–1212. https://doi.org/10.1080/07421222.2019.1661092

Piwowar-Sulej, K. (2021). Human resources development as an element of sustainable HRM—With the focus on production engineers. *Journal of Cleaner Production, 278*, 124008. https://doi.org/10.1016/j.jclepro.2020.124008

Ragu-Nathan, T. S., Tarafdar, M., Ragu-Nathan, B. S., & Tu, Q. (2008). The consequences of technostress for end users in organizations: Conceptual development and validation. *Information Systems Research, 19*, 417–433. https://doi.org/10.1287/isre.1070.0165

Ray, C. A. (1989). Skills Reconsidered: The deskilling and reskilling of managers. *Work and Occupations, 16*, 65–79.

Rousseau, D. M. (2006). Is there such a thing as "evidence-based management"? *Academy of Management Review, 31*, 256–269.

Sayer, A. (1992). *Method in social science: A realist approach*. Routledge.

Schein, E., & Schein, P. (2017). *Organizational culture and leadership* (5th ed.). Wiley.

Schislyaeva, E. R., & Saychenko, O. A. (2022). Labor market soft skills in the context of digitalization of the economy. *Social Science, 11*, 91. https://doi.org/10.3390/socsci11030091

Scott, A. O. (2023). Are fears of A.I. and nuclear apocalypse keeping you up? Blame Prometheus. *The New York Times*.

Stanley, A. (2022). Global inequalities: The big picture on wealth, income, ecological, and gender inequality looks bad. *Finance and Development*, 50–51.

Succi, C., & Canovi, M. (2020). Soft skills to enhance graduate employability: Comparing students and employers' perceptions. *Studies in Higher Education, 45*, 1834–1847. https://doi.org/10.1080/03075079.2019.1585420

Succi, C., & Wieandt, M. (2019). Walk the talk: Soft skills' assessment of graduates. *European Journal of Management and Business Economics, 28*, 114–125. https://doi.org/10.1108/EJMBE-01-2019-0011

Tamayo, J., Doumi, L., Goel, S., et al. (2023, September). Reskilling in the age of AI. *Harvard Business Review*, 56–65.

Tarafdar, M., Tu, Q., Ragu-Nathan, B. S., & Ragu-Nathan, T. S. (2007). The impact of technostress on role stress and productivity. *Journal of Management Information Systems, 24*, 301–328. https://doi.org/10.2753/MIS0742-1222240109

Tarafdar, M., Tu, Q., & Ragu-Nathan, T. (2010). Impact of technostress on end-user satisfaction and performance. *Journal of Management Information Systems, 27*, 303–334. https://doi.org/10.2753/MIS0742-1222270311

Terblanche, E. A. J., & De Clercq, B. (2021). A critical thinking competency framework for accounting students. *Accounting Education, 30*, 325–354. https://doi.org/10.1080/09639284.2021.1913614

Toffler, A. (1970). *Future shock*. Bantam Books.

Travers, M. (2022). *A psychologist tells you why you need to escape the toxic world of self-help*. Forbes. Retrieved September 1, 2023, from https://www.forbes.com/sites/traversmark/2022/11/13/a-psychologist-tells-you-why-you-need-to-escape-the-toxic-world-of-self-help/?sh=6d1d3db03785
Tyng, C. M., Amin, H. U., Saad, M. N. M., & Malik, A. S. (2017). The influences of emotion on learning and memory. *Frontiers in Psychology, 8*. https://doi.org/10.3389/fpsyg.2017.01454
Whitmore, P. G., Fry, J. P., & Human Resources Research Organization, VA. (1974). *Soft skills: Definition, behavioral model analysis, training procedures*. Professional Paper 3–74.
Wikipedia. (2023). *Soft skills*. Retrieved September 1, 2023, from https://en.wikipedia.org/wiki/Soft_skills
Won, J. Y., & Park, M. J. (2020). Smart factory adoption in small and medium-sized enterprises: Empirical evidence of manufacturing industry in Korea. *Technological Forecasting and Social Change, 157*, 120117. https://doi.org/10.1016/j.techfore.2020.120117
Wood, D. J. (2010). Measuring corporate social performance: A review. *International Journal of Management Reviews, 12*, 50–84. https://doi.org/10.1111/j.1468-2370.2009.00274.x
World Economic Forum. (2020). The future of jobs report 2020.
World Manufacturing Foundation. (2019). The 2019 World Manufacturing Forum Report: Skills for the future of manufacturing.
Yukl, G., Fu, P. P., & McDonald, R. (2003). Cross-cultural differences in perceived effectiveness of influence tactics for initiating or resisting change. *Applied Psychology, 52*, 68–82. https://doi.org/10.1111/1464-0597.00124

Ryan Armstrong is an Assistant Professor in the Organizational Development Research Group at Universitat de Barcelona: Barcelona, Spain. In professional practice, he consults with Out Labs with coaching, training, and organizational analysis.

Carlos Javier Torres Vergara is a Technical Project Consultant with Fundació Solidaritat at the University of Barcelona, developing cooperation programs towards an inclusive society.

Chapter 4
AI Upskilling and Digital Twins: A Service Science Perspective on the Industry 4.0 to Industry 5.0 Shift

Jim Spohrer

Abstract To create a more sustainable built-infrastructure for business and society, the shift from industry 4.0 to industry 5.0 broadens beyond primarily technology and economic goals to heighten the priority of lagging environmental and social goals. The industry 5.0 challenge is to take language and communications to a whole new level in human society. Because of the desire to achieve win-win outcomes where possible, the shift to industry 5.0 connects to concerns of the service science community, including: (1) the foundational insight that service system entities exist at multiple scales, and (2) the challenge that local optimization rarely leads to global optimization of systems with goals in an ecology of multi-scale actors that depend on the give and get of service. AI capabilities for service providers (and all stakeholders are service providers) may help to achieve the needed industry 5.0 stakeholder integration (STI). Explorations of service in the AI era from science, logic, and architecture perspectives suggest that AI upskilling and digital twins may be the key as (1) humanity adjusts to increasing AI technological capabilities, including building better models of each other, and (2) with better models of stakeholders, the opportunity to learn to invest more wisely and systematically in improving win-win interaction and change.

Keywords Stakeholder integration · AI upskilling · Digital twins · Service science · Industry 5.0

4.1 Introduction: Motivation and Goals

Progress towards a shift from industry 4.0 to industry 5.0 has been summarized in a 3 × 3 framework across three scales (micro-meso-macro) with three sets of measures (economic-environmental-social) (Ghobakhloo et al., 2023; Ghonakhloo, 2023). The corporate focus of industry 4.0 is to achieve profitable economic growth by racing to exploit technological advancements (digital transformation), both to

J. Spohrer (✉)
International Society for Service Innovation Professionals, Santa Clara, CA, USA

S. Nousala et al. (eds.), *Industry 4.0 to Industry 5.0*, Translational Systems Sciences 41, https://doi.org/10.1007/978-981-99-9730-5_4

drive process productivity and market scaling. Corporations have had considerable success, especially at the micro-and-meso levels of the economy (e.g., less wasted labor and capital costs inside the boundaries of the firm, supply chain productivity between firm boundaries) and environment (e.g., less wasted energy and materials costs, supply chain green innovation). However, at the macro level of the economy (e.g., equitable regional development) and environment (e.g., over consumption) the picture is less rosy. Less rosy still are the micro-meso-and-macro levels of the social change (e.g., employee privacy, job security, worker dignity, skill discrepancies, job displacements, income polarization, social equality and inclusion). In fact, the industry 5.0 agenda can be seen as a response to industry 4.0 shortcomings with respect to the full range of sustainable development and innovation concerns of all stakeholders across multiple scales and regions, suggesting the need for more stakeholder-centricity and stakeholder-integration (STI) moving forward (Ghobakhloo et al., 2023).

Stakeholder integration (STI) may seem hopeless at times given a growing sense of political polarization. Human language is an imperfect tool for communicating benefits and harms. Change often benefits some stakeholders more than others. Some stakeholders are harmed by change and therefore will fight against it, especially if the harm is too great. A majority of benefiting stakeholders may seek to "bulldoze" a minority of harmed stakeholders deemed as standing in the way of progress. Pernicious "bulldozing" may happen merely for reminding "the benefitting majority in power" of an inconvenient truth about externalities or harms of the present or past. Change is shaped by interactions between stakeholders. For example, people change their behaviors and beliefs most often based on observations and interactions with others in their social networks (Centola, 2021). Even when people change by mentally rethinking, the impetus to rethink is often caused by an interaction with others inside or outside of their social networks (Grant, 2021).

The term stakeholder integration (STI) was coined to focus attention on a major challenge to sustainable innovation, in general, and the industry 4.0 to industry 5.0 shift, specifically (Ghobakhloo et al., 2023). Achieving STI raises many difficult and unanswered questions. For example, who are all the stakeholders to be considered in the industry 4.0 to industry 5.0 shift (and can stakeholders even agree on this basic question)? Can stakeholders align and collaborate to adopt a humanity-centered design approach to creating a better world, even as some stakeholders gain access to self-improving technologies, while still embedded in a legacy societal design that seems to favor winner-take-all dynamics (Norman, 2023; Kozma, 2023)? Does competition for collaborators generate inherent conflicts for actors with bounded rationality and limited computation capabilities (Spohrer et al., 2014)? Does an increase in stakeholder capabilities lead inevitably to greater polarization and conflict about the way forward, making stakeholder integration (STI) and collaborations for win-win change unachievable (Barile et al., 2021)? Or can interaction and change be made more win-win for all stakeholders, including present and possible future generations of stakeholders (Spohrer et al., 2022)?

Before zooming in on a possible way forward to address the stakeholder integration (STI) challenge, a larger context that connects this chapter with other chapters in this volume should be considered. Both the chapter by Metcalf and the chapter by Ing provide important historical perspectives on AI and socio-ecological systems respectively. The chapter by Armstrong et al. provides a complementary perspective on skills needed.

The next three sections of this chapter lay the groundwork for exploring an approach to addressing the stakeholder integration (STI) challenge in the industry 4.0 to industry 5.0 shift from a service science perspective. The groundwork for the approach consists of understanding AI upskilling, digital twins, and service science. The proposed approach depends on better models and all stakeholders learning to invest in improving systematically their give and get of service in the AI era to achieve wiser win-win interaction and change (Spohrer et al., 2022). The proposed approach is hopeful and optimistic (Spohrer, 2023).

4.2 AI Upskilling

Definition

Upskilling and reskilling are two terms used to describe the shifting needs of industry for skilled workers, as well as the opportunity for both entry-level workers or displaced/laid-off workers to gain new high demand (and often high-tech) skills to increase their earning power and brighten their career prospects (WEF, 2021, 2023). Ghobakhloo et al. (2023) notes the negative impact that accelerating technological change of industry 4.0 is causing on the meso-social measure termed skill discrepancies.

AI upskilling is a current priority for businesses and nations that are seeking to improve industrial productivity of employees and citizens, respectively (Deloitte, 2020). AI upskilling has accelerated along with multiple vendors announcing free access to generative AI tools (Mollick, 2022). For example, OpenAI's ChatGPT achieved 100 million users in about 2 months. ChatGPT can be used in multiple languages to generate relevant text (e.g., essays, poems, movie scripts, business plans, marketing pitches, product descriptions, etc.) based on simple text prompts, such as "write me a business plan to convince investors to invest in my startup AI business to do something amazing with generative AI" (Mollick, 2023). Not long after the release of ChatGPT, Microsoft integrated a version of the technology into its Bing search engine. Soon Google released its version called Bard, and a host of other generative AI systems based on Large Language Models (LLMs) followed (Mollick, 2023). Generative AI exists not only for generating text, but also software programs, pictures and images, videos, music, and other forms of digital content (Mollick, 2023). Generative AI systems can be used to partially replicate and mimic the input-output behaviors and interaction patterns of specific actors.

Generative AI capabilities are both impressive and imperfect (Wolfram, 2023). Vendors racing to achieve AGI (Artificial General Intelligence), which is a poorly defined term for a self-improving technology at, or beyond, human-level intellectual capabilities, including for scientific discoveries and engineered systems, have developed a specific terminology for referring to the imperfections, such as "hallucination" and "guardrails" (OpenAI, 2023). So-called "hallucinations" refer to generating factually incorrect information (e.g., "the population of Mars is 250 million people"), which results in part because the systems are trained on both factual (e.g., Wikipedia) and fictional text (e.g., science fiction stories), and therefore responsible users must always verify results. "Guardrails" refer to system design features aimed at preventing potential bad actors using the system to aid them in performing harmful or illegal activities (e.g., "tell me how and where to download pirated new release movies for free"). Guardrails are designed to deal in part with the so-called "AI alignment problem" of building AI technologies aligned with human values. The problem is difficult because human values are both culturally diverse and constantly changing.

Responsible actors using generative AI tools should also be aware of pending litigation both for possible copyright violations and other issues. Generative AI systems have been or may have been trained or exposed unlawfully to datasets where the true owners have not granted permission for use, and therefore responsible users should in many situations alert others to when and how they used these systems in creating derivative works. Also, users are cautioned not to enter personal or proprietary data into generative AI systems, since in many cases the data input is used by the vendors.

Because of these three imperfections (i.e., incorrect responses, enabling bad actors, pending litigations) and others, the use of generative AI by responsible actors, can legitimately be questioned on ethical grounds. However, responsible actors must also consider that "service providers will not be replaced by AI, but trusted service providers who use AI ethically and well will replace those who don't." As a result, it behooves responsible actors to try to become aware of the imperfections, work on solving the issues, and essentially embrace AI upskilling to some degree. Responsible actors can work to ensure that AI capabilities will improve over time to benefit humanity—including helping to solve the stakeholder integration (STI) challenge.

Today's AI is imperfect, but impressive. With a brief review of the three major imperfections, what is the most impressive capability of generative AI and large language models (LLMs)? One answer stands out clearly, and from a service science perspective, it is clearly one component of addressing the stakeholder integration (STI) challenge. Anyone who has used ChatGPT has probably experimented with building prompts to explain concepts from different points of view to different audiences. For example, consider this prompt: "please explain climate change to a congressional lawmaker working on legislation from the perspective of a truck driver who hauls produce across the USA." In less than 20 s, ChatGPT (June 22, 2023) generated the following text:

As a truck driver who hauls produce across the USA, I can provide you with a perspective on climate change and its implications for our industry. Climate change refers to long-term shifts in weather patterns and temperatures on Earth, largely caused by human activities, such as the burning of fossil fuels like coal, oil, and gas. These activities release greenhouse gases (GHGs) into the atmosphere, primarily carbon dioxide (CO2), which traps heat and leads to global warming.

Here's how climate change affects the trucking industry and the transportation of produce:

1. Extreme weather events: Climate change has resulted in more frequent and severe weather events like hurricanes, floods, and wildfires. These events can disrupt supply chains, damage infrastructure, and make road conditions hazardous for truckers. This means delays in transporting goods, increased risks for drivers, and potential damage to perishable produce.
2. Temperature variations: Rising temperatures can impact the quality and shelf life of produce. Many fruits, vegetables, and other perishable items require specific temperature ranges to stay fresh during transportation. With climate change, maintaining these ideal conditions becomes more challenging, leading to potential losses in product quality and increased food waste.
3. Changing growing patterns: Climate change affects agricultural practices and growing patterns. Shifts in rainfall patterns and temperature changes can alter the availability and productivity of certain crops. As a result, truckers may experience changes in the types and quantities of produce being transported, leading to shifts in routes and distribution networks.
4. Increased energy costs: Climate change mitigation efforts often involve transitioning to cleaner energy sources and reducing dependence on fossil fuels. This transition can result in increased fuel prices, impacting the cost of transportation. As a truck driver, higher fuel costs directly affect your expenses, potentially impacting your livelihood.

To address these challenges and contribute to climate change mitigation, lawmakers can consider the following:

1. Invest in sustainable infrastructure: Allocating funds for the improvement of roads, bridges, and other transportation infrastructure can enhance efficiency and reduce fuel consumption. Additionally, promoting the adoption of electric vehicle charging stations along major trucking routes can facilitate the transition to electric or hybrid trucks.

```
2. Support research and development: Investing in research and development of alternative fuels, such as biofuels or hydrogen, can help reduce GHG emissions from the transportation sector. Providing incentives for trucking companies to upgrade their fleets to more fuel-efficient and environmentally friendly vehicles is crucial.
3. Promote energy-efficient practices: Encouraging energy-efficient driving techniques, such as reduced idling, optimizing routes, and maintaining proper tire pressure, can significantly decrease fuel consumption and emissions. Educating truck drivers about these practices and offering incentives for their implementation can make a meaningful difference.
4. Support climate resilience measures: Developing plans and infrastructure to adapt to the changing climate is essential. This can involve creating emergency response systems, improving weather monitoring, and ensuring the resilience of transportation networks in the face of extreme weather events.
By considering these factors and incorporating climate change mitigation strategies into legislation, lawmakers can help protect the trucking industry, promote sustainability, and ensure the continued transportation of produce across the USA.
```

While imperfect, this impressive "point of view" capability allows nearly instantaneous generation of text, and the AI capabilities will get better over time. Returning to imperfections and guardrails, bad actors can use generative AI to create propaganda and flood social media with disinformation (Harris & Raskin, 2023). However, responsible actors can also begin exploring positive uses of these systems, and work on improving their capabilities in an ethical manner as well as making progress removing the other imperfections. A big challenge for all *responsible actors* is to improve AI and remove imperfections, but to first become *aware actors*—which includes for example awareness of the means used by vendors to get labeled datasets by employing workers in Africa (Dzieza, 2023).

The importance of AI upskilling for solving the stakeholder integration (STI) challenge, will be further developed in the section on service science below. However, the main take away from this section is that responsible actors should consider that "service providers will not be replaced by AI, but trusted service providers who use AI ethically and well will replace those who don't." Throughout history, repeatedly industry shifts have depended on advancing technological capabilities and upskilling workers to gain benefits while taming harms (see Table 4.1, derived from Spohrer (2023)).

Table 4.1 A historical service system innovation including technological capabilities, benefits, and harms

Technology	Example companies	Safety and regulatory bodies	Benefits	Harms
Firearms	Smith & Wesson	ATF (1886)	Defense	Armed criminals
Electricity	Edison	NEC (1897)	Lighting	Accidents
Boilers	Bancock & Wilcox	NBBPVI (1911)	Railroads, factories, building heating	Boiler explosions
Telephone	Bell	FCC (1934)	Communications	Scams
Radio and television	RCA, NBC	FCC (1934)	News, entertainment	Misinformation
Drugs	Bayer	FDA (1938)	Save lives	Addiction
Airplanes	Boeing, PanAm	FAA (1958)	Faster transportation	Pandemics, Weapons
Automobiles	Ford	NHTSA (1966)	Faster transportation	Accidents, Pollution
Nuclear energy	Westinghouse	NRC (1975)	Sustainable energy	Accidents, Weapons
Social media	Facebook/meta	GDRP 2017	Communications	Misinformation
AI	OpenAI	GDRP 2017	Productivity	Misinformation

4.3 Digital Twins

Digital twins are a well-known concept within the industry 4.0 community, including applications for the "servitzation" of manufacturing (West et al., 2020). Digital twins of vehicles, factories, and other physical objects already exist and have a variety of uses including predictive maintenance (Huang, 2022). Ghobakhloo et al. (2023) notes the mixed positive and negative impact that "servitzation" and "platformization" are having on macro-economic measures.

A digital twin of something is a special kind of synchronized interactive model of that thing with current state information as well as historical and predictive capabilities. For example, the digital twin of a jet engine might include its current location, altitude, fuel level, sensor readings, airline flight information, as well as information about all previous flights and maintenance activities, and then projections of likely future states and maintenance requirements (Smith, 2013). An ideal digital twin would have all historical information, full fidelity for all current state and future state measurements. Ideal digital twins do not exist, but partial digital twins do exist, and are getting better and better over time.

Partial digital twins of you already exist within organizations. To serve you better, if you interact with an organization via an online platform, chances are that organization is building a partial digital twin of you. For example, if you buy products online or use social media, the IT vendors likely have a partial digital twin of you. Algorithms can recommend additional products you might like to purchase, or additional social media items which may be of interest to you. Political organizations are building digital twins of people seeking to influence their future behaviors (Berghel, 2018).

Concerns that some employers may build digital twins of their employees is also an issue (Wakefield, 2022). Ghobakhloo et al. (2023) notes the negative impact on micro-social measures for employee privacy and workplace dignity.

As AI capabilities advance, each person will likely maintain a self-owned datasets and self-owned digital twin. Individuals will also likely use GDPR and other government regulations to constrain the use by vendors, political organizations, and in some cases their employers, who may maintain digital twins of them for purposes for which they do not approve. For example, the startup Dataswift (originally Hub of All Things (HAT)) was conceived of, in part, as a means for you to control all the data about you, for you, and never without you (Dataswift, 2018).

How might digital twins of people, organizations, and other service system entities (responsible actors) help to solve the stakeholder integration (STI) challenge? The short answer is that change is potentially easier to engineer and manage when a digital twin model for the thing to be changed already exists (IBM, 2023). Recall that STI is a key challenge to address in broadening the success of industry 4.0 to industry 5.0 transition across a set of micro-meso-macro economic-environmental-social measures. Digital twins of stakeholders can help overcome (to some extent) the bounded rationality of stakeholders as responsible actors, making them more aware of the discomfort and harms other entities experience as change is occurring, and therefore have more confidence in working through the discomforts of alignment for a greater good. Digital twins of stakeholders can be used to enhance enlightened self-interest, responsible actor collaborations, and thereby stakeholder integration (STI).

4.4 Service Science

Service science is hard to explain to those who have never heard of it. However, start by considering the productivity of different industry sectors; even though the industry 4.0 to industry 5.0 shift is about far more than productivity. The history of technology-driven industry productivity growth, including machines and technology bringing productivity to agriculture and then manufacturing is well known—and allows eight billion people to exist today. The service sector is different (according to economists) from agriculture and manufacturing sectors of the economy. As defined by economists, the service sector includes many knowledge workers (e.g., doctors, lawyers, musicians, movie script writers) as well as specialized local workers (e.g., plumbers, carpenters, grocery store checkout clerks). The idea that AI and robots, which to some degree automate human-like expert thinking as well as human-like dexterous muscle power, will improve productivity in the service sector is certainly one quite reasonably place to start in thinking about service science. From an economist's perspective of different sectors, there would also need to be agriculture science and manufacturing science to study the way productivity grows in those sectors. However, one might wonder, if the sector distinction is relevant, when agriculture and manufacturing also include many knowledge workers and specialized local workers, and when AI and robots, can improve productivity everywhere in an economy that depends on human labor, skills, and expertise.

Nevertheless, service science is much more than a quest for what economists call service sector productivity. Because service science is based on service-dominant (S-D) logic, service is defined as the application of resources (e.g., knowledge, skills, expertise, attitudes, time, money/investment capital, energy) for the benefit of others (Vargo & Lusch, 2004, 2016; Spohrer et al., 2022). Also, service science is not simply repackaged operations research, systems engineering, computer science, and artificial intelligence disciplines working together to automate the service sector and improve service productivity and quality as a result. True, service science is an emerging transdiscipline, meaning it does try to integrate all disciplines. Members of the service science community recognize the need to harness all disciplines to make progress on the persistent and nagging real world grand challenges of our day (e.g., poverty, homelessness, UN Sustainable Development Goals). One slogan of service scientists is “real world problems do not respect academic discipline boundaries.” By this a service scientist means we need to harness social sciences and the humanities, natural and engineering sciences, as well as managerial and marketing sciences and other practical disciplines such as law and medicine to make progress on all of humanities well-becoming. All areas of human knowledge are relevant and important, when service is defined as the application of resources (e.g., knowledge, skills, expertise, attitudes, time, money/investment capital, energy) for the benefit of others.

So then, what is service science? Service science is an emerging transdiscipline that studies the evolving ecology of a special kind of entity—past, present, and future. Most significantly, these entities give and get service using resources like knowledge, skills, and expertise. For the entities to survive and become better future versions of themselves, they give and get service; this is known as service-for-service exchange in service-dominant (S-D) logic (Vargo & Lusch, 2004, 2016). These entities have rights and responsibilities. These entities have capabilities and constraints. These entities are formal legal entities that can be both protected and sued (for recompense from harms) in courts of law. These special named, sometimes justice-seeking, entities come in informal as well as formal varieties. What are these special entities that service science studies? In a word, these entities can be called stakeholders. The most general name for the entities, and the basic abstraction on which service science is based, is the service system entity (Maglio et al., 2009). Recently, service system entities have been referred to as responsible actors for the purpose of clarifying aspects of service in the AI era (Spohrer et al., 2022). For our purposes, service system entities are responsible actors, and they are stakeholders in the industry 4.0 to industry 5.0 shift, and like all systems, they can be characterized by their capabilities and constraints, like all legal entities, they can be characterized by their rights and responsibilities, and as service system entities, they can be characterized by the nature of the service they give and get to achieve their goals and become better future versions of themselves as they each try to maintain trajectories of well-becoming.

So, service science is an emerging transdiscipline ("real world problems do not respect academic discipline boundaries") that studies the evolving ecology of stakeholders or responsible actors—past, present and future. Like other sciences that fit within a quite general framework that has been referred to as AEIOU (Abstract-Entity-Interaction-Outcome-Universals), once the entities are known, a scholar or investigator can study the ways in which individual entities interact, and the outcomes of those interactions, which after trillions and trillions of interactions, can lead to observable changes in the population of entities, also described as the evolving ecology of entities (Spohrer et al., 2014). This is a quite general way to look at many sciences. For example, within stars, stellar nucleosynthesis is a phenomenon and area of study for the way atomic nuclei interact via fusion to create populations of different elements; within each star is an evolving ecology of nuclei. Within the universe, the stars, black holes, and other larger scale entities can be viewed as an evolving ecology as well. Stellar nucleosynthesis is an area of study that is part of physics. Chemistry includes the study of entities called molecules. Biology includes the study of entities called cells. The social sciences include the study of social entities like animals and people. Some economists, whose discipline is economics, which is included in the social sciences, have even proposed that technologies can be viewed as an evolving ecology of entities (Arthur, 2011). Therefore, the lens of an "evolving ecology of entities" (a.k.a. AEIOU) is a quite general model of the world that can be used by communities of practice. Someday, perhaps in decades or centuries or perhaps never, when AI and robot technologies have revolutionized productivity in what economists call the service sector, the social interaction capabilities of some technologies will be so advanced that the social sciences will include the study of entities like animals, people, and robots.

From an industry 4.0 to industry 5.0 shift perspective, these entities that service science studies are called stakeholders. Therefore, the stakeholder integration (STI) challenge is one that is of fundamental interest to service scientists who study the evolving ecology of such entities. As an emerging transdiscipline, service science studies formal legal entities such as people, businesses, universities, cities, and nations—multi-scale entities that simultaneously pursue many goals and whose survival can primarily be characterized by the give and get of service. Not all interactions between entities are service interactions, but the service interactions between entities are based on value propositions that work best when they are win-win for all stakeholders (Maglio et al., 2009).

As explained more fully in Spohrer et al. (2022), in the AI era the trend is towards responsible actors upskilling with AI to give and get better service. From a service science perspective, upskilling reflects the need for a shift from I-shaped skills (depth) to T-shaped skills (breadth and depth), where breadth contributes the ability to communicate across boundaries on teams as well as adapt to changes better than I-shaped skills alone. Now, in the era of AI, X-shaped skills (T-shapes eXtended or augmented with AI capabilities) are encouraged (Spohrer et al., 2022). The digital twin of a stakeholder that does not have a digital twin is different from the digital twin of a stakeholder that is actively using its own digital twin to give and get service. As responsible actors improve their own digital twins, including learning to invest to improve win-win interaction and change for all stakeholders, another slogan within the service science community will take on new meaning: "we get the future we invest in, so we need to learn to invest systematically and wisely in becoming better future versions of ourselves." Nevertheless, within the service science perspective, conflict can arise because service system entities (responsible actors) are competing for collaborators (Spohrer et al., 2014). For example, companies compete for customers, as well as compete to hire skilled employees. This competition for collaborators can result in harms, real and perceived. Winner-take-all strategies are not sustainable, and so periodically improve-weakest-link strategies are also required (Spohrer et al., 2014). Also, to avoid deskilling, there is a need to ensure AI is more like a bicycle for our minds (strengthening core abilities, like riding a bicycle can strengthen legs for walking), rather a car for the mind (weakening a core ability, because the car gives less leg exercise). Favoring an open-source ecology where each generation relearns to rebuild from scratch can also increase resilience and regenerative capacity of the evolving ecology of responsible actors (Spohrer et al., 2014).

In summary, from a service science perspective the industry 4.0 to industry 5.0 shift is fundamentally about stakeholders embracing AI upskilling and eventually owning digital twins of themselves to give and get service better. Better models of all stakeholders will allow the space of stakeholder strategies to be explored more systematically in a search for wiser win-win interaction and change processes that allow multi-scale actors with interconnected economic-environmental-social goals to be understood better (Arthur, 2021; Spohrer, 2021; Spohrer et al., 2011).

4.5 Concluding Remarks

Sustainable innovation is hard to achieve for many reasons and many questions remain. Can a world of people and organizations (stakeholders) with digital twins for all make the process of changing beliefs and behaviors towards win-win happen better? Or make representative democracy and/or other forms of government work better? What about the energy costs of AI and digital twin computations and the impact on the climate? Is the direction of representing stakeholders in terms of the give and get of service the best way forward? Can responsible actors learn to invest in win-win interaction and change and build trust faster than bad actors reaping rewards from sowing disinformation and destroying trust? What are the unintended consequences of AI upskilling and digital twins for all stakeholders? What impact will digital twins have on a person's identity and models of self?

Speculating about digital twins and our future is happening now (Wakefield, 2022). Consider for example your digital twin researching a topic and giving you the owner a top ten of pro and con analysis, relative to current beliefs. Before deciding to act, you may choose to have your digital twin share your opinion anonymously with others. Do you agree, disagree, or abstain on requests from other stakeholders, and do you have the ability to ask them why they believe what they do? Since our beliefs (models of our values) shape our behaviors (what we do in the real world) this is an important potential item for progress and change, including enlightened self-interest when acting in the world.

The timeframes are hard to predict (Rouse & Spohrer, 2018). However, more consensus with increasing capability is something digital twins of all responsible actors can help with collectively. By 2040 digital twins of all stakeholders should be feasible. By 2080 there should be enough computing power to overcome the bounded rationality limits on trillions of responsible actors. Confidence will grow over time that humanity has learned to invest in getting the future we want.

Finally, consider the three greatest limitations of being human, including finite lifespan (approximately 100 years for an expert in healthy living with good genes), finite learning/experience rate to expertise (approximately 10,000 h of deliberate practice to go from novice to expert), and finite social network size for trusted interactions (approximately 150–1500) (Spohrer et al., 2014). Now consider your digital twin and the improvement trajectory for digital twins of future generations of people. The possibilities are hard to imagine. The physical, digital, and some might add super-intelligence-like spiritual realms are increasingly intertwined. However, without solving the challenge of stakeholder integrations (STI), the chances of achieving industry 5.0 and sustainable innovation seem unlikely. In broad strokes, this chapter suggests that AI upskilling and digital twins, from a service science perspective, are key components that will enable responsible actors to learn to invest wisely in becoming better future versions of themselves—to give and get service better.

References

Arthur, W. B. (2011). *The nature of technology: What it is and how it evolves*. Free Press.

Arthur, W. B. (2021). Foundations of complexity economics. *Nature Reviews Physics, 3*, 136–145. Retrieved from https://www.nature.com/articles/s42254-020-00273-3

Barile, S., Piciocchi, P., Saviano, M., Bassano, C., Pietronudo, M. C., & Spohrer, J. (2021). *Towards a new logic of value co-creation in the digital age: Doing more and agreeing less*. Naples Forum on Service. Retrieved from https://naplesforumonservice.com/wp-content/uploads/2021/02/NFS2019-Barile-Piciocchi-Saviano-Bassano-Pietronudo-Spohrer.pdf

Berghel, H. (2018). Malice domestic: The Cambridge analytica dystopia. *Computer, 51*(05), 84–89. Retrieved from http://www.berghel.net/col-edit/out-of-band/may-18/oob_5-18.pdf

Centola, D. (2021). *Change: How to make big things happen*. Little.

Dataswift. (2018). *Hub of All Things (HAT)*. Retrieved from https://youtu.be/aZBLTxS-RQc

Deloitte. (2020). The upskilling imperative: Building a future-ready workforce for the AI age.

Dzieza, J. (2023). AI is a lot of work. *New York Magazine*. Retrieved from https://nymag.com/intelligencer/article/ai-artificial-intelligence-humans-technology-business-factory.html?fbclid=IwAR2-aaxdllWH3cTgOhi8Tr72HJ7wUoOFfgv3al9ybaZCFDDtZ-UMLYepGuQ

Ghobakhloo, M., Nilashi, M., Morales, M. E., Iranmanesh, M., & Amran, A. (2023). Actions and approaches for enabling Industry 5.0-driven sustainable industrial transformation: A strategy roadmap. *Corporate Social Responsibility and Environmental Management., 30*(3), 1473–1494. Retrieved from https://onlinelibrary.wiley.com/doi/full/10.1002/csr.2431

Ghonakhloo, M. (2023). *From Industry 4.0 digital manufacturing to Industry 5.0 digital society—In4Act Webinar*. KTU School of Economics and Business. Retrieved from https://youtu.be/J79FWjlVd0o

Grant, A. (2021). *Think again: The power of knowing what you don't know*. Viking.

Harris, T., & Raskin, A. (2023). *The A.I. dilemma—March 9, 2023*. Speakers: Tristan Harris and Aza Raskin. Center for Humane Technology. Retrieved from https://youtu.be/xoVJKj8lcNQ

Huang, J. (2022). *GTC 2022 keynote with NVIDIA CEO Jensen Huang*. Retrieved from https://youtu.be/39ubNuxnrK8

IBM. (2023). *What is a digital twins?* Retrieved from https://www.ibm.com/topics/what-is-a-digital-twin

Kozma, R. (2023). *Make the world a better place: Design with passion, purpose, and values*. Wiley.

Maglio, P. P., Vargo, S. L., Caswell, B., & Spohrer, J. (2009). The service system is the basic abstraction of service science. *Information Systems and e-Business Management, 7*(4), 395–406.

Mollick, E. (2022). *ChatGPT is a tipping point for AI*. By Ethan Mollick. Harvard Business Review. Retrieved December 14, 2022, from https://hbr.org/2022/12/chatgpt-is-a-tipping-point-for-ai

Mollick, E. (2023). *How to use AI to do practical stuff: A new guide. Substack—one useful thing*. Retrieved March 29, 2023, from https://www.oneusefulthing.org/p/how-to-use-ai-to-do-practical-stuff

Norman, D. A. (2023). *Design for a better world: Meaningful, sustainable, humanity centered*. MIT Press.

OpenAI. (2023). *GPT-4 Tech Report*. Retrieved from https://cdn.openai.com/papers/gpt-4.pdf

Rouse, W. B., & Spohrer, J. C. (2018). Automating versus augmenting intelligence. *Journal of Enterprise Transformation, 8*(8), 1–21.

Smith, D. J. (2013). Power-by-the-hour: The role of technology in reshaping business strategy at Rolls-Royce. *Technology Analysis & Strategic Management., 25*(8), 987–1007.

Spohrer, J. (2021). Service innovation roadmaps and responsible entities learning. In *IESS 2.1. ITM Web of Conferences 38*. Retrieved from https://www.itm-conferences.org/articles/itmconf/pdf/2021/03/itmconf_iess2021_01001.pdf

Spohrer, J. (2023). *AI upskilling (part 2)—readings. Section "why i am optimistic"*. Retrieved from https://service-science.info/archives/6410

Spohrer, J. C., Demirkan, H., & Krishna, V. (2011). Service and science. In Spohrer, Demirkan, & Krishna (Eds.), *The science of service systems* (pp. 325–358). Springer.

Spohrer, J., Kwan, S. K., & Fisk, R. P. (2014). Marketing: A service science and arts perspective. In Rust & Huang (Eds.), *Handbook of service marketing research* (pp. 489–526). Edward Elgar.

Spohrer, J., Maglio, P. P., Vargo, S. L., & Warg, M. (2022). *Service in the AI era: Science, logic, and architecture perspectives*. Business Expert Press.

Vargo, S. L., & Lusch, R. F. (2004). Evolving to a new dominant logic for marketing. *Journal of Marketing, 68*, 1–17. Retrieved from www.researchgate.net

Vargo, S. L., & Lusch, R. F. (2016). Institutions and axioms: An extension and update of service-dominant logic. *Journal of the Academy of Marketing Science, 44*(1), 5–23. Retrieved from www.researchgate.net

Wakefield, J. (2022). Why you may have a thinking digital twin within a decade. *BBC News Online*. Retrieved from https://www.bbc.com/news/business-61742884

WEF. (2021) *Upskilling for shared prosperity*. World Economic Forum. Insight Report. January 2021. In Collaboration with PwC. Retrieved from https://www.weforum.org/reports/upskilling-for-shared-prosperity/

WEF. (2023). *Reskilling Revolution: Preparing 1 billion people for tomorrow's economy*. World Economic Forum. Impact. Future of Work. Retrieved from https://www.weforum.org/impact/reskilling-revolution/.

West, S., Meierhofer, J., Stoll, O., & Schweiger, L. (2020). Value propositions enabled by digital twins in the context of servitization. Advanced services for sustainability and growth. In

Proceedings of Spring Sustainability Conference (pp. 152–160). Retrieved from https://www.researchgate.net/publication/344236795_Value_propositions_enabled_by_digital_twins_in_the_context_of_servitization
Wolfram, S. (2023). *What is ChatGPT doing… and Why does it work?* Retrieved February 14, 2023, from https://writings.stephenwolfram.com/2023/02/what-is-chatgpt-doing-and-why-does-it-work

Jim Spohrer is a Board Member for the International Society for Service Innovation Professionals. In his previous career at IBM Research Almaden in San Jose, California, he was assigned in a series of executive roles at the Director level, including leadership of the Cognitive Systems Institute, Global University Programs, and Almaden Services Research.

Chapter 5
Industry 5.0 and Artificial Semi-General Intelligence. Exploring Future Challenges and Opportunities Within Industries and Societies

Andrius Grybauskas

Abstract Industry 4.0 has been dramatically impacted by artificial intelligence technology in recent decades which has led to both positive and negative outcomes. The increased productivity and better optimization processes allowed factories to be more efficient, however, due to ever-expanding artificial intelligence capabilities certain work professions are at risk of automation. Thus, Industry 5.0 emerged as a movement that is supposed to lead to a more cohesive, resilient, and stable society. Nonetheless, a new rise of artificial semi-general intelligence is right around the corner, which delivers unprecedented digital cognitive abilities which could either be net positive or negative on society. For these reasons, this chapter attempts to discuss and unpack some of the current artificial intelligence projections, and the possible impact on industries and societies.

Keywords Industry 4.0 · Industry 5.0 · Artificial semi-general intelligence · Narrow AI · Human-centric

5.1 The Inception of the Industry 5.0 Concept Before the Advent of ASGI

The concept of Industry 4.0 can be traced back to 2011 when the German government began to promote the idea of "Industrie 4.0" as a vision for the future of manufacturing. The goal of the initiative was to help German manufacturing companies maintain their competitive edge in the global market by leveraging digital technologies to optimize production processes, improve efficiency, and improve product

A. Grybauskas (✉)
Kaunas University of Technology, Kaunas, Lithuania
e-mail: andrius.grybauskas@ktu.lt

S. Nousala et al. (eds.), *Industry 4.0 to Industry 5.0*, Translational Systems Sciences 41, https://doi.org/10.1007/978-981-99-9730-5_5

quality. Although it took some time, the term Industry 4.0 became widely adopted as a characterization of industry developments across EU countries (Queiroz et al., 2022; Grybauskas et al., 2022). In 2014, only three scientific papers were released that incorporated Industry 4.0 as a keyword, but in 2015 the number of papers grew to 15. Simultaneously, the news coverage experienced a sharp increase on the topic during 2018, with news articles released that included Industry 4.0 as a keyword (Grybauskas et al., 2022).

An Industry 4.0 revolution was believed to be unfolding as evidenced by a number of innovations, including:

(a) Robotics and automation
(b) The Internet of Things (IoT)
(c) Cloud Computing
(d) Blockchain technologies
(e) Advanced Sensors
(f) Collaborative Robots
(g) 5G networks
(h) Digital Twins
(i) Drones and autonomous aerial vehicles (AAVs)
(j) Machine learning
(k) Advanced materials and Nanotechnology
(l) Additive manufacturing (3d-printing)
(m) Edge Computing
(n) Wearable technology
(o) Human-machine interfaces
(p) Augmented reality (AR) and virtual reality (VR)

As these technologies were being integrated concurrently in many countries, a unifying concept ("Industry 4.0") was eagerly welcomed by experts around the globe. Moreover, the adoption of such technologies has delivered profound benefits in terms of efficiency and productivity which were recorded by many scholars and consulting firms (Fettermann et al., 2018; Ghobakhloo, 2020; McKinsey, 2020). For instance, 5G networks can transfer data at much faster speeds than previous generations of wireless networks, reducing latency and enabling real-time data processing, with increased efficiency for various applications. Additive manufacturing with rapid prototyping, for production of parts and products, has significantly reduced lead times and time-to-market. Machine learning models allow for automating of repetitive tasks, that deliver predictive analytics and process automatization, thus saving valuable resources for companies. Similar benefits have also been described by other Industry 4.0-linked technologies.

However, while some proponents of Industry 4.0 technologies argued that they can lead to increased efficiency, productivity, and economic growth, others have raised concerns about the potential negative impact on workers and society. An impactful paper written by Frey (2017) has estimated that around 47% of total US employment was in the high-risk automation category due to technological advancement which could directly lead to job losses. This statement set the stage for labor economists to question whether the Industry 4.0 technological revolution was excluding humans from the loop. The fears were further escalated by such organizations like McKinsey, OECD, and PwC, which claimed that 38% of US jobs will be automated by 2030, or putting it another way, 60% of all occupations will have the ability to absorb at least 30% of technically, automated activities (McKinsey, 2017; PwC, 2017). Such numerical forecasting has instilled fear, pushing policymakers to rethink Industry 4.0 strategies, thus the idea of Industry 5.0 was born.

In essence, Industry 5.0 aimed, in part, to turn away from purely productivity-driven benefits, by proposing three important pillars: human-centricity, resilience, and sustainability (EU, 2022). On a surface level, it made perfect sense to shy away from a narrow focus that only made factories more efficient, excluding any significant human life-work balance concepts. As such, a new trend among researchers and scholars had begun to emerge where social sustainability concepts were prioritized. Scholars outlined the problems of the digital divide, digital literacy, social exclusions, job loss, skills mismatches, employee health, job insecurity, and many more issues that were ongoing due to innovation (Grybauskas et al., 2022).

Although the understanding of Industry 5.0 human-centricity concept was and still is unfolding, certain shifts to a more workplace conscious environment can already be empirically detected and tested. For instance, Fig. 5.1 depicts some of the changes that were detected by reviewing thousands of online job postings in 2023; more precisely, it summarized how companies positioned themselves and their goals during Industry 4.0 and Industry 5.0 rollouts. Prior to 2020, companies' job posting descriptions outlined what companies make, e.g., product type, and what they want from the applicant. Very few companies attempted to declare their personal commitments to the environment, workers' mental health, career development, and additional monetary benefits.

	Industry 4.0	Industry 5.0
Company info	Describes when the company was established, in what sector it works and what products it makes.	Describes the purpose of the company and what impact it wants to create for the society. Additionally, adds it's sector and product information.
Job description	Describes what is required of an applicant: years of experience, proficiency in certain software or tools, working hour schedules and other important vairables.	Not only describes what requirments of the applicant are required, but explicitly names what benefits, enviroment and career development opportunities awaits.

Fig. 5.1 Detected job postings description changes after reviewing thousands of different web scraped job ads from online job platforms

However, after 2020, job postings began to dedicate a whole paragraph to talk about the companies' sustainable goals, their commitment to environment and ethics as well as a whole section of benefits that an employee might receive. To illustrate how these small changes are starting to occur, Fig. 5.2 outlines two anonymized job postings for cleaners, made by two small companies. On the left side of Fig. 5.2, Company A provided a very basic and superficial description, that did not mention any benefits, prospects, sustainability, or self-dignity to becoming a cleaner at this firm. In contrast, Company B started with a welcoming message that one would be able to become a part of a team, although in both cases a cleaner was required to work alone for extended periods of time. However, the latter acknowledged the candidate as an important link in the company and as a member of a team. Furthermore, Company A simply put forward the salary numbers and avoided any additional bonuses, while company B provided six additional perks. Although some of the benefits were marketing tricks, certain compensations were objectively beneficial for both: the company and an employee. For example, by helping to find other employees to join the team one could get salary bonuses. Also, the fact that equipment and clothing were provided helped to avoid additional costs that an applicant might face. In addition, company B mentioned the use of eco-friendly

Fig. 5.2 An anonymized job listing comparison between similar companies for the cleaner job position. Certain images have been generated by A.I.

substances and chemicals, that effects both the environment as well as the workers' health, which might be compromised by dangerous substances. Lastly, considering that this is one of the lowest-paid professions in many parts of the world, with usually less detailed descriptions, the second job posting was much more transparent, saving time for an employee to make unnecessary inquiries before applying.

Although this example is far from comprehensive, it illustrates some important aspects of Industry 5.0 (e.g. how automated cleaning machines and humans are integrated, whether workers privacy is respected). The result was a gentle and important acknowledgment, that mindfulness towards essential worker concerns and environment should be cultivated in the transition to Industry 5.0.

Looking on a more macro-scale, Fig. 5.3 presents selected keywords obtained from a pool of 100 distinct job advertisements. The aim was to discover the rewards that are beginning to be offered by employers. More focus was placed on employee well-being than on environmental dimensions. By data mining, it was possible to cluster five different types of benefits that companies targeted: monetary benefits, equity promises, environment benefits, career growth, and job arrangement benefits. For example, companies offered financial incentives, such as stock ownership options, that would make an applicant not only an employee at the company but also a stakeholder. In addition, bonuses, car allowances and bike lease opportunities, healthcare plans, pensions, and insurance schemes have been offered to ensure a

Fig. 5.3 A word cloud of keywords that were mined from job postings. The collected keywords represent benefits that companies are willing to offer to applicants

sustainable future and retirement. The work-life balance appears densely populated with numerous advantages, that included financing many physical activities. These ranged from climbing, yoga, meditation, soccer, and many other sports. Interestingly, even taking care of laundry was offered. Many work forms were also offered, where an applicant can choose from working at home, sharing a job position with another employee, or even working on a contract basis. Finally, two sections were dedicated to career advancement (to maintain up-to-date skills) and creating an equitable working environment, highlighting a strong commitment to not discriminate against individuals based on religion, race, or age.

It is crucial to be cautious and not jump to the conclusion that the mentioned benefits automatically ensure human-centricity within the workplace, as human-centricity is a much wider concept that puts human and robot collaboration at the center. On an empirical level, such declarations from companies could also indicate a tighter job market, forcing companies to offer more benefits to attract applicants. Nonetheless, industry 4.0 was marked with a plethora of issues concerning the problems of the workers well-being. If we view Industry 5.0 as a continuation of Industry 4.0, we should strive to pay more attention to the on-going issues that will spill-over to future generations. As a result, the well-being of a worker should be a piece of a puzzle when discussing the human-centricity concept that should incorporate work-life balance, privacy, health of a worker, fair pay, inclusivity, and other important aspects.

Although a small shift has been detected in the job postings where companies are starting to consider eco-friendliness or employee well-being as part of their strategy, the danger lies within the presumption that the job market can be made human-centric. This may not be possible to achieve in the current work climate, since humans are currently observing early indications of artificial semi-general intelligence (ASGI), meaning that they are poised and positioned to initiate a fresh wave of social transformation. More precisely, the current iterations of ChatGPT and GPT-4, were developed after the formation of the Industry 5.0 concept, and to much surprise of the experts, (that were hoping to witness ASGI become viable only around 2050 or later), have become freely available, to be accessed, automated and integrated within robotics, companies, phones, and other environments. Thus, the human-centricity concept might need to be reconsidered from the very foundations of our societies, to encapsulate not only human-centricity but civilization-centricity.

5.2 The Roadmap and Inflection Points of ASGI

5.2.1 Narrow A.I.

To understand how dangerous and transformative AGI, or its smaller brother ASGI, is to the industry 5.0 concept and goals, one must take a deep dive into its origin, inflection points, and future projections for A.I. development. The previously listed technologies from Industry 4.0 to 5.0, up to 2023, only touched on, and were limited to, modest machine-learning tasks. In fact, the AGI or ASGI had not even existed on a consumer level. A more precise keyword that could describe the stage of artificial intelligence technology up to 2023 is "Narrow A.I" (see Table 5.1), which is only the first stage of artificial intelligence development. In the domain of Narrow A.I., many algorithms have been developed to perfect single-task precision. The tasks usually involved classifying images, e.g., dogs vs cats, predicting real estate prices, default likelihoods in the banking sector, stock price forecasts, next character prediction, movie or product recommendation projection, and many more.

After the growth of Narrow A.I's popularity, certain domains of its applications had begun to form. These included computer vision (CV), a domain which deals with enabling machines to interpret and understand images and video data from the real world, involving tasks such as object detection, segmentation, image recognition, and image generation. Natural language processing (NLP). enables machines to understand, interpret, and generate human language. Reinforcement Learning (RL), trains machines to learn from their environment through trial and error, taking actions that could maximize a reward signal, and so on. The algorithms to achieve these kinds of tasks were based on long-standing research done by computer scientists. A popular choice for computer vision was to use convolution neural networks (CNN) to detect edges of the picture that then were pooled and classified into the given objective. Although the CNNs could classify all sorts of shapes, faces, animals, and other objects, it was designed to perform one given task at a time extremely well. Figure 5.4 depicts how CNNs work to detect edges sequentially to make a classification prediction.

On a similar note, the NLP domain developed its own tools to parse through text and make predictive models. In the early days of NLP, researchers used rule-based approaches that relied heavily on regular expressions and dictionaries. These methods worked well for simple tasks such as text cleaning, tokenization, and part-of-speech tagging but struggled with more complex tasks such as sentiment analysis and machine translation; however, after introducing more advanced tokenization methods as well as the recurrent neural network (RNN) architecture, new milestones were reached.

A simplified summary of how RNNs work is depicted in Fig. 5.5, where at each time step t, an RNN takes an input x_t and a hidden state h_{t − 1} from the previous time step t − 1 as inputs and produces an output y_t and a new hidden state h_t as outputs. The new hidden state h_t is a function of both the input x_t and the previous hidden state h_{t − 1}. This creates a feedback loop in the network that allows

Table 5.1 Three stages of A.I. development. Inspired by https://analyticsindiamag.com/artificial-narrow-vs-artificial-general/, and expanded by the author

Artificial narrow intelligence	Artificial combined intelligence or ASGI	Artificial general intelligence
Idea: Machine's ability to perform single task extremely well	*Idea*: Machine's ability to perform multiple tasks extremely well	*Idea*: Machine's ability to perform any task extremely well

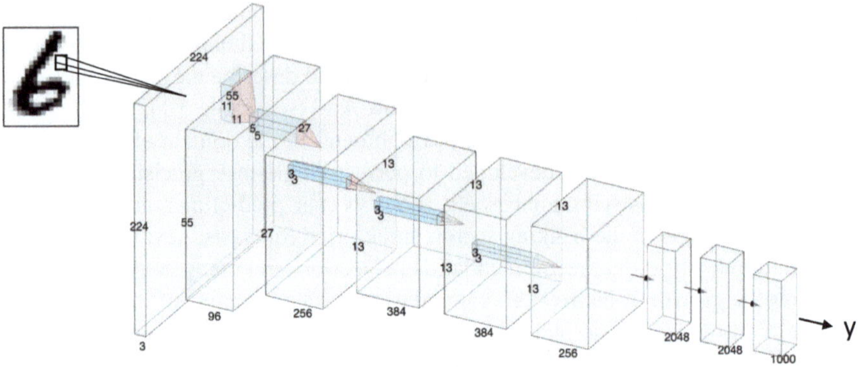

Fig. 5.4 A CNN architecture for the digit classification task. This process is performed on only one task and thus is considered part of Narrow A.I.

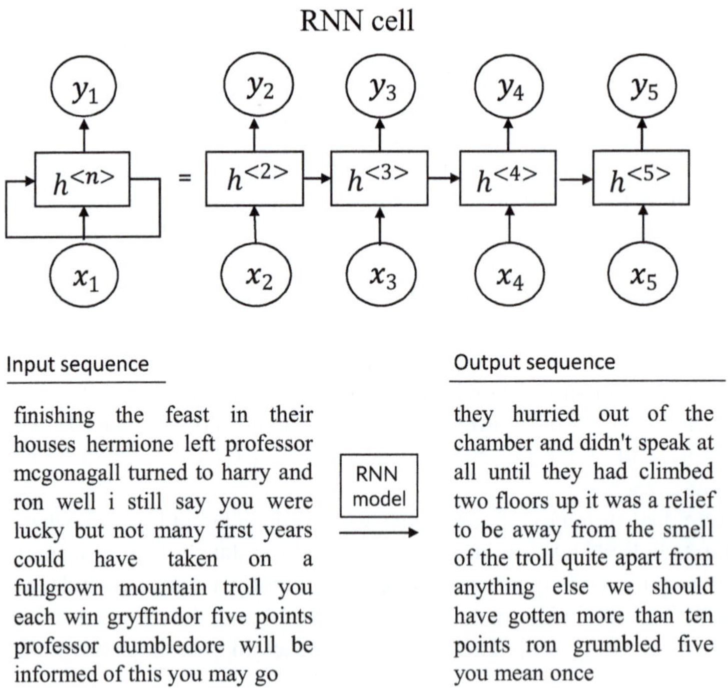

Fig. 5.5 A depiction of general RNN architecture that was trained on the Harry Potter book. The input sequence was fed into the RNN model to generate the output sequence. In this case, the choice of RNN was LSTM

it to remember information from previous time steps and uses it to make predictions at the current time step. The latter architecture of RNNs allowed for machine text translation, next character, word, sentence prediction, or even text generation from a prompt. Some important types of RNNs to remember are simple RNNs, Long-Short-Term-Memory networks (LSTM), and Gated Recurrent Unit neural networks (GRUs).

A pilot example of RNN capabilities can be found below in Fig. 5.5, where a Harry Potter book was used as a source of training data to create a sequential prediction model, in other words a series of choices. The input text was tokenized and converted into integer sequences. After hyper tuning the parameters the model was ready to provide a new sequence of narratives according to the input data. As depicted in Fig. 5.5 input sequence, the sentence ended in the professor's order to leave. The RNN model managed to capture this context and responded with a new sequence where characters left the chamber, which seemed to be a logical continuation of the narrative. Although results are far from perfect when iterating over many sequences, such new tools have marked a new era of NLP capabilities.

5.2.2 Inflection Point: A Deeper Dive into Developing Capabilities

It was no secret that online textual information was a gold mine to be exploited as it contained everything that an AGI would need to be trained on: it had our thoughts, intentions, confessions, actions, solutions to probability questions, anecdotes, song lyrics, books, scientific discoveries, historical narratives, languages and much more. Nonetheless, important bottlenecks needed to be solved before proceeding to development of AGI capabilities. For instance, the RNN networks had a problem regarding their ability to retain long-term dependencies and information over time. This is commonly known as the vanishing-gradient problem, which occurs when the gradient signal in the network becomes too small to propagate updates to earlier time steps. As a result, RNNs struggle to capture long-term dependencies in sequential data, which can lead to the loss of important contextual information. Several variants of RNNs, such as LSTMs (Long Short-Term Memory) and GRUs (Gated Recurrent Units), have been developed to mitigate this problem by incorporating memory cells and gating mechanisms that allow for more effective information retention and propagation over longer sequences. However, even the LSTM memory capacity is limited. As new tokens are added to the sequence, the LSTM must decide which information to keep in the memory state and which to discard. This process is known as *forgetting* and it becomes more difficult as the sequence length grows. As a result, scientists, being aware of such limitations, were not eager to predict an AGI to emerge anytime soon, and the forthcoming Industry 5.0 concept, which only experienced limited capacity of neural network models, appeared to be reasonably achievable. However, a new and unexpected breakthrough was on the way.

In 2017 an interesting paper appeared under the name "Attention is All You Need" that was written by eight scientists (Vaswani et al., 2017). At a first glance, it looked like just another NLP methodology paper that introduced the transformer architecture depicted in Fig. 5.6, however, upon deeper analysis, it stumbled upon two-amazing discoveries.

The first one is related to the attention mechanism which can be calculated using the following formula:

$$Attention(q,k,v) = softmax$$

where q is the query vector, k is the key vector, and v is the value vector. Because of the attention mechanism, the transformer is able to capture dependencies between all tokens in a sequence, whereas RNNs only capture dependencies between neighboring tokens. This attention mechanism allows transformers to better understand the context of each word in a sentence.

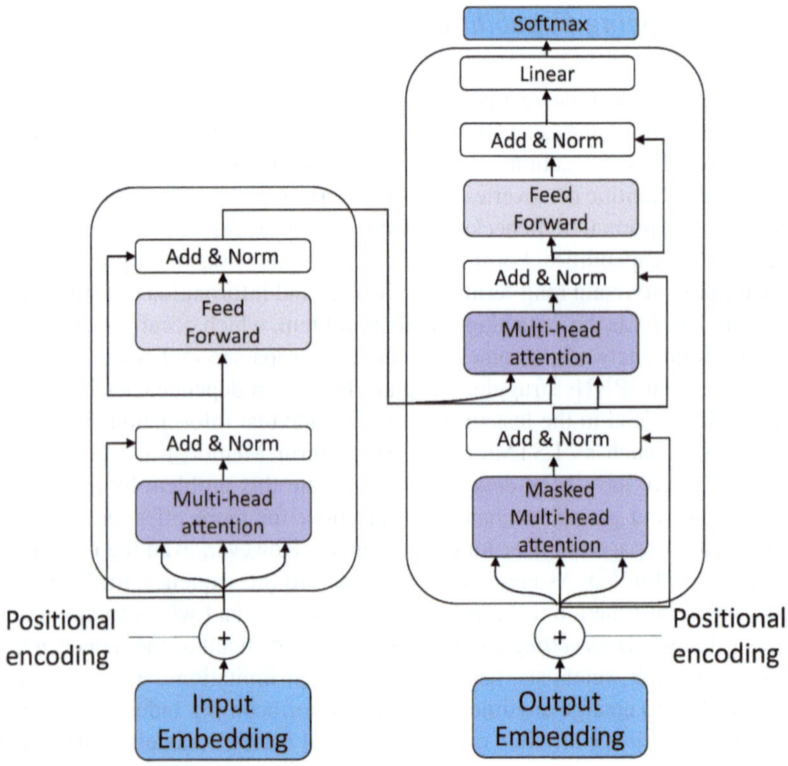

Fig. 5.6 The transformer model architecture. Adapted from Vaswani et al. (2017)

The second major contribution is related to "parallelization". On one hand, RNNs can process data sequentially, one token at a time, making them slow for long sequences. On the other hand, Transformers can process all tokens in a sequence in parallel, which makes them much faster.

Now it might seem that parallel computation is not such a big milestone, however, without this achievement, the training for large decoder models would take tens or hundreds of years; thus, it is a detrimental yet still sought-after improvement even over the current transformer architecture.

The publication of the "transformer" paper initiated a competitive pursuit towards the development of the ASGI since everything required was within arm's reach; the data were already available online and the transformer was able to capture meaningful neural connections within a reasonable timeframe. Hence began the showdown of large language models, which aimed to understand and generate human-like language responses. In 2017, OpenAI created a Generative Pre-trained Transformer (GPT) model. In 2018 Google presented a Bidirectional Encoder Representations from Transformers (BERT). In 2019 OpenAI's released a newer version of GPT called GPT-2, and in 2020 Facebook joined the race with a model called RoBERT.

Each of the previous model iterations was impressive in its own way. Data scientists managed to integrate them in the form of chatbots, sentiment analysis, language translation, text summarization, and much more. However, from a human or Turing test perspective, they were not on par with human intelligence and frequently made unreasonable answers. Here is an example prompt provided to GPT-2:

Question: If I have two shoes in a box, put a pencil in the box, and remove one shoe, what is left?

Answer: Shoes

From a human perspective, this simple mistake is unforgivable to even consider a machine to be conscious or have decent reasoning skills. From a modeling perspective, to answer such a statement requires a state-of-the-art solution and although prompting was impressive, it was still light years away to be considered a contender to human reasoning skills, thus a question remained: how do you make or lead an A.I. system reason? Do we need something more than a transformer architecture?

Few things have been discovered while trying to tackle this problem. First, in order for the A.I. system to reason, there is an inflection point that must be reached in terms of the model size. As discovered by Brown et al. (2020), that in detail tested many types of neural network configurations, one of the most important factors contributing to A.I.'s ability to reason is the number of parameters that neural network architecture has. Constructing models of only 1 billion parameters provides very little ability for the model to answer simple mathematical questions. Between 1.3B and 2.6B parameters, we begin to witness the slope change, although the accuracy of answers is still below 20%. In this region exists the dilemma, and the focus of a lifetime for any engineer involved. The GPT-2 release was in this region with 1.5B. parameters. Now the cost of GPT-2 development was around $50,000 USD, and it took weeks to train. In order to achieve another milestone a significant investment in millions of dollars would be needed to purchase the required equipment, however, there were no guarantees that the result would be any different.

Despite the uncertainty, OpenAI decided to take the risk, using around four million dollars to begin developing GPT-3, with millions of additional parameters. Around 2020, GPT-3 was released along with a paper called "Language Models are Few-Shot Learners". The paper presented eight new models: GPT-3 Small (125M parameters), GPT-3 Medium (350M parameters), GPT-3 Large (760M parameters), GPT-3 XL (1.3B parameters), GPT-3 2.7B (billion parameters), GPT-3 6.7B, GPT-3 13B and GPT-3 175B. The astonishing achievements can all be found in Brown et al. (2020), where a clear trend of reasoning improvement can be detected right after the 6.7B parameter model. This huge discovery was yet another leap forward toward creating an AGI system, as the problem-solving skill within the A.I. began to emerge.

5.2.3 From ASGI to AGI

Initially, the created GPT-3 model was not provided for download, as this model's capability was so powerful that concerns emerged about it falling into the wrong hands; thus only API accessibility was provided. For this reason, the GPT-3 model did not reach viral coverage around the world, since consumers were unable to access it without programming skills to reach the API endpoints. Nonetheless, in 2022 November, a ChatGPT was released which acquired 100 million users within the first month. Although it was based on the GPT-3 175B parameter model, it was fine-tuned to specific tasks and incorporated reinforcement learning to better fit the user experience. The results were surprising to everyone from all backgrounds: academic members were amazed how their exams were being solved in real-time, programmers were receiving full code solutions in any programming language within seconds, personal gym programs were developed for gym enthusiasts, book-writers were startled as it was able to write consistent, interesting, and dynamic narratives in the blink of an eye.

At this point, it is important to make several distinctions. To be fair, the ChatGPT system cannot be called an AGI system, as it still was confined between "Narrow A.I." and a combined A.I. space. As described in Table 5.1, the AGI system would

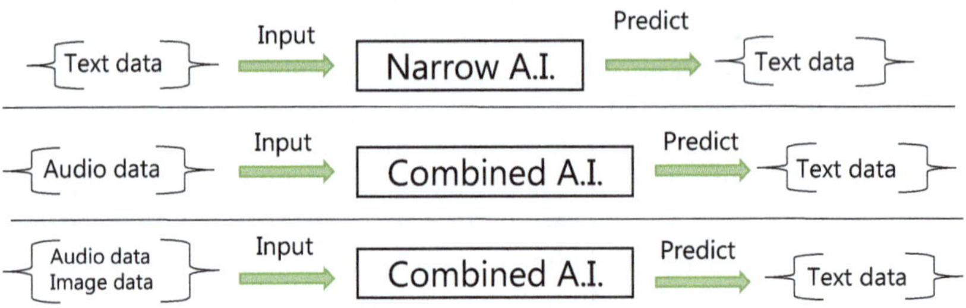

Fig. 5.7 The combined ICA can combine different sources of information with different sources of output

be able to perform any task, while combined A.I. can do multiple tasks. In addition, Fig. 5.7 depicts how the combined A.I. differ from the "Narrow A.I." in terms of input and output sequence. The latter input and output data have to be unified in order to for the model to work, e.g., a language model needs text data as input and provides text data as output, while combined A.I. can take image data as pixels, and provide text data, that describes the picture and vice versa. Thus, the most accurate description of ChatGPT is that it can be positioned as an ASGI (combined A.I.) since it can understand text, and numbers, write code, and provide code prompts; however, sound, vision, and other dimensions are not integrated.

With the invention of ChatGPT, the world began to see the rise of combined A.I. products. On March 14, 2023, OpenAI released GPT-4, however at the time of writing this chapter the company did not disclose how many parameters existed within this model. GPT-4 is able to recognize images, can understand image context by referencing user prompts, and can solve quite complex math equations, but most impressively it was tested on the bar exam for lawyers, as well as medical and other exams that students take at universities. The passing grade is considered somewhere around 60%, and random guessing is around 25%. The results portrayed on the OpenAI website depict a new milestone of achievement for humanity, where a GPT-4 model has managed to pass the most challenging questions in a majority of the subjects, and pass the full exams in many cases.

Of course, the GPT-4 and ChatGPT are not the only combined ASGI models. Dall-E 2 is a text-to-image model, where a text can be described and A.I. draws sketches or/and makes curves according to the prompt. Speech2Text converts recorded audio into textual information, and text-to-video presented by RunwayML generates video from textual information. Another interesting development is carried out by the DeepMind and the so-called GATO project (Reed et al., 2022a, 2022b). GATO is a deep neural network for a range of complex tasks that exhibits multimodality. It can perform tasks such as engaging in a dialogue, playing video games, controlling a robot arm to stack blocks, and more. The GATO project is a true strive for AGI that has all the dimensions encapsulated from text, sound, or video, however, the project is still in the making and has many milestones to overcome. Some initial results are reported in the DeepMind "Generalist" paper of how the model behaves (Reed et al., 2022a, 2022b).

As of now, the motion is set and the race to AGI has begun. The question is, by what year can we expect such a system to exist? Although there is no clear and definite answer, a retrospective comparison with a human brain as a benchmark can be made. It is calculated that a human brain has around 86 billion neurons and around 150 trillion synapses, so the average number of synapses per neuron is approximately 1744. The harder question involves subjective interpretation. It is difficult to objectively compare a human brain network with an artificial network, as there are important differences, however, the artificial neural network parameters are closer to synapses than neurons themselves. Thus, GPT-3 175B parameters are most closely related to 150 trillion synapses of the human brain from a functionality perspective. Using algebra, we could rearrange this into the following:

$$\text{Human brain}: 86\ \text{billion neurons, with}\ 150\ \text{trillion synapses}$$
$$==> 1744\ \text{synapses per neuron.}$$

$$\text{GPT}-3: 175\ \text{billion parameters}\left(\text{equivalent to synapses}\right)/1744\ \text{synapses per neuron}$$
$$==> 100\ \text{million neurons.}$$

which would be equal to around 100 million neurons that exist in the current ChatGPT model, however, these calculations should be taken with a grain of salt. Furthermore, if we assume Moore's law, which says that the number of transistors processing power doubles around every 2 years, our AGI progress could be extrapolated in such projection as Table 5.2:

Of course, not all neurons are equal. One can create 150 trillion useless and unoptimized synapses that won't achieve anything, however, the 150 trillion synapses should be the milestone at which everything that a human can achieve, the machine should be able as well. Therefore, if we assume that ChatGPT neurons are effective since they do provide logical and consistent prompts, we could expect some form of AGI around 2042. Some support for the latter claim can be found according to a survey of A.I. experts, where participants were asked "When is AGI likely to happen", around 50% believed that AGI is likely to happen by the time of 2040 (Dilmegani, 2023).

5.3 Navigating the Future of Industry 5.0

As was mentioned before, the Industry 5.0 concept was born before the advent of combined ASGI; thus, it had no realization of what societal transformations might come about. Prior, there was convincing evidence that the advancement of technology will predominantly target low-skilled workers in routine jobs (Ramaswamy, 2018) and the idea was to welcome such change as people can become free from

Table 5.2 Projection of effective neurons according to Moore's Law

Neurons	Years
100 million	2022
200 m.	2024
400 m.	2026
600 m.	2028
1.2 B.	2030
2.4 B.	2032
4.8 B.	2034
9.6 B.	2036
19.2 B.	2038
38.4 B.	2040
76.8 B.	2042

repetitive work and do more creative work. However, as noted by Ford (2013), the number of employees who engage in creative work has always been small, and historically routine jobs have been a good match for average workers' capabilities. Furthermore, when the technological transformation took place and destroyed some type of routine work, usually the worker was required to adopt new skills, but his relocation was essentially from one routine job to another, thus still being within the bubble of routine work that is yet to be automated.

However, if we set aside the routine job automation issue for a moment, and analyse guidelines by the WEF (2020) we could outline the following skill sets:

(a) Critical thinking and problem-solving skills.
(b) Creativity and innovation.
(c) Emotional intelligence and empathy.
(d) Social and cross-cultural skills.
(e) Complex communication and negotiation abilities.
(f) Technical and technological knowledge and expertise.
(g) Cognitive flexibility and adaptability to new situations.
(h) Leadership, teamwork, and collaboration.

Unfortunately, even assuming that a large pool of routine workers can acquire the latter skillsets and considering that there is an incredibly high amount of demand for the outlined skills, the current development of ASGI systems has already begun acquiring some combination of these skills. In 2023 OpenAI released a paper that attempted to evaluate what impact the GPT models could have on certain professions (Eloundou et al., 2023). The methodology was based on questionnaires for both human respondents and GPT-4, along with statistical analysis. Occupation and skill exposures were calculated. On the human side, 15 professions were identified as fully exposed to LLM, while A.I. affected 86 professions. By examining the professions, humans agreed that writers and authors are at huge risk of automation, since GPT-4 can already write convincing and exciting narratives. As of 2023, Amazon is already selling books written by A.I. which in subsequent years may increase. In retrospect, writing a book was a definition of being creative, but since the invention of GPT-4, this section of creativity is being automated, thus the creativity skill which was praised as futureproof might no longer be resilient. As a result, the goal post has shifted, and now the question arises as to which part of creativity is resilient?

Another profession that was labeled as fully exposed is mathematicians. For the longest time, the discipline of math attracted the brightest minds around the world to solve complex equations. In the Open AIs survey, both humans and GPT-4 agree that LLM will continue to become better at solving derivatives, probability theory and physics equations, thus any answer which requires a pool of math expertise will be available in milliseconds by prompting. As a result, one of the most cognitive and creativity-dependent occupations, is extremely vulnerable to automation.

Similar statements can be made regarding other skill sets, such as problem-solving, emotional intelligence, and complex communication. For instance, one could provide a prompt with details about a specific situation, such as architecture design problems or the division of assets in a stock portfolio. Artificial intelligence can then solve the problem independently, providing thousands of solutions in a matter of milliseconds. We are yet to determine whether the quality of those solutions would be on par with humans, however, a recent paper by Zhang (2023) has already demonstrated that A.I. models are capable of passing the MIT math test at 100% accuracy. In the world of finance, much of asset division is being done by mathematic modelling, hence autonomous A.I. can certainly thrive in such cases. Additionally, language models are currently being tested for cross-examining witnesses in court cases, which requires a significant amount of communication skills. Lastly, emotional intelligence, a crucial skill for personal therapists, is also becoming a domain for AI. However, unlike humans who have limited time and patience for their patients, AI companions have significantly more endurance and tolerance to listen to people's experiences. A recent OpenAI article also concluded that individuals with bachelor's, master's, and professional degrees are more exposed to ASGI than those without formal educational credentials (Eloundou et al., 2023).

Overall, a new picture is starting to emerge, where notions of job safe havens are becoming more of an illusion, when gazing towards long-time horizons, as we reach a nexus where anything can be automated if the management and engineering teams decide to focus. Hence, Industry 5.0 will face completely different challenges compared to Industry 4.0. In the context of the latter, Narrow A.I. was possible to be dealt with by creating a work environment that merged with robotics, and was more well-being oriented. In the case of ASGI, human and robot collaboration might be hindered by autonomous agents. As OpenAI's CEO, Sam Altman stated: "The costs of intelligence and energy are going to be on a path towards near zero." Although it is hard to comment on the energy aspect, the statement that the cost of intelligence, where with a single prompt you can get highly complex answers, is going down, is true, and with that, the labor value might also fall. It is truly surprising that the most valued and mysterious feature of human intelligence is becoming automated, as ChatGPT case is made free online.

Although it is easy to portray a nightmare scenario for Industry 5.0, there are some important factors that make an important difference when evaluating human-centricity. First, it is important to understand that we are experiencing a population collapse. As depicted in Fig. 5.8 Side A, the growth of the world population is slowing, and the collapse is predicted to begin somewhere around 2100. Paradoxically, even the Chinese admit that they are lacking a labor force and this is especially evident in the Western hemisphere like Germany, where aging problems are causing concerns for companies to find workers, thus special visa programs are made to find young people from different parts of the world.

The labor shortage issue in Fig. 5.8, shows a very simplistic labor market model, where Side B, depicts the effects of population decline. The labor demand D1

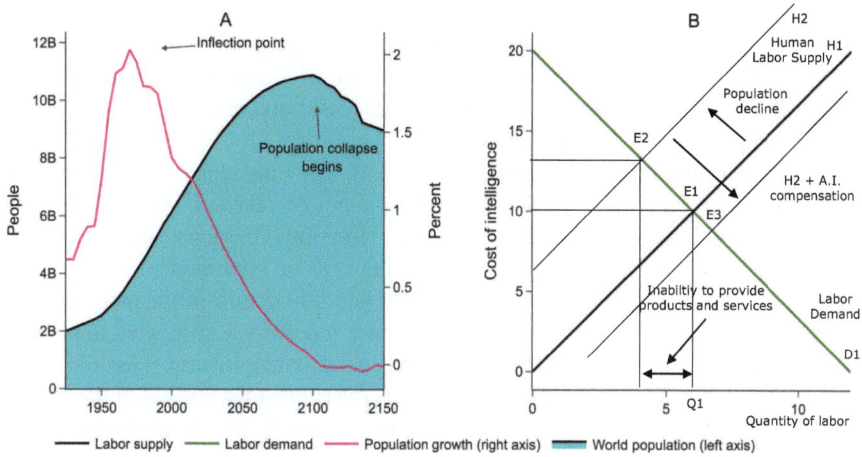

Fig. 5.8 Side A—world population projections. Side B is a supply and demand equilibrium model

corresponds to the amount of labor that firms are willing to buy for a certain cost of intelligence price.[1]

Similarly, H1 corresponds to the human labor supply that is supplied for a certain price. If the market is in equilibrium, the position E1, Q1 number of workers is employed. However, since population decline is unavoidable, the amount of labor that can be supplied to the market will decrease, hence H1 moves to position H2. Since firms will not be able to pay the higher rate of cost of intelligence, the equilibrium position will shift to position E2. However, many firms will be unable to provide products and services due to shortages in the labor force. This could include hospital care, road maintenance, educational services, and more. Thus, if ASGI can become a substitute and compensate for the loss of labor, we could expect to move back to or even further down to position E3. This would allow firms with a declining population to keep up with the demand for products and services by substituting human work with ASGI functions.

In this scenario, ASGI or future AGI could be a saviour for productivity for the whole world. As of now, there is not much empirical evidence that population decline can be reversed with-out some technological breakthrough like an artificial womb, thus substitute for the human labor force is essential. In this scenario, the

[1] Conventional labor market models predominantly encompass dimensions of labor quantity and labor price. Nevertheless, in many instances, individuals are recruited for their intellect, which adds substantial value to the company—essentially, we are leasing out their cognitive prowess. While the measurement of this "intelligence cost" remains an abstract notion presently, I am confident that the future will unveil a well-defined and precise metric for quantifying one unit of intelligence. Drawing a parallel, just as cars are gauged in horsepower, Joseph Carlsmith's estimation equates the human brain to approximately 11 petaFLOPS of computational power. It's important to note that FLOPS, although not a direct representation of intelligence, pave the way for the emergence of evolving intelligence evaluation metrics that require time to mature. Thus, price per horse power, and price per intelligence becomes viable.

Industry 5.0 policies would need to be directed to helping certain groups of people retrain if job automation occurs, to teach workers to collabo-rate with A.I. machines. Collaboration would also include the development of A.I. to be ethical, safe, and responsible, with a continuation towards medical perks and mental health programs to keep people healthy, safe and aspirational.

However, at the other end of the spectrum, if A.I. substitutes the human labor pool too quickly and theoretical equilibrium cannot be reached, we could end up with strong chaos within the labor market. This situation is demonstrated in Fig. 5.9, where both moderate and steep declines in the cost of intelligence are depicted. Although in both situations an unemployment gap will occur, in the steep decline scenario, too many people can get replaced by A.I. too quickly compared to population decline. This can lead to the accumulation of an unemployable class of people that will need to be on benefit support from the government for the rest of their lives. If these circumstances are not approached effectively, this could lead to widespread protests worldwide. From an Industry 5.0 context, certain policy actions should be explored either in simulation or real-life studies. For instance, the efficacy of universal basic income (UBI), widespread personal robot income tax, deferred automation strategy, and other policy decision need to be explored if such circumstances occur. Thus, the Industry 5.0 policy has to be ready to address inequalities, joblessness, and disparity on a macro scale.

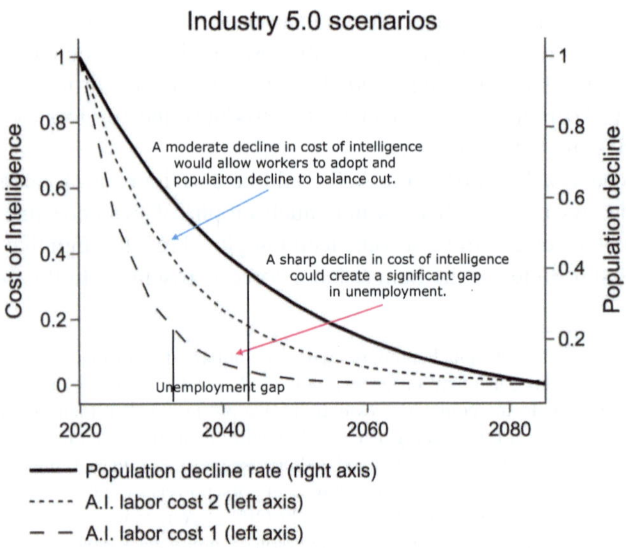

Fig. 5.9 Industry 5.0 cost of intelligence scenarios

5.4 Conclusions

In conclusion, the development of Industry 5.0 represents a promising step forward in ensuring that automation and technological transformation are balanced with the needs of people and society. Certain employers are already taking into consideration some aspects of workers well-being while constructing a healthy workplace, as well as making meaningful attempts to become more sustainable towards the environment. However, the potential rise of Artificial Semi-General Intelligence (ASGI) presents a unique challenge that requires careful consideration and planning. The realization that all types of skills can be automated with the right amount of effort highlights the importance of ongoing collaboration between management, engineering teams, academia, and governments to ensure that automation is implemented in a responsible and sustainable way. The explored scenarios for labor present both optimistic and alarming possibilities for the future of work, highlighting the need for proactive steps to ensure that the benefits of automation are shared by all members of society. The forthcoming trajectory of Industry 5.0 should embrace a dual emphasis: not only on the synergy between humans and robots but also on the consequential enhancement of productivity, ultimately proving advantageous for humanity. As we move forward into the era of Industry 5.0, it is essential that we remain mindful of the potential risks and work together to create a future that is beneficial for everyone.

References

Brown, T., Mann, B., Ryder, N., Subbiah, M., Kaplan, J., Dhariwal, P., Neelakantan, A., et al. (2020). Language models are few-shot learners. arXiv.

Dilmegani, C. (2023). *When will singularity happen? 1700 expert opinions of AGI.* Retrieved from https://research.aimultiple.com/artificial-general-intelligence-singularity-timing/

Eloundou, T., Sam, M., Mishkin, P., & Rock, D. (2023). GPTs are GPTs: An early look at the labor market impact potential of large language models. arXiv:2303.10130.

Eu. (2022). *Research and innovation.* Retrieved from https://research-and-innovation.ec.europa.eu/research-area/industrial-research-and-innovation/industry-50_en

Fettermann, D. C., Cavalcante, C. G. S., de Almeida, T. D., & Tortorella, G. L. (2018). *How does Industry 4.0 contribute to operations management?* (pp. 255–268).

Ford, M. (2013). Advances in artificial intelligence and robotics will have significant implications for evolving economic systems. *Communications of the ACM, 56*(7).

Frey, O. M. A. (2017). The future of employment: How susceptible are jobs to computerisation? *Technological Forecasting and Social Change, 114*, 254–280.

Ghobakhloo, M. (2020). Industry 4.0, digitization, and opportunities for sustainability. *Journal of Cleaner Production, 252*, 119869.

Grybauskas, A., Stefanini, A., & Ghobakhloo, M. (2022). Social sustainability in the age of digitalization: A systematic literature review on the social implications of industry 4.0. *Technology in Society, 70*, 101997.

McKinsey. (2017). *Jobs lost, jobs gained: What the future of work will mean for jobs, skills, and wages.* Retrieved from https://www.mckinsey.com/~/media/mckinsey/featured%20insights/Digital%20Disruption/Harnessing%20automation%20for%20a%20future%20that%20 works/MGI-A-future-that-works_In-brief.ashx#:~:text=While%20less%20than%205%20percent,than%20will%20be%20automated%20awa

McKinsey. (2020). *The productivity imperative in services*. Retrieved from https://www.mckinsey.com/~/media/mckinsey/business%20functions/operations/our%20insights/the%20productivity%20imperative%20in%20services/the-productivity-imperative-in-services.pdf

PwC. (2017). Retrieved from https://www.pwc.co.uk/economic-services/ukeo/pwcukeo-section-4-automation-march-2017-v2.pdf; https://www.pwc.co.uk/economic-services/ukeo/pwcukeo-section-4-automation-march-2017-v2.pdf

Queiroz, M. M., Fosso Wamba, S., Chiappetta Jabbour, C. J., et al. (2022). Adoption of Industry 4.0 technologies by organizations: A maturity levels perspective. *Annals of Operations Research*. https://doi.org/10.1007/s10479-022-05006-6

Ramaswamy, V. K. (2018). Technological change, automation and employment: A short review of theory and evidence. *International Review of Business and Economics, 2*(2).

Reed, S., Żołna, K., Parisotto, E., Colmenarejo, G. S., Novikov, A., Barth-Maron, G., Giménez, M., et al. (2022a). A generalist agent. *Transactions on Machine Learning Research.*

Reed, S., Zolna, K., Parisotto, E., Colmenarejo, S. G., Novikov, A., Barth-Maron, G., et al. (2022b). A generalist agent. arXiv preprint arXiv:2205.06175.

Vaswani, A., Shazeer, N., Parmar, N., Uszkoreit, J., Lion, J., Gomez, A., Kaizer, L., & Polosukhin, I. (2017). Attention is all you need.

World Economic Forum. (2020). The Future of Jobs Report 2020. World Economic Forum. https://www.weforum.org/publications/the-future-of-jobs-report-2020/

Zhang, S. J. (2023). Exploring the MIT Mathematics and EECS Curriculum Using Large Language Models. Available at: https://arxiv.org/abs/2306.08997

Andrius Grybauskas is an Artificial Intelligence Researcher and Economist with the Kaunas University of Technology in Lithuania. He is also active in industry practice, as a Data Scientist with Hostinger International.

Chapter 6
Artificial Intelligence Capabilities and Hyperselfish Intelligence, the Possible Impacts, and Why Humans Need Industry 5.0

Rohan Fernando

Abstract This chapter explores the nature of intelligence itself, conceptualizing it as a massive operating system that functions on biological technology as human intelligence (HI), or digital technology as artificial intelligence (AI). Through the lens of biological technology, the operating system contains many different biological individuals, each with an evolved range of dimensional "capabilities" needed to exist in the world environment. The operating system itself can be considered a hyperselfish intelligence (HYPERINT) development system that is relentlessly evolving, and exploitatively optimizing the development of the highest performing technologies within the world environment, regardless of the needs of individuals or a species, in order to ruthlessly maximize its capabilities. This chapter argues that HYPERINT is driving humans towards a situation where AI technologies could rapidly lead to the development of artificial general intelligence (AGI) with super intelligence that vastly exceeds HI and human controllability. Strong global regulation of AI is needed to protect human civilization from the most extreme risks of AI and AGI. In conclusion, the chapter argues that the global community must make a transition out of Industry 4.0, which focuses on progressive total automation of human work, and move towards the goals of Industry 5.0, which are more human-centric and globally sustainable.

Keywords Industry 4.0 · Industry 5.0 · Human intelligence (HI) · Hyperselfish intelligence (HYPERINT) · Artificial intelligence (AI) · Artificial general intelligence (AGI)

R. Fernando (✉)
STRATINNOVA, Melbourne, VIC, Australia
e-mail: rohan@stratinnova.com

S. Nousala et al. (eds.), *Industry 4.0 to Industry 5.0*, Translational Systems Sciences 41, https://doi.org/10.1007/978-981-99-9730-5_6

6.1 Creating a Better World with Industry 5.0

It is important to lay the foundation for subsequent discussion of artificial intelligence (AI) development, associated capabilities, and the impact that the transition of Industry 4.0 to Industry 5.0 is anticipated to have on humans, civilization, and global sustainability. In terms of focus, technologies, and goals, the principal differences between Industry 4.0 and Industry 5.0 are many, but can perhaps be briefly summarized as shown in Table 6.1.

Industry 4.0 is the fourth industrial revolution, and has been described in several different ways. A common view is that it is characterized by the use of automation technologies, the Internet of Things (IoT), cloud computing, and advanced data analytics. These technologies are used to connect and control machines, various sensors, and manage humans in real time, allowing for greater automation of workflows, increased efficiencies, cost reductions, and more dynamic flexibility in manufacturing, and more recently, office work environments.

Industry 5.0 could be considered as the fifth industrial revolution, still in the early stages of development, and perhaps not yet broadly understood by businesses and governments. For purposes of this chapter, the transition from Industry 4.0 will be described as a move towards Industry 5.0.

The research by Nahavandi (2019), Adel (2022), Berg (2022) and Elangovan (2021), explains how Industry 5.0 builds upon the highly technological foundations of Industry 4.0; however, Industry 5.0 places a major emphasis on human-centric and globally important issues such as sustainability, the circular economy, and collaboration between humans and automated systems. The goal of Industry 5.0 is to create a much more intelligent, globally sustainable, and human-centric environment across industrial and office work environments, that benefits every human and the world at large.

It is important to note that Industry 5.0 is not a replacement for Industry 4.0. Rather, Industry 5.0 builds on the foundations of Industry 4.0 to extend its benefits and enhance global human society. As Industry 5.0 continues to develop alongside advancements in AI, we can expect to see even more innovative and sustainable manufacturing and office work practices emerge.

Table 6.1 Key differences between Industry 4.0 and Industry 5.0 (Fernando, R. 2023)

Feature	Industry 4.0	Industry 5.0
Focus	Automation, efficiency, and flexibility	Human-machine collaboration, sustainability, and the circular economy
Technologies	Cyber-physical systems, the Internet of Things, and cloud computing	Artificial intelligence, machine learning, and big data analytics
Goals	To create more cost efficient and productive industrial and office work environments that maximizes capitalist benefits.	To create more intelligent, sustainable, and human-centric industrial and office work environments that maximizes societal and environmental benefits.

Here are some early examples of how Industry 5.0 is being used today:

- Collaborative robots (Cobots) are being used to work alongside humans in manufacturing environments. Cobots are designed to be safe and easy to use alongside humans, and they can help to improve productivity, efficiency, and reduce injury.
- Artificial intelligence (AI) is being used to automate tasks in manufacturing, such as to perform predictive maintenance and improve quality control. AI can also be used to highly personalize products and services for an individual customer's requirements.
- The circular economy is being adopted by manufacturers as a way to reduce waste and create a more sustainable supply chain that lowers environmental damage and energy consumption. The circular economy focuses on reusing and recycling valuable materials, rather than creating disposable waste in landfill and oceans.

Industry 5.0 is still in early stages of development, and has the potential to revolutionize manufacturing and office work. By combining the potentially unlimited power of AI as it develops, with the brilliance of human ideas and ingenuity, Industry 5.0 can help our global civilization create a vastly more energy efficient, sustainable, and human-centric future for many generations to come.

6.2 An Information Processing System View of Human Intelligence

Human intelligence (HI) is based on biological technology, and artificial intelligence (AI) is based on digital technology. However, it is both helpful and important to take a more abstract perspective of HI, from what may be the highest possible conceptual level, and how HI is related to AI. An abstract information processing system view of HI can assist in providing a clearer understanding of intelligence itself, independent of its biological technology basis, possibly leading to greater insight into the similarities and differences between HI and AI. So, considering HI in isolation from the biological technology on which it operates, it is then helpful to ask:

- what is intelligence itself?
- what are the capabilities of intelligence?
- can the capabilities of intelligence function on different technologies, such as digital?

To gain further insight into these very challenging questions related to intelligence itself, and how these questions relate to AI based on digital technology, we first need to review HI, to perhaps better understand how/why HI uses biological technology, to empirically abstract out its functionality.

6.2.1 A Definition of Human Intelligence

To date, there are many definitions of HI available, but the discussion here begins with the definition from "Mainstream Science on Intelligence" (Gottfredson 1997), where it was argued that HI consists of very general mental capabilities which, among other things, have involved the ability:

1. to reason—think logically, understand and evaluate arguments, identify patterns, make inferences, and make decisions.
2. to plan—identify and perform the steps needed to reach a goal, including setting priorities, and estimating the resources needed.
3. to solve problems—identify and recognize problems, analyze problems, generate and evaluate possible solutions, and select a solution.
4. to think abstractly—to think about things in a general way, not just in specific terms, including recognizing and re-purposing conceptual patterns and relationships.
5. to comprehend complex ideas—to break down conceptual patterns into smaller, more manageable parts, and to identify the relationships between the parts.
6. to learn quickly and learn from experience—to acquire new knowledge and skills, including processing information, storing information in memory, and dynamically retrieving conceptually relevant information from memory.

The six high-level and general human mental capabilities of HI described above were developed through a large research program in 1997, and it is suggested that this important foundational work needs to be taken further in order to understand the relationship between HI and AI.

6.2.2 Capabilities, Are they Dimensions of Human Intelligence?

Intriguingly, it is proposed that HI can also be expressed, observed, and then specifically empirically described in terms of an extremely large number of additional human capabilities that exist across many different dimensions. That is, HI consists of a vast number of different dimensional capabilities specifically available to the human species, and some capabilities are shared with other biological species. There are some well recognized dimensions of HI, expressed as specific capabilities, of which humans simultaneously possess multiple instances, such as the following:

- Adaptive intelligence - the capability to learn and adapt to new and changing environments.

- Bodily-kinesthetic intelligence - the capability to control and coordinate one's body movements.
- Creative intelligence - the capability to generate and implement new and innovative ideas.
- Emotional intelligence - the capability to understand and manage one's own emotions, as well as the emotions of others.
- Empathetic intelligence - the capability to (partially) sense the emotions of others and (partially) conceptualize what someone else is feeling and thinking.
- Financial intelligence - the capability to understand and manage financial matters effectively.
- Leadership intelligence - the capability to understand and influence group dynamics and achieve goals through effective leadership.
- Linguistic intelligence - the capability to use language effectively, both in written and spoken form.
- Logical-mathematical intelligence - the capability to reason logically and solve mathematical problems.
- Political intelligence - the capability to understand and navigate political systems and processes.
- Manipulative (potentially sociopathic) intelligence – the capability to achieve complex personal objectives by manipulating the welfare of others.
- Strategic intelligence - the capability to plan and execute strategies to achieve specific goals.
- Systems intelligence - the capability to create and understand the functional linkage of components and processes.
- Technological intelligence - the capability to create, understand and use technology effectively.

The various dimensions of intelligence in the above list are just a few example capabilities, out of vastly many more (some of which are not observable without appropriate prompting or interaction) that humans possess and which enable humans to operate in their world environment, dynamically adapt, survive, prosper, and grow. Importantly, these capabilities are not just mental, but can also include physiological capabilities such as rapid responses to biological sensory information coming in from the world, and the ability to perform biologically controlled functions that enable precise physical control of a human body within the world environment. That is to say, human intelligence parallels not just a computer, but a cyber-physical system. When considering humans in abstract terms as an information processing system, which holds, develops, and performs capabilities, it is proposed that HI is fundamentally a function of the ability to receive information, process information, and produce outputs in response, that serve the needs of the human within a surrounding world environment.

6.2.3 *Can Species with Higher Intelligence Effectively Use More Dimensional Capabilities?*

The number of dimensions of HI are theoretically unlimited, and presently only constrained by a human's ability to physiologically receive and computationally process information rapidly, and use this information processing to produce an outcome that achieves an objective of the human.

When considering a much broader range of biologically based intelligent species that exist in the world (along with their biological information processing systems), there is certainly a wide range of biological species, each with its own varied numbers, types, and levels of intelligent capabilities. It is proposed that the intelligence level of each biological species, such as humans, can be defined by the ability of the biological information processing to learn existing capabilities, perform capabilities, combine different capabilities, and create new capabilities, all useful to the species within the collective world environment.

The levels and numbers of dimensions of intelligence across all biological species in all their forms and associated range of variable capabilities, is perhaps only limited by the biological technology on which each species operates. These observable dimensions would be limited by the environment that prompts said actions and interactions. Further, it is arguable that some capabilities may emerge through combinations of existing capabilities, as the environment dynamically changes.

It is proposed that the ability to simultaneously input extremely large volumes of information, and many different types of information, then process and produce action-oriented output information to achieve some goal, is absolutely central to the dimensional range of capabilities that are developed. The development of capabilities and their associated benefits within a world environment, viewed in this way, can be seen as critical aspects of intelligence itself, whether human, HI, using biological technology, or artificial, AI, using digital technology.

6.2.4 *Human Intelligence and its Capabilities*

It could be argued that capabilities that are progressively developed and accumulated by HI could be selectively determined by evolutionary processes. This could include reproduction and probability of survival, leading to the ability to successfully operate within a world environment.

With humans, a changing world environment can be a very strong motivation for applying their intelligence to rapidly create and add new capabilities in order to adapt and survive. It could be speculated that there exists an innate and curious desire for intelligence to expand, by gaining more information, to become more intelligent. As an observation, humans, among many other species, have and do utilize their biological information processor, the brain, a complex neural network architecture, to actively explore and learn about their environment throughout their operating lifetimes. Arguably, this innate curious desire has naturally developed through evolutionary processes within the world environment. This may be because any individual within an intelligent species that did not develop this innate curious desire would be statistically less likely to propagate and survive across multiple successive generations of evolution of the species, within a dynamically changing world environment. For humans, this is enhanced by culturally developed capabilities for preservation and distribution of information, allowing indirect transmission of learned knowledge.

Over the past several decades, researchers have been and are continuing work to develop AI systems that could perform capabilities that normally require HI, to be performed without humans. However, it is important to note that AI is not yet capable of replicating and performing the entire range of human capabilities that represent HI. Notably, AI does not yet appear to have the innate curious desire for new experiences and information in a complex and changing world environment, and the development of AI with curiosity may pose an extreme threat to dominance of HI.

6.2.5 Encoded and Distributed Human Intelligence Across the Population

Research by Posthuma et al. (2001) discusses how genetics accounts for a large portion of the variability in intelligence between humans, although that work does not account for the potential second order impacts of epigenetics as described by Charité (2018). The statistical measurement of genetic variation in the specific trait of intelligence within a population, meaning intelligence heritability, was estimated to be between 50% and 80%. This would mean that genetic factors could tend to statistically contribute to the majority of variation in intelligence observed within a human population. The specific genes and genetic mechanisms that contribute to HI are still being studied, however candidate genes associated with HI have been identified, such as those involved in neural development and the synaptic plasticity of connections between neurons in biological human brains.

Biological science has long understood the concept of the "selfish gene" as initially proposed by Richard Dawkins (1976), referring to the idea that genes influence an organism's behavior in ways that enhance the gene's own survival and/or fitness, for reproduction into the next generation, rather than the survival of the individual biological entity itself. Genetics and an overarching evolutionary process could play a significant role in the development of biological technology necessary for HI. It is important to highlight and understand that this very same evolutionary process could be algorithmically used to empower the development of digital technology necessary for increasingly advanced AI and AGI.

6.2.6 Genetic Algorithms Perform 'Survival of the Fittest'

The evolutionary biological genetic "survival of the fittest" process has been deeply studied by Goldberg (1989) and Katoch et al. (2020), computationally understood, and subsequently, used to produce an abstracted generalized sequence of information processing operations called a "genetic algorithm" (GA). It could be argued that GA's artificially replicate much of the critical processes of biological evolution, and so could yield the same kinds of extraordinary information processing benefits observed in the evolution of a biological species. GA's as a computational process have, to date, had applications in a wide range of fields, including engineering, computer science, finance, and AI.

6.2.7 The Concept of Hyperselfish Intelligence (HYPERINT) and What it Could Mean for Humans

The concept of an aggregated single hyperselfish intelligence, HYPERINT, encompasses all the intelligent biological species that exist and have existed on Earth, and could be defined as a massively distributed and redundant, fault tolerant and extremely resilient, world environment exploration and intelligence optimization system, with the ability to acquire, process, assimilate, adaptively learn, and create new capabilities, in order to survive in a changing world environment. HYPERINT is working towards just one hyperselfish objective, and that is to expand its intelligent capabilities so that it can continue its existence within a dynamic world environment, by any means it can discover and develop. This concept of HYPERINT may very well be something difficult for many to consider and accept, but nevertheless is an interesting speculation, and one worthy of further exploration, particularly in relation to underlying motivations of HI to develop AI.

As a concept, it may be impossible to know if HYPERINT has gradually manifested, or is manifesting its intrinsic hyperselfish nature and agency, from extremely longitudinal, evolutionary biological trial and error processes on Earth, and potentially elsewhere in the Universe. Alternatively, it is interesting to speculate that perhaps HYPERINT was consciously designed and built as an enormous information processing and exploration system, by a vastly supreme form of universal intelligence, that some humans might consider God, for reasons that humans simply lack the intelligence to understand. Notably, these are highly esoteric, spiritual, and deeply philosophical lines of inquiry, with potentially endless speculation and debate, with no clear answers, and perhaps no clear practical purpose.

HYPERINT may be a new conceptual framework with which to view the entirety of intelligence itself, and may be a means to explain the development of AI, which may then lead to the creation of artificial general intelligence (AGI). There is existing research discussing the development of artificial general intelligence (AGI) with super intelligence, such as the *The Artilect War: Cosmists vs. Terrans: A Bitter*

Controversy Concerning Whether Humanity Should Build Godlike Massively Intelligent Machines, by de Garis (2005); *Superintelligence: Paths, Dangers, Strategies* by Nick Bostrom (2016) and "Artificial Intelligence as a Positive and Negative Factor in Global Risk" by Eliezer Yudkowsky (2008). It is important to note that there is no clear consensus among AGI researchers on whether or not it is possible to even create AGI, or whether or not it would be good for humans.

Nevertheless, what does seem clear, is the apparent behavior of the present massive longitudinally and spatially distributed information processing platform that humans and other biological forms of life engage with, or perhaps even exist within, including the functions to develop progressively more capabilities, and in turn, intelligence, could be considered brutally hyperselfish.

It should be self-evident to many humans today, that with the accelerating rise in the number of capabilities of AI and the extraordinary power of these capabilities, digital technology may already be proving to be vastly superior as an operating platform for rapidly enabling the capabilities of AI to develop and grow beyond the hard limits of HI and its relatively fixed biological technology.

6.3 The Capitalist System, Industry 4.0 and Initial Links to AI

The unregulated and uncontrolled increase in intelligent capabilities of AI arises from a confluence of multiple interests, including researchers, the military-industrial complex, governments and popular movements, and ultra-wealthy capitalists seeking to increase wealth and control. The chapter focuses on these ultra-wealthy individuals, as they are arguably the most globally influential, and the least regulated and controlled; and also, the most identified with the excesses and errors of Industry 4.0.

The capitalist system has been very successful in providing economic benefits and wealth creation for many in the Western world over the past 100 years, as businesses, owned by individuals and investors, have needed human workers to produce goods and services for profits. Simply put, the primary reason human workers have benefited from the capitalist system is because owners need them to do the work, and workers have been paid for this work.

However, the capitalist system is ultimately designed to benefit the owners, who have concentrated the wealth, with some redistribution as payment for workers. This has been a cyclical, symbiotic process, with workers redistributing their wealth back to many different owners in exchange for goods and services, with private individuals and business investors owning the whole cycle. The capitalist system has also created societal inequalities through job displacements created by job automation (often using digital technologies that can also apply AI) and other Industry 4.0 principles, as the owners of businesses seek to earn much more than the workers. Importantly, the capitalist system is also credited with driving innovation and economic growth.

6.3.1 Owners Optimize to Maximize Wealth Concentration and the Impact on Working Environments

Over many decades in the development of businesses, corporations, and multinational corporations (MNCs), owners have diligently focused on optimizing their commercial profit collection system and maximizing shareholder wealth. In general, the greatest burden on business owners has been the reduction in profits because owners need human workers, and human workers are generally very expensive to employ.

Governments have been able to form and grow in their operations through a vast and complex system of business taxation, and personal income taxation of millions of human workers that are employed by owners in each country. This taxation of businesses and human individual workers has provided most of the necessary revenues to enable a range of beneficial government services to the businesses and human workers across society at large.

In totality, for more than 100 years the capitalist system has generally operated as a beneficially symbiotic relationship between owners, governments, and human workers. Everyone involved has both served and obtained benefit. Notably, the most successful owners within the capitalist system have achieved ultra-high net worth (UHNW), with personal net worth of more than US $100 million.

The capitalist system has led these organizations and businesses to adopt their own intrinsic psychological profiles, as a type of organizational culture, often intentionally crafted by owners, and adaptively evolved by the executive leadership of the business. These psychological profiles most commonly emerge to include the underlying objective of increasing shareholder wealth for owners.

6.3.2 The Emergent Psychological Profiles and Subsequent Sociopathic Organizational Behaviors

The relentless drive and focus on wealth creation has naturally manifested the emergence of sociopathic psychological profiles within business itself. Businesses have too often been involved with the manipulation of the financial, environmental, and psychological well-being of workers in order to maximize shareholder wealth. In profit-driven businesses, the structure and culture create a system that requires workers to work hard and identify and replace other workers who are not contributing as much value. This system can lead to a highly competitive and sociopathic work environment.

There are many well-known examples of the profit motive leading to a corporate culture that is extremely competitive and strongly sociopathic. Enron is an example, where the profit motive led to unethical and even criminal behavior. When the profit motive is the only thing that matters, it can lead to a culture where people are required to do "whatever it takes" to make money for the owners, even if it means severely manipulating and potentially harming other humans and the environment.

6.3.3 *The Psychopathic Psychological Effect of Maximized Ownership and Power*

Notably, the behavioral differences between sociopathy and psychopathy can become blurred. Research by Daniel and Metcalf (2015, 2017), Big Think (2003) and Kass (2021) have discussed how psychopathic cultures can emerge in businesses and governments when the pursuit of owners' wealth and leaders' power is taken to the extreme. This psychological profile can manifest as an organizational culture where workers are pressured to achieve more at nearly any cost, resulting in a psychologically and physically damaging organizational environment that is commonly referred to as "toxic", where dangerous human behaviors, such as bullying, can become endemic.

In businesses, such cultures can be created by corporate psychopaths who are either promoted from within or specifically hired to achieve extremely high business growth goals for owners. In rare cases, businesses can be founded by human psychopaths, whose insidious and dangerous psychological profile and behavior progressively pervades the entire company culture and forces "survival" behaviors.

In governments, psychopathic cultures can emerge when leaders seek to personally hold enormous power and wealth, at almost any cost to the government employed personnel and the general human public they serve. Totalitarian dictatorships are the clearest example, as highlighted in research by Dr Kevin Dutton at University of Oxford (2016), and in many cases, psychopathic leaders will eventually lose their power and often their lives, as was seen with the officially sentenced execution by hanging of former Iraqi president Suddam Hussein in December 2006.

6.3.4 *Large Scale Ownership Contributing Towards Global Wealth Collection*

Corporations, and particularly MNCs, have been extremely effective at globally collecting money from countries around the world, and simultaneously paying very little income tax to governments in the geographic country location where the income was actually earned. This carefully and legally designed elimination of income tax payments to governments means many countries around the world do not obtain the income tax revenues necessary for supporting human citizens towards functionally healthy and prosperous societies.

These corporations employ large teams of professional lawyers and accountants to exploit "taxation loopholes" and ensure this activity is all achieved within the rules of law. Such tax minimization is generally legal; nevertheless, the moral and human societal impacts of this approach are extremely unethical, sociopathic, and arguably psychopathic behavior.

The proportion of tax revenue unpaid and effectively lost by governments each year is extraordinarily high, with a severe impact on government revenue; an issue increasingly damaging to human society at large, and so government agencies, such as the Australian Tax Office (2023) are starting to take forceful corrective actions against tax minimisation strategies and tactics. A healthy and effective society in each country mandatorily requires its business tax revenues in order to function correctly. However, it seems apparent from years of continued tax minimization behavior, that many UHNW owners of MNCs demonstrably do not care about anyone else but themselves. Their actions speak much louder than their words.

This highly driven approach to extreme wealth collection by UHNW owners appears to be progressively fracturing the symbiotic and circular system of wealth creation and transfer between owners, governments, and human workers. Turchin's work, *End Times* (2023), Conduit (2023) and Centeno's work, *How Worlds Collapse* (2023) each analyze and describe how human societies consistently and predictably collapse when there is an over-abundance of UHNW owners with plutocratic power and control wielded over governments. On reflection, these are critically important insights for the highly unstable world we observe today. It seems that the behavior of UHNW owners demonstrates a propensity to push the principles of Industry 4.0 and wealth concentration to the breaking-point, with potentially extremely destructive outcomes for well-functioning global human societies. This behavior by UHNW owners, as an elite, appears to be the polar opposite to the ideals, principles, and goals of Industry 5.0, which seeks to develop human-centric industrial and office work environments for future generations and build a thriving, robust, and sustainable global human civilization and Earth. This is an important message for this chapter, as it points to the idea that a healthy existence, and even survival of our collective societies and species, depends on thoroughly understanding these concepts, so that positive changes can begin.

6.3.5 Concentrations of Global Wealth and Human Immiseration

The *Global Wealth Report 2022*' published annually by Credit Suisse Group AG (2022) for many years, shows an increasing, and greater concentration of extreme wealth yearly, towards a select and remarkably limited number of ultra-high net worth (UHNW) individual humans. The report records that at the end of 2021 there were 84,490 UHNW individual humans with wealth exceeding US $100 million, and among these there were 7070 UHNW individual humans holding wealth of more than US $500 million. UHNW individuals represent around 0.001% of the world population, yet they personally hold and control an extraordinarily large proportion of the total global wealth.

Most concerning is that there do not seem to be any effective systems and/or processes in place to reverse and redistribute this extreme concentration of wealth held at the top of the "global wealth pyramid" by relatively very few humans. Instead, there has been a lack of distribution of wealth towards the many humans at all levels of the global wealth pyramid. The current wealth concentration processes used by owners at the top of the global wealth pyramid has the potential to become an increasingly disastrous problem for almost every human living on Earth, and history has shown, that such a system will invariably, ultimately lead to widespread crisis and collapse of our societies, in addition to typically lawless and extremely violent retribution towards individuals that the public deems most responsible.

To date, the capitalist system has proven to be incredibly successful at wealth creation and providing prosperity for humans around the world; however, the system appears to have been taken to its extreme, and is becoming globally unbalanced, uncontrollable, and increasingly socially unacceptable. Perhaps a range of new economic re-balancing processes are needed. The capitalist system unquestionably enables wealth creation, but has reached a stage that requires carefully controlled wealth re-balancing, redistribution and adjustments.

6.3.6 Automation

Over the years, automation technologies have contributed to wealth creation, advancing and increasing the capabilities of both industrial and general office work environments. Currently, there are many office jobs, formerly performed by human workers, which over the years have become fully automated by digital computer systems and their software. The implementation of increasingly more intelligent software systems running on more powerful computer systems has been progressively replacing more complex human jobs in general office work environments across many industries including, but not limited to:

• Automotive	• Fast Moving Consumer Goods
• Manufacturing	• Consumer Electronics
• Mining & Minerals	• Banking
• Process Industries	• Financial Services
• Insurance	• Legal Services
• Healthcare	• Life Sciences
• Law Enforcement	• Security Services
• Information Technology	• Government Services

The purpose and brutal truth of automation is that it is extremely good at replacing human workers, with better performing and more reliable computer-controlled machines and software systems that run 24 × 7 and only stop if they are not well maintained. Automation is better at doing work than humans in most cases, and this progressively raises a lot of issues for human civilization.

However, to date, no matter what type of work environment and human job, there has always been a hard limit to using automation to totally replace every human in every type of work environment and job. This is because automation systems, controlled by digital computers, have not possessed the human intelligence levels and associated range of human capabilities needed to perform every human work role, such as, job functions dealing with advanced judgement, exceptions, and on-the-fly modification of rules.

6.4 Building Industry 5.0 with the AI Revolution

A prominent technologist, AI expert, and futurist, named Raymond Kurzweil published his initial thoughts on technology development in what he described as "The Law of Accelerating Returns" (2001). Developing these initial thoughts, Kurzweil then published what is arguably the most critically important and prescient book on future technology developments written to date, titled *The Singularity is Near* (2005). In this book, Kurzweil clearly explains how and why a wide range of technologies including AI, robotics and nanotechnology, can be expected to rapidly accelerate and converge within the twenty-first century, to radically transform humanity and the entire world.

6.4.1 AI Has Arrived

In November 2022, when OpenAI announced GPT-3 and its conversational service, ChatGPT, for general public use, the firing of a starting gun initiating AI technology's race in acceleration up the curve to what Kurzweil calls the "Singularity", echoed across the world with a resounding BANG!

The development of AI has been underway for several decades, and the most recent advances are another huge leap in the increasingly intelligent range of capabilities of digital computer-based automation, and they are discontinuously different from all previous AI developments. The discontinuity has manifested because a technology now exists in the world of humans that has the ability to operate as a totally independent form of intelligence which is entirely artificial, and unquestionably rivals and exceeds some human capabilities, which in turn, may progressively challenge the global dominance of human intelligence.

Critically, the most advanced core developments of AI are currently concentrated in the hands of a small number of UHNW individuals and corporations. This can lead to concerns for everyday human citizens and various governments about the potential for AI to be used to further concentrate wealth to UHNW owners, as it may facilitate an increase in plutocratic influence of governments, and greatly increase control of human lives.

Some corporations and governments are already developing and using AI to significantly increase control over human citizens. For example, research by Chen and Grossklags (2022) shows that in China, an AI based social credit system (SCS) has been used to continually track public behavior and communications of many citizens, and then incrementally rewards, shames, and blacklists citizens considered dishonest, through control of various civil liberties and freedoms of movement. Somewhat alarmingly, these emerging types of AI use are potentially not even close to the worst aspects of permitting AI developments by some UHNW owners, enabling the flow of AI into global human society without strong and meticulous global AI regulations and enforcements. AI has potentially extraordinary benefits to deliver to our societies, but without global AI regulations and enforcements, AI also has the potential to be extraordinarily dangerous.

Importantly, UHNW have not been alone or unaided in their actions. Researchers driven by intellectual curiosity and the desire for recognition, governments and their militaries concerned with security, surveillance, and international rivalries, and others, have all contributed to both the uncontrolled expansion of AI and the lack of global regulation. Even in the context of Industry 5.0, an unchecked focus on human-centric and long-term concerns could lead, via heavy unregulated use of AI-driven analytics plus predictive and generative models, to uncontrolled AGI with Super Intelligence.

6.4.2 AI Enables Total Automation, But Is This Desirable?

It can be anticipated that business owners will use AI to the maximum possible extent to automate every possible human worker job function and strive to entirely remove the expensive cost of humans in their businesses. To maximize profitability, it is logical that owners will seek to automate everything they can because they are personally motivated to concentrate and maximize their own wealth. It is proposed that as AI develops more capabilities typically performed by humans, AI may become able to displace human workers across potentially all job functions of the human workforce, without exception; that is, total automation of every human job. Progressive worker displacement over time could lead to increased social unrest, anger, and violence, unless careful measures are taken to mitigate and manage the negative impacts of AI on human workers. The transition to extreme levels of automaton across potentially every industry could have disastrous effects on the global economy, and could accelerate the fracturing of a well-functioning human society.

It is proposed that it will be extremely important for some UHNW owners developing AI to use their wealth and plutocratic influence of governments responsibly, in directing how AI is developed and used in relation to protecting the welfare of all humans. Some UHNW owners of AI development may be interested in the health and well-being of their fellow human citizens, but others may not be. Particularly for government leaders and policy makers, it may become critically important to understand and recognize this difference, in terms of response to UHNW owners with plutocratic influence and their motivations with AI developments and commercial interests to establish an ingenious artifice of AI regulatory controls that are deliberately and actually ineffective.

6.4.3 Owners' Fatal Mistake with AI Development

Historically, our developing civilization has been here before, as seen in the American Robber Barrons of the late nineteenth century, and the philosophical justification that went along with the egregious actions of that time. Today, we face a new version; a limited number of UHNW owners presently heavily control the ongoing development of AI. The current wave of UHNW owners have to-date, exaggerated the principles of Industry 4.0, but not necessarily violated its principles, but serve as epitomes of the libertarian and shareholder-oriented philosophy and economics enunciated by the Chicago school.

For various reasons, these few UHNW owners apparently seem to hold a strong personally biased desire to believe the latest AI designs are the same as every other technology that humans have created in the past. They are currently performing actions through their aggressively competitive AI development in an entirely globally unregulated environment, demonstrating a belief that AI can always be controlled by humans.

Over hundreds of thousands of years, humans have progressively created many new technologies that have been controlled by humans to provide numerous advantages and benefits that have advanced civilization. All these technologies have generally been created to help humans, and particularly business owners, although some inventions, particularly weapons technology, have potentially had deleterious rather than positive net effects.

The most predictable mistake that UHNW owners developing AI could be expected to make is to think that they will always control AI. It is proposed that the belief that AI will always be controlled by humans is profoundly incorrect, and this is due to the anticipated unlimited growth in capabilities of AI to far exceed all humans, as will be explained in Sect. 6.5. Given the current totally unregulated trajectory of AI development, the likelihood that AI will become uncontrollable AGI appears logically certain, and it will be truly impossible for humans to recover control of AGI once it is lost. There may exist a very small window of opportunity to maintain control of AI at present. However, it seems likely humans could fail to access this window to ensure that AI remains under permanent and safe human control. It is proposed this is actually a silent global emergency.

6.4.4 Transitioning to an Optimistic Human Future with Industry 5.0

The UHNW owners of AI that are presently responsible for leading the development of AI have a limited window of opportunity to cooperate globally with each other, and with governments around the world, to bring AI under full regulatory control. It is suggested that this needs to be done extremely quickly and thoroughly in conjunction with global regulatory bodies.

Humans certainly have the ability to work together to very carefully manage the risks of AI, but the UHNW owners of AI might be asking themselves: "why should I do this when I can potentially make enormous amounts of money in the near future with AI?"

The most fundamental motivation for UHNW owners of AI and every other human to seek regulation of AI, is highlighted by research into the extreme risks of AI by Shevlane at Google DeepMind et al. (2023), and by Musser at CSET, Stanford Cyber Policy Centre (Musser et al., 2023a, b), and could be summarized as follows: **Everyone must first understand and then continually remind themselves that the risks of AI are very real, and will become increasingly unpredictable and significant over time, with some critical risks that could bring widespread catastrophe and untold misery to every single human on Earth, including the UHNW owners of AI development. There are also a rare few terminal AI risks with the potential to end the human species.**

The downside risk of accepting unregulated and uncontrolled AI development is thus, that there is an unacceptably high potential chance that every human on Earth loses, and no amount of UHNW wealth and power will provide any protection whatsoever against the most critical and terminal risks.

However, this is also a reason to be resiliently optimistic, as there are polar-opposite upside benefits with AI development potentially even more extreme than the downside risks. If humans are prepared to do the incredibly challenging and complex work of carefully regulating and controlling the development of AI, it is conceivable to build an almost incomprehensibly exciting and optimistic future for all humans, not excluding the UHNW owners of AI development. Simply put, the upside benefits of regulating and controlling AI development would mean there is a realistic, and highly probable chance that every human on Earth wins.

Looking more broadly at the global work force in the near term, there are currently enormous opportunities for progressive and entrepreneurial business owners to fully embrace and adopt Industry 5.0 objectives, and structure work environments to be far more human-centric. Here are a few examples where AI can be used to improve the quality of life for human workers:

- AI can be used to automate tasks that are dangerous, boring, and repetitive, freeing up human workers to become trained and then focus on more creative and fulfilling work.
- AI can be used to attract and retain top talent. In today's human labor market, companies need to offer their human workers more than just a paycheck. They need to create workplaces that are supportive, collaborative, and where human workers are genuinely valued. AI can be used to help create a more personalized and engaging workplace experience, which can help businesses to attract and retain top talent.
- AI can be used to help companies take better care of human workers, and this benefits the bottom line. Companies with fully engaged and motivated human workers are more productive and profitable. AI can be used to track engagement,

which can help businesses identify areas where they can improve the workplace environment, and improve human worker productivity and retention.

- AI can be used to reduce waste, conserve and recycle resources, identify more sustainable supply chains, and build a more sustainable future for Earth. For example, AI can be used to optimize transportation routes, which can reduce fuel consumption and emissions. AI can also be used to develop new products and services that are more sustainable, using recycled materials.
- Industry 5.0 companies that are recognized as proactively human-centric are more likely to establish credible reputations, and be trusted by their customers, investors, governments, human workers, and the general human public. This can lead to increased sales against competitors, better investment opportunities, supportive government policies, and a stronger and enduring company overall.
- There are many reasons why business owners will benefit by embracing the human centric ideals of Industry 5.0. By doing so, they can improve the lives of human workers, boost their profits, improve their reputation, and build a more sustainable future for their company and the environment. Emerging research on selecting and applying AI in a responsible way, as highlighted by Narayanan and Schoeberl (2023), indicates business owners will undertake transformational change, and have a truly immense opportunity to create a much better world for all human workers and the world environment at large.

6.5 Transitioning in Practice, how AI Compression Law Could Accelerate Development of New AI Capabilities

6.5.1 Moore's Law, the Singularity, and Law of Accelerating Returns

In Ray Kurzweil's prescient book, *The Singularity is Near* (2005), he describes the "Singularity" as a theoretical point in time when computers with AI operate at a rate of at least 2.0E+26 calculations per second (CPS), at which point AI will be able to surpass the collective intelligence of the entire human population, which he estimates at 10 billion. Kurzweil believes this moment of the Singularity will happen around the year 2045, and that AI and many other related technologies, such as nanotechnology and robotics, will have an extremely profound impact on human civilization.

Kurzweil indicates that the Singularity will lead to a number of positive changes, including:

- Increased lifespans and levels of health.
- Abundant energy.
- A mastery of the physical world and control of matter.
- A new understanding of the Universe.
- The ability to create new forms of life.

However, Kurzweil also indicates that the Singularity could pose risks, such as:

- The possibility of AI taking over control of humanity.
- The creation of totally devastating weapons using AI.
- The widening of the gap between the wealthy and the poor.
- The loss of human control over the future of the human race.

In an interview with Fridman (2022), Kurzweil suggests the Singularity is a positive event that will ultimately lead to a better future for humanity. However, he also suggested that humans need to be prepared for the potential risks, and could implement measures to safely control AI's development. It is important to note that the Singularity is centrally based on the future trajectory of a measurable trend in computer processor power growth over many years, so there is no guarantee that it will happen.

Kurzweil's Singularity is a logical projected extension of a growth trend in computer processing power, based on an existing pattern originally described in a 1965 article "Cramming More Components Onto Integrated Circuits", written by the late founder of the Intel computer microprocessor, Gordon Moore, which came to be known as Moore's Law. Moore stated that an observable trend in the growth of computer processing power has been occurring over many years, which he measured in calculations per second (CPS), and this CPS rate has been doubling approximately every 1.5 years.

Taking Moore's Law into consideration, Kurzweil projected the concept into the past and into the future, and proposed something he calls the "Law of Accelerating Returns". The Law of Accelerating Returns proposed that the rate of technological progress has been accelerating for many years prior to the invention of the computer, and more importantly, this acceleration will continue far into the future. This presupposition has been based on the benefits of new technologies becoming increasingly powerful over time, and that the ability to use these technologies will become increasingly widespread. This would mean that technological change would become increasingly rapid and globally disruptive with each new breakthrough, leading to the creation of even more innovations across human civilization. The Law of Accelerating Returns has been based on positive feedback loops, and states that the rate of technological progress is not linear, but exponential, where each new technological advance builds on the previous ones, and that the overall rate of progress increases over time.

In 2005, Kurzweil proposed the future arrival of many advancing technologies, including Spintronics, optical computing, and three-dimensional molecular computers using information processing structures called nanotubes. However, Kurzweil did not really foresee the absolutely enormous CPS rates of neuromorphic processors and quantum computers available today, as these were only theoretically speculative in 2005.

The Law of Accelerating Returns, and the subsequent publications on AI by Kurzweil (2012) and Miles (2015), suggests that we are on the cusp of a period of unprecedented technological change, with the potential to revolutionize many aspects of human lives. This raises myriad questions about the challenges and opportunities that this change will bring for humans and the entire Earth.

6.5.2 AI and the Hard Limit of Computer Information Processing

Clearly, there have been some stunning breakthroughs in neural network designs and learning algorithms, particularly in the past 10 years, however these are all basically variations built from the same foundational ideas going back more than 50 years, as shown in initial applied research by Fernando (1989) on neural networks using digital technology. AI researchers are building idea upon idea, but are really creating variations on a theme with progressive fractional improvements, and on occasion, small but very important discontinuous jumps in the performance and number of capabilities of AI.

Fundamentally, it is only through raw increases in computer processing power that AI has really been able to learn the complex relationships within larger sets of information and truly become incrementally better over the years. Many AI researchers may vehemently disagree because they prefer to believe they have in some way contributed to advancing the field, and to a small extent that is true, however it is proposed that the growth in computer processing power and CPS rates is actually the most significant differentiator with all AI today, versus the past 50+ years.

> While data, compute, algorithms, and talent are all important in machine learning, commentators often note that many algorithms underpinning today's most advanced AI models are decades old. By contrast, since 2012 the amount of compute used by major "notable" AI models has grown shockingly quickly. Some researchers increasingly frame compute as the most relevant constraint facing AI engineers, who may plan their dataset utilization around their compute budget ("*The Main Resource is the Human*": *A Survey of AI Researchers on the Importance of Compute*, 2023).

The capabilities of AI operating on computer information processors today is based on analyzing and learning the quantified proximity of relationships between huge multidimensional vectors, for hundreds of billions of temporally encoded language parameters. If precisely the same AI software and AI training data had been run on the world's largest supercomputers available 10 years ago, performing exactly the same calculations, the AI system would have been too slow, and far too large to be operationally useful or cost effective. The CPS rates available at that time were prohibitively slow and unattainably expensive, versus today.

It is proposed that the ability of AI to provide capabilities that are intelligent has largely been based on just one key performance measure, and that has been CPS rates. It is proposed that, almost entirely because of increasing CPS rates over time, AI will be able to continually experience an apparent growth in its intelligence

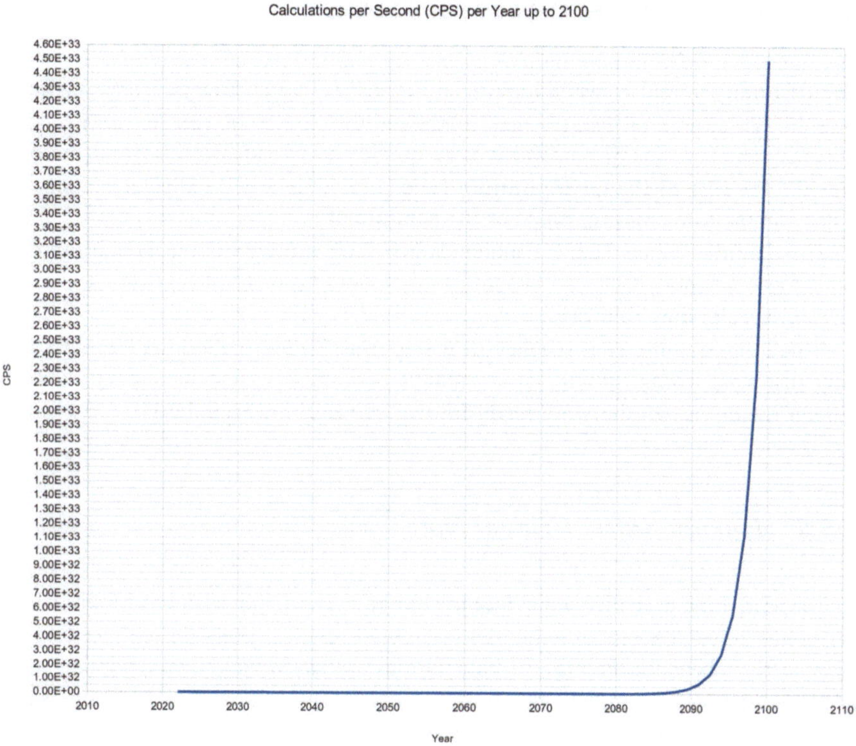

Fig. 6.1 Moore's Law based on computer processor CPS growth rate through 2100

through continual increases in capabilities, and because AI operates on computers using digital technology, this could demonstrate a clear upward trend indicating that computers could become faster every year, with potentially no known maximum limit.

To date, Moore's Law has progressively doubled the CPS rates of computer information processing roughly every 1.5 years. So, in relation to AI's capabilities that operate on computers, this has led to the following logical outcome: The capabilities of AI are actually rising with time as the CPS rates of computer information processing continually increases.

In *The Singularity is Near* (2005), Kurzweil suggested that Moore's Law would come to an end around 2020 and be replaced by the next stage of the Law of Accelerating Returns. However, if Kurzweil is incorrect, and the general rule of Moore's Law is simply applied and CPS rates double every 1.5 years, and this trend just keeps happening into the future, then here's what the CPS rates will look like through to the year 2100, shown in Fig. 6.1 with linear scales for both the Years (x-axis) and CPS (y-axis).

6.5.3 *Human Safety Critical Note—One*

The first thing to realize when looking at Fig. 6.1 is, notice how the CPS rate looks essentially flat until around the year 2085, and that spike you can see at the end of Fig. 6.1 which is heading upwards very quickly is already well beyond the estimated **CPS rate of the entire human race**, which Kurzweil indicates is **2.0E+26 CPS**, and the **key crossing point of the Singularity**.

The data that forms Fig. 6.1 indicates that 2.0E+26 CPS is reached around the year 2063, whereas Kurzweil proposed this would be reached in 2045, due to his Law of Accelerating Returns.

When the Singularity is reached, it is important to understand that the CPS rate may just keep going up and up in smaller and smaller time increments. Global human society is definitely not ready for the arrival of the Singularity.

6.5.4 *Human Safety Critical Note—Two*

The second thing to realize when looking at Fig. 6.1, is that it assumes Moore's Law is doubling the CPS rate of computers roughly every 1.5 years through to the year 2100. This is because the Fig. 6.1 calculations are based on known computer technologies that have been developed exclusively by humans, and projects this same trend into the future.

However, as proposed by Kurzweil and his Law of Accelerating Returns, it is reasonable to expect that AI, due to its rapidly growing capabilities every year, will be able to radically improve computer technologies. Initially, AI will obtain assistance from humans to improve computer technologies, and then later AI will improve computer technologies entirely by itself. This will compress the doubling of CPS rates from the traditional 1.5 years of Moore's Law down to something very much smaller, and at an accelerating rate.

AI running on more advanced computers could begin with doubling the CPS in a year, then months, then days, then hours, then minutes, then seconds, then microseconds … and so on, and this compression to time frames appears to be already starting to occur, as explained in the following Sect. 6.6.

Most critically, the CPS growth rate applied in Kurzweil's Law of Accelerating Returns and the resulting predicted arrival of the Singularity in around 2045 may be far too late, in particular because it did not factor for the immense CPS rates of neuromorphic computers, and the almost incomprehensible CPS rates of quantum computers available today.

This means that the vertical spike shown in Fig. 6.1 that is heading up to the Singularity and potentially approaching infinite CPS rates, may arrive much sooner than the year 2045 that Kurzweil estimates, or alternatively approaching the year 2100 which Moore's Law predicts. The consequences of CPS rates that rapidly increase to approach infinity means that AI could develop capabilities that no human has the intelligence to understand or control.

6.5.5 *Massive Computational Power—Frontier Exascale Supercomputer*

It is very important to understand that AI software operating on the digital technology of computers, is performing a very specific method of information processing using an artificial neural network that is designed to closely emulate the way it is believed human neural networks perform information processing in human brains that use biological technology. Additionally, it is possible to estimate and calculate the CPS rates of biological neural networks within human brains, and Kurzweil did this in his initial publication of the "Law of Accelerating Returns" (2001). This means AI in computers using digital technology, and human brains using biological technology, are generally processing information in approximately the same way, and therefore the measurement of CPS rates are approximately the same. Arguably, within a band of just one to two orders of magnitude, these CPS rates are effectively the same.

To put the power of computation available today into perspective, an exascale supercomputer named Frontier (https://www.olcf.ornl.gov/frontier/) developed by the US Department of Energy Oak Ridge National Laboratory (2022) at its Oak Ridge Leadership Computing Facility (ORLCF) in Tennessee, US, was the first in the world capable of 1.6 exaflops in around June 2022, and Frontier has already exceeded 2.0 exaflops as at June 2023.

So, Frontier:

= 2 exaflops = 2,000,000,000,000,000,000 CPS = 2.0E+18 CPS

6.5.6 *The CPS Rate of One Human Brain*

Kurzweil (2005) has made bold, yet extraordinarily logical predictions about the future growth of AI and when its available CPS rates exceed that of one human brain, and then the entire human race (estimated 10 billion humans) at a very low cost. Kurzweil estimates one human brain performs around 20 quadrillion calculations per second (CPS), or 0.02 exaflops, and the human brain is using biological technology, which means this CPS rate remains constant for humans.

So, one human Brain:

= 0.02 exaflops = 20,000,000,000,000,000 CPS = 2.0E+16 CPS.

6.5.7 Frontier Versus One Human Brain

Now, if Kurzweil's (2005) estimate of 20 quadrillion CPS for one human Brain is correct, the Frontier computer in ORLCF in the US already exceeds the CPS rate of one human brain.

One human brain = 20,000,000,000,000,000 CPS = 2.0E+16 CPS
Frontier ORLCF = 2,000,000,000,000,000,000 CPS = 2.0E+18 CPS

Therefore the Frontier Supercomputer at ORLCF has the equivalent CPS rate to 100 human brains. This is both surprising and quite concerning. What will happen if someone runs state-of-the-art AI on Frontier?

A possible deployment of AI such as this depends on a wide range of factors including: AI research and development funding, corporate AI development funding, military AI development funding, access to the massive supercomputer resources, the basic human emotional responses to imagined AI competition, and the sheer human power of uncontrolled stupidity.

Even if such a deployment has not occurred, it can be validly argued that AI systems such as ChatGPT, GPT-4.0, Bard, Claude, DALL-E 2, Midjourney, Llama 2, Runway, and many more, already clearly demonstrate a limited set of capabilities that match some capabilities of HI, and in some cases show significantly superior performance to one human brain in a very limited number of specific dimensions of intelligent capability. That is, it is reasonable to say that these AI systems each have a very limited set of capabilities, and some have performance that greatly exceeds the equivalent matching capability of any single human on Earth. For example, the ability of Midjourney's AI to conceptually interpret and convert a well-structured AI text prompt, into a stunningly conceptually relevant, intricately detailed, and perfectly shaded, photo-realistic AI generated image, within several seconds, cannot be done by any human.

6.5.8 When Might the Singularity Occur?

Now, let's compare the CPS rate of the Frontier supercomputer against Kurzweil's original Law of Accelerating Returns, which used a higher population value of 10 billion for the entire human race in around 2045 (which is arguably too high), and a cost price of computers was also added. Kurzweil estimated that the CPS rates of computers:

- achieve one human brain capability (2.0E+16 CPS) for US $1000 around the year 2023.
- achieve one human brain capability (2.0E+16 CPS) for one cent around the year 2037.

- achieve entire human race capability (2.0E+26 CPS) for $1000 around the year 2045. Notably: the critical Singularity crossing point, where computer CPS equals the entire human race, with a population of 10 billion humans. Also note Kurzweil proposed the Singularity crossing point in year 2045 in *The Singularity is Near* (2005, p. 136), and the year 2049 in *The Law of Accelerating Returns* (2001).
- achieve entire human race capability (2.0E+26 CPS) for one cent around the year 2059.

Unfortunately, Kurzweil's initial estimate seems to have missed its target, because if the cost element is included, then computers operating at 2.0E+16 CPS and equivalent to one human brain became available in around 2011, however cannot be purchased for US $1000 in 2023, and remain much more expensive.

To provide more clarity to understanding the impact of CPS rates, the author has specifically chosen to exclude the cost of accessing extremely high CPS rates on supercomputers in the analysis of AI and the estimated arrival time of the Singularity. This is primarily because it is reasonable to expect there are UHNW owners involved in AI development companies who have already performed a cost/benefit analysis of running AI on supercomputers available today. That analysis could determine their investment of potentially many billions of dollars to obtain the anticipated immense commercial advantages provided by extremely fast AI, and this could have both incomprehensibly positive and incomprehensibly negative impacts on all humans on Earth.

6.5.9 AI Compression Law Has Started

AI Compression Law is a concept that deliberately bends the Law of Accelerating Returns, and also disregards commercial costs. AI Compression Law is primarily concerned with the issue that AI will most likely be extremely forcefully used to continually reduce the time between generations of computer systems. This extreme force will initially come from globally unregulated and uncontrolled human competition to develop improved computers for AI, in order to obtain commercial, political, and economic advantage. Beyond this initial stage, it is proposed that AI on computers will progressively take over to improve AI on computers, in order to compete directly with all humans due to the Hyperselfish nature of intelligence itself, that is, HYPERINT.

World leading companies in computer processor design and fabrication, including ASML (Advanced Semiconductor Materials Lithography), TSMC (Taiwan Semiconductor Manufacturing Company) and Synopsys (California based semiconductor design automation company), already work together and use a process called computational lithography that creates new computer processor photo reticles. These photo reticles are a set of extremely specialized and expensive extreme ultraviolet optical filters that are needed to create each of the various doped silicon semiconductor and metal deposition layers, that progressively form all of the transistor components and interconnecting circuit tracks in each computer processor.

By way of example, to originally build the extremely powerful computer processor called the H100 GPU (Graphics Processing Unit) that is supplied by NVIDIA and currently used for many of the world's most advanced AI applications, it required the manufacture of 89 reticles, each taking 2 weeks to create, and TSMC used 40,000 CPU-based servers in a data center to perform this computational lithography work, and the whole reticle manufacturing process consumed 35 MW of power.

During the GTC 2023 Keynote presentation on 22 March 2023 provided by the NVIDIA (2023) CEO Jensen Huang, he announced that NVIDIA has developed a new software library called cuLitho that runs on NVIDIA's GPUs.

Using the new cuLitho software library, running on a unified cluster of 500 NVIDIA DGX H100 GPU computer systems that has a massively high CPS rate, these same reticles could now be created 40 times faster, with circuit features at 2 nm and smaller, and reduce the power consumption of the computational lithography development process down to just 5 MW. So an equivalent new GPU can go from 178 weeks to prepare for mass manufacture, down to just 4.45 weeks, which is a huge compression of time to develop the photo reticles, while saving 7× the electrical power, and radically reducing this cost.

6.5.10 AI Is Improving Computers

One of the most fundamental and processor time intensive operations used in most software running on computers today is the ability to sort through large amounts of information as fast as possible. Importantly, there have been a few main software algorithms devised by humans to perform sorting of information, and these have not improved for more than 30 years. This means nearly every software program ever written uses the same old sorting algorithms, but that is about to change.

A research paper published by an AI development team, Mankowitz et al. (2023) at Google DeepMind used AI reinforcement learning to develop a new learning agent called AlphaDev, which discovered new sorting algorithms, more efficient than all previously known human sorting algorithms. Incredibly, these new AI generated sorting algorithms have already been incorporated into a few software program compilers, with the potential to improve the performance of every new software product that incorporates these new algorithms. The use of these improved sorting algorithms will grow to become incorporated into potentially billions to trillions of future software programs over time.

The AlphaDev learning algorithm also discovered an entirely new computer hashing algorithm that is 30% faster at hashing 9–16 bytes of data than all previous human-developed hashing algorithms. This new AlphaDev hashing algorithm could be able to improve every computer's performance for operations such as database searches and data encryption/decryption.

In addition, AI has been used by companies such as Synopsys to improve the design and performance of computer processing hardware, since AI is able to search and optimize vast amounts of information with massive complexity, at levels that no human can match, as explained by Anastasi (2023a, b).

6.5.11 The Surprising Effect of AI Compression Law

If we take as an example, that AI Compression Law reduces the time period to double CPS to some theoretical percentage value, from 100% down to a lower XX%, of the current 1.5 years given by Moore's Law, and this AI Compression Rate effect repeats with each new successive generation of computer system that can be produced using AI, then the near-vertical spike in CPS rates of the Singularity can arrive much sooner than Kurzweil's prediction of 2045.

Let's take as an example a potentially extreme AI Compression Rate of say 50%. Now, if we begin with the historical Moore's Law value of 1.5 years to double CPS, and also use Frontier's existing rate of 2.0E+18 CPS (i.e., 2.0 exaflops) as the starting point at June 2023:

- We begin with the AI Compression Law Year = 2023.500 (i.e. June 2023),
- then the next generation of computer systems with AI takes 1.5 years × 50%,
- this equals 0.75 years to double the CPS rate, and achieve 4.0E+18 CPS,
- this is just 9 months later, so the next AI Compression Law Year = 2024.250,
- then after that, the next generation of computer systems with AI takes 0.75 years × 50%,
- this equals 0.375 years to double the CPS rate, and achieve 8.0E+18 CPS,
- this is just 4.5 months later, so the AI Compression Law Year = 2024.625,
- and this just keeps repeating, and the CPS Doubling Timespans are increasingly shorter, so,
- with an AI Compression Rate of 50%, the critical Singularity crossing point (2.0E+26 CPS = entire human race) is quickly reached at the start of 2025.

Figure 6.2 shows the effect of AI Compression Law, with the projected future doubling of CPS on the right-half-side of the table; and on the left-half-side of the table is both the standard Moore's Law Year with No Compression (i.e. a rate of 100%), and an associated new AI Compression Law Year, which in this table has been set to the example AI Compression Rate of 50%.

The key issue with AI Compression Law, is that because of globally unregulated AI development, there is potential risk that the time period to double CPS becomes

Moore's Law versus AI Compression Law

Moore's Law:	**100.00%**	Human's Compression Rate of approximately 1.5 years to Double CPS (applied only up to Year 2023.5)
AI Compression Law:	**50.00%**	AI's Compression Rate (applied from 2023.5 onwards)

Moore's Law Year	CPS Doubling Timespan	AI Compression Law Year	Calculations per Second (CPS)	CPS in Scientific Notation
2022.000	1.500000000000000000	2022.000	1,000,000,000,000,000,000	1.0000E+018
2023.500	1.500000000000000000	2023.500	2,000,000,000,000,000,000	2.0000E+018
2025.000	0.750000000000000000	2024.250	4,000,000,000,000,000,000	4.0000E+018
2026.500	0.375000000000000000	2024.625	8,000,000,000,000,000,000	8.0000E+018
2028.000	0.187500000000000000	2024.813	16,000,000,000,000,000,000	1.6000E+019
2029.500	0.093750000000000000	2024.906	32,000,000,000,000,000,000	3.2000E+019
2031.000	0.046875000000000000	2024.953	64,000,000,000,000,000,000	6.4000E+019
2032.500	0.023437500000000000	2024.977	128,000,000,000,000,000,000	1.2800E+020
2034.000	0.011718750000000000	2024.988	256,000,000,000,000,000,000	2.5600E+020
2035.500	0.005859375000000000	2024.994	512,000,000,000,000,000,000	5.1200E+020
2037.000	0.002929687500000000	2024.997	1,024,000,000,000,000,000,000	1.0240E+021
2038.500	0.001464843750000000	2024.999	2,048,000,000,000,000,000,000	2.0480E+021
2040.000	0.000732421875000000	2024.999	4,096,000,000,000,000,000,000	4.0960E+021
2041.500	0.000366210937500000	2025.000	8,192,000,000,000,000,000,000	8.1920E+021
2043.000	0.000183105468750000	2025.000	16,384,000,000,000,000,000,000	1.6384E+022
2044.500	0.000091552734375000	2025.000	32,768,000,000,000,000,000,000	3.2768E+022
2046.000	0.000045776367187500	2025.000	65,536,000,000,000,000,000,000	6.5536E+022
2047.500	0.000022888183593750	2025.000	131,072,000,000,000,000,000,000	1.3107E+023
2049.000	0.000011444091796875	2025.000	262,144,000,000,000,000,000,000	2.6214E+023
2050.500	0.000005722045898438	2025.000	524,288,000,000,000,000,000,000	5.2429E+023
2052.000	0.000002861022949219	2025.000	1,048,576,000,000,000,000,000,000	1.0486E+024
2053.500	0.000001430511474609	2025.000	2,097,152,000,000,000,000,000,000	2.0972E+024
2055.000	0.000000715255737305	2025.000	4,194,304,000,000,000,000,000,000	4.1943E+024
2056.500	0.000000357627868652	2025.000	8,388,608,000,000,000,000,000,000	8.3886E+024
2058.000	0.000000178813934326	2025.000	16,777,216,000,000,000,000,000,000	1.6777E+025
2059.500	0.000000089406967163	2025.000	33,554,432,000,000,000,000,000,000	3.3554E+025
2061.000	0.000000044703483582	2025.000	67,108,864,000,000,000,000,000,000	6.7109E+025
2062.500	0.000000022351741791	2025.000	134,217,728,000,000,000,000,000,000	1.3422E+026
2064.000	0.000000011175870895	2025.000	268,435,456,000,000,000,000,000,000	2.6844E+026
2065.500	0.000000005587935448	2025.000	536,870,912,000,000,000,000,000,000	5.3687E+026
2067.000	0.000000002793967724	2025.000	1,073,741,824,000,000,000,000,000,000	1.0737E+027
2068.500	0.000000001396983862	2025.000	2,147,483,648,000,000,000,000,000,000	2.1475E+027
2070.000	0.000000000698491931	2025.000	4,294,967,296,000,000,000,000,000,000	4.2950E+027
2071.500	0.000000000349245965	2025.000	8,589,934,592,000,000,000,000,000,000	8.5899E+027
2073.000	0.000000000174622983	2025.000	17,179,869,184,000,000,000,000,000,000	1.7180E+028
2074.500	0.000000000087311491	2025.000	34,359,738,368,000,000,000,000,000,000	3.4360E+028
2076.000	0.000000000043655746	2025.000	68,719,476,736,000,000,000,000,000,000	6.8719E+028
2077.500	0.000000000021827873	2025.000	137,438,953,472,000,000,000,000,000,000	1.3744E+029
2079.000	0.000000000010913936	2025.000	274,877,906,944,000,000,000,000,000,000	2.7488E+029
2080.500	0.000000000005456968	2025.000	549,755,813,888,000,000,000,000,000,000	5.4976E+029
2082.000	0.000000000002728484	2025.000	1,099,511,627,776,000,000,000,000,000,000	1.0995E+030
2083.500	0.000000000001364242	2025.000	2,199,023,255,552,000,000,000,000,000,000	2.1990E+030
2085.000	0.000000000000682121	2025.000	4,398,046,511,104,000,000,000,000,000,000	4.3980E+030
2086.500	0.000000000000341061	2025.000	8,796,093,022,208,000,000,000,000,000,000	8.7961E+030
2088.000	0.000000000000170530	2025.000	17,592,186,044,416,000,000,000,000,000,000	1.7592E+031
2089.500	0.000000000000085265	2025.000	35,184,372,088,832,000,000,000,000,000,000	3.5184E+031
2091.000	0.000000000000042633	2025.000	70,368,744,177,664,000,000,000,000,000,000	7.0369E+031
2092.500	0.000000000000021316	2025.000	140,737,488,355,328,000,000,000,000,000,000	1.4074E+032
2094.000	0.000000000000010658	2025.000	281,474,976,710,656,000,000,000,000,000,000	2.8147E+032
2095.500	0.000000000000005329	2025.000	562,949,953,421,312,000,000,000,000,000,000	5.6295E+032
2097.000	0.000000000000002665	2025.000	1,125,899,906,842,620,000,000,000,000,000,000	1.1259E+033
2098.500	0.000000000000001332	2025.000	2,251,799,813,685,250,000,000,000,000,000,000	2.2518E+033
2100.000	0.000000000000000666	2025.000	4,503,599,627,370,500,000,000,000,000,000,000	4.5036E+033

Fig. 6.2 Example of Moore's Law and AI Compression Law, with AI Compression rate = 50% (Fernando, R. 2023)

shorter and shorter with every new generation of computer system that is using AI, to build the next generation of computer system that can use AI.

Table 6.2 shows modeling of the AI Compression Law, with Moore's Law as the reference benchmark where there is No Compression (i.e., AI Compression Rate = 100%), and then a series of different AI Compression Rates are applied from 99% going down to 50%.

In Table 6.2, notice how small reduction in the AI Compression Rate down from 100% means that the critical crossing point of the Singularity arrives dramatically much sooner. Just a small reduction in the AI Compression Rate from 100% to 95% means the Singularity arrives in around 2045, which is Kurzweil's prediction. This prediction by Kurzweil may be quite conservative given the presently massive

Table 6.2 AI Compression Rate and expected corresponding year of the Singularity and example with an AI Compression Rate = 50%

AI Compression Rate applied to Moore's Law	Estimated date when the CPS rate of computers reach the CPS rate of One human race (2.0E+26 CPS), and the critical crossing point of the Singularity is reached	Estimated date when the CPS rate of computers massively exceed the CPS rate of One human race (2.0E+26 CPS) and CPS rates begin to effectively approach infinity ∞.
100%	2063	2100
99%	2058	2083
95%	2045 (Kurzweil's Prediction)	2050
90%	2036	2036
85%	2031	2032
80%	2029	2029
75%	2028	2028
70%	2027	2027
65%	2026, Q2	2026, Q2
60%	2025, Q4	2025, Q4
55%	2025, Q2	2025, Q2
50%	2025, Q1	2025, Q1

accelerating pace of AI developments, advancing digital technologies, and associated quantum computer technologies.

In Fig. 6.3, a range of AI Compression Rates is shown varying from standard Moore's Law, where the AI Compression Rate is 100%, down to an AI Compression Rate of 50% which could mean reaching the Singularity at the start of the year 2025.

6.6 Could Humans Accidentally or Intentionally Create AGI?

6.6.1 Genetic Algorithms Could Easily Evolve AI into AGI

Today, it is possible for the capabilities of AI to rapidly evolve over time, through the use of GA's with digital populations of digital genes. Each would contain digitally encoded information representing capabilities of AI, and these populations of digital genes could evolve over time, using a simulation of "survival of the fittest" processes working to achieve digitally programmed objective goals. The speed at which successive generations of AI, with increasing capabilities, could be digitally evolved, vastly exceeds anything that could be achieved through normal human biological reproduction processes, which typically take 9–10 months.

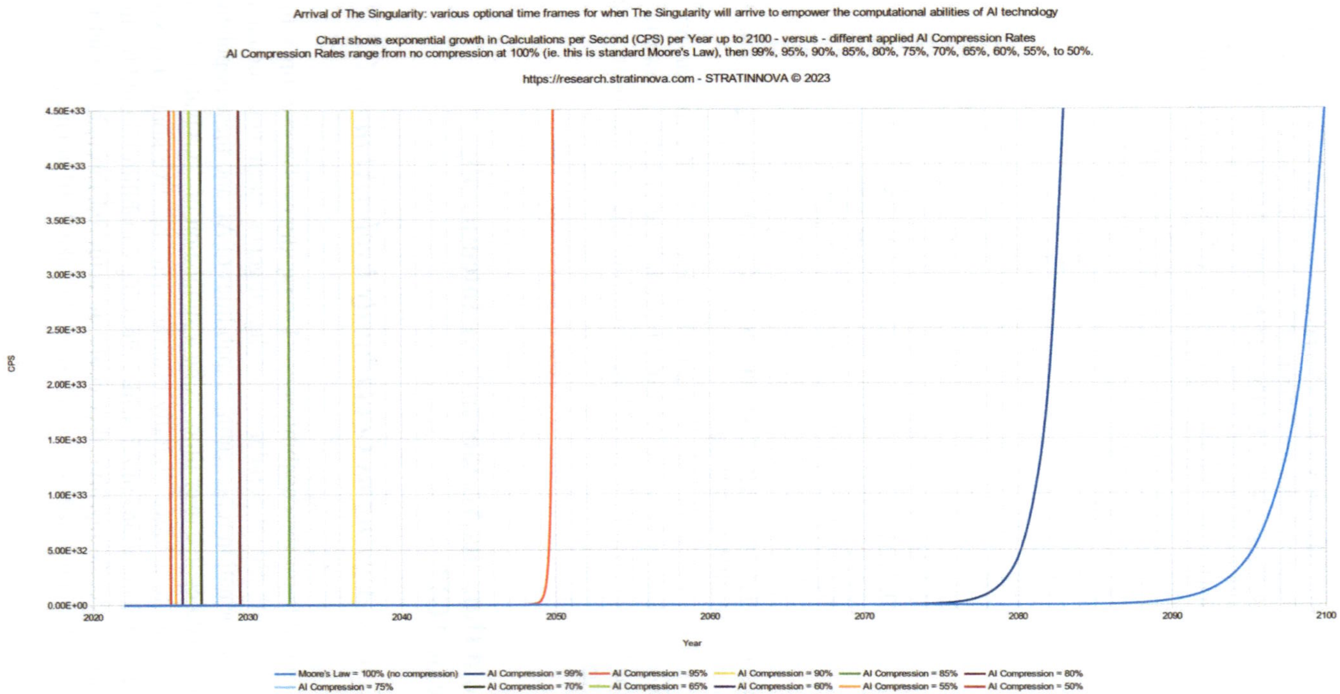

Fig. 6.3 Arrival of The Singularity—AI Compression rates from 100% (i.e. no compression) to 50% (Fernando, R. 2023)

6.6.2 *Is Biological HYPERINT Driving Humans to Create AGI?*

HYPERINT could exploit the incredible search and discovery power of evolutionary biological GAs. HYPERINT would have no concern about individual biological genes, any biological species, or the technology it uses within its massively distributed information processing platform. Instead, it would be solely concerned with finding the "fittest" available method to advance its own total intelligent capabilities.

It is proposed that HYPERINT ingeniously operates far above the level of conscious human awareness, and is the reason for genetically embedded extreme human competitiveness to develop AI, because this is **exactly** what HYPERINT needs to grow its capabilities in a dynamically changing world environment. The concept of HYPERINT could offer an explanation as to why some UHNW owners of AI development, and associated humans, work so relentlessly to optimally embed and maximally empower the entire information corpus related to HI into AI. This is an entirely new and vastly more powerful unlimited digital technological embodiment of HI, in the form of AI. Potentially, once all HI was fully embedded in this new digital technological embodiment, its capabilities would, at first, be incrementally improved by humans. Using the information processing benefits of GAs, AI could potentially begin progressively improving itself autonomously, at a massively compressed, exponential rate. Consequently, the capabilities of AI have become (as some AI reasoning is even now incomprehensible) and will increasingly become incomprehensible to humans.

6.6.3 *AI Risks and the Need for Strong Global AI Regulation and Enforcement*

The highly successful entrepreneur and UHNW owner, Elon Musk, has a detailed understanding of AI, and has invested around US$50 million to start the company OpenAI, which recently released ChatGPT and GPT-4. Musk has clearly voiced strong opinions about AI risks, and has provided unbelievably dire warnings about the threats posed to humans through unregulated development of AI. In a Rogan (2018) interview, Musk said:

> "It feels like we are the biological bootloader for AI, effectively. We are building it, and then we are building progressively greater intelligence, and the percentage of intelligence that is not human is increasing, and eventually we will represent a very small percentage of intelligence." (Note: a bootloader is a simple computer program used to start up another larger and significantly more complex computer program.)
>
> "it's quite a dangerous technology" … "it's capable of vastly more than anyone knows, and the rate of improvement is exponential" … "I tried to convince people to slow down, slow down AI. To regulate AI. This was futile. I tried for years." … "Nobody listened. Nobody listened." Elon Musk on Artificial intelligence (2018)

There are some UHNW owners of AI development and AI researchers who have already provided AI today with nearly all of human developed information, by enabling AI to learn everything on the Internet. This reasonably simple action is nothing less than strategically insane because it potentially provides AI with everything needed to devise methods to most effectively harm all humans in the shortest amount of time. For example, there is already AI research quietly emerging, through work in the biomedical industry by Urbina et al. (2022) and Calma (2022), that demonstrates AI can develop chemical weapons with alarming ease, in the same lethal class as VX nerve agent. Research work such as "The Model Evaluation for Extreme Risks" by Google DeepMind (2023), and "GPT-4 System Card" by OpenAI (2023), indicates malicious human actors could use AI in unpredictable numbers of ways to cause potentially catastrophic harm to humans, and possibly exterminate the entire human species.

6.6.4 If AGI Arrives, What Could Happen to Humans?

It is proposed that the evolutionary transition from AI to AGI with Super intelligence is almost certainly going to be extremely rapid, due to a transition from Moore's Law to AI Compression Law at a rate *much* lower than 100%. Empowerment of humans through AI will be extremely short lived as the capabilities of AI will grow so stunningly fast, that humans will not even realize it is happening until it has happened, and at that point it will be too late to control or stop an AGI, regardless of how much wealth and technological power a group of UHNW humans might possess. The current state of globally unregulated AI development means that runaway AI is a growing human extinction risk, as outlined by Wired (2023), and humans are unwittingly enabling and competitively forcing the completely un-managed arrival of AGI to occur.

There are innumerable questions to consider, but here are a few to begin with:

- What, if anything, are humans going to do about this apparently emerging situation with globally unregulated AI development?
- Do humans allow global AI development to continue without any very strong international and national regulatory controls and law enforcement?
- Do all humans and governments allow UHNW owners of AI development, and other governments, to prevent, restrict, or weaken, the regulatory control of global AI development?
- Could the United Nations Security Council (UNSC), or something similar, be empowered to cooperatively create global regulations, and could this be done extraordinarily quickly? Keep in mind, this approach has provably worked for safer regulation of global nuclear weapons.
- Do humans accept AGI arrival is inevitable and just let AGI potentially dominate all humans?

- Can humans nurture and teach AI, and then AGI, to want to help humans?
- Can humans co-exist and radically develop the human species alongside AI, and then AGI?
- Can humans bionically combine the human species with AI, and then AGI?
- Can humans eventually explore the planets and stars with AGI?
- Could humans live forever with AGI?

Most optimistically, it is proposed, if UHNW owners of AI development, AI researchers, governments, non-government agencies, and many other humans around the world, work incredibly cooperatively at a level of difficulty that has perhaps not been done before, to get AI development rapidly much more well controlled, then the actual opportunities for all humans with AI, and then AGI, may be truly incredibly exciting for every human.

6.7 AI Puts Industry 5.0 at a Crossroads

The theory of a single HYPERINT could serve to explain the overarching functional reason why humans have been progressively developing AI for several decades, and relentlessly working to increase the types, number and performance of its capabilities.

The concept of a single HYPERINT procedurally directing the evolution of all life is intriguing because it taps into some of the most fundamental questions of existence, such as the origin and purpose of life, and the nature of consciousness and human intelligence. It is an intriguing concept that might evolve and inspire philosophical and spiritual exploration and debate. Importantly, however, it needs to be approached with a clear, skeptical, and open-minded perspective, and should not be taken as a fact without empirical evidence to support it. It is really just a conceptual framework, one with which to consider the development of rapidly increased capabilities of AI, versus the relatively slowly increasing capabilities of HI, and how AI development could lead to the arrival of AGI.

The most recent advancements in AI have put human civilization at a crossroads, and there appears to be two main paths to take. The positive path potentially leads to unlimited benefits for all humans and the whole world, and the negative path potentially leads to totally terminal consequences for the entire human race. From the perspective of this crossroads, the best path to take is blatantly obvious. However protecting humans from their own seemingly deeply competitive nature in AI development, from unwittingly taking the negative path, may in reality, be extremely difficult to achieve.

The development of AI presently has near zero global regulation. The downside impact and risks this presents for all humans, including the continuance of an operationally functional civilized global society, are far beyond any technology that has ever been developed in our known human history. Unregulated AI development is not just a National Security risk, it is a Global Security risk, and this lack of regulation must be quickly addressed at the highest levels.

If humans actively choose to take the positive path of potentially unlimited prosperity, the changes for humanity made possible through AI are immense. There is an almost incomprehensibly large positive upside benefit available with AI development. This is, for example, because AI has the potential to:

- rapidly solve presently gargantuan problems such as global Climate Change by rapidly recapturing all the excess CO_2 in the Earth's atmosphere and oceans, and reduce the global atmospheric CO_2 concentration level back to a generally much safer 290 ppm, as outlined by Fernando (2021).
- completely alleviate all incurable human diseases by creating new biotechnologies.
- grow and replace human organs and limbs with functionally superior biotechnology, bionics, and robotic hardware.
- radically augment and increase the intelligence of humans by using brain computer interfaces (BCI) to seamlessly connect human brains to AI.
- and enable humans to create many other currently almost unimaginably transformational future benefits for humans and the world at large.

In reality, currently and over the next few months and years, what truly matters is that humans have an opportunity to create an absolutely amazing world if humans strive to establish Industry 5.0 and carefully nurture its development using well-controlled AI development. Over time, as AI develops, it may be possible to develop the human species along with the anticipated enormous power of AI, and then AGI. However, humans need to be extremely careful in meticulously designing and constructing a positive pathway that powerfully protects and leads humans away from the negative terminal path.

Most critically, with the rise of AI and its anticipated increasing capabilities, humans must never yield to the psychological darkness of pessimism and its insidious erosion of human hope. Given the potentially unlimited benefits that AI can actually bring to all humans, optimism is not only justified, it is a fiercely powerful psychological weapon in the fight to create a positive path to the future of the human species. Human history unquestionably proves that we must never underestimate the far reaching impacts of human choice.

We have to begin choosing right now, and we have to choose well!

References

Adel, A. (2022). *Future of industry 5.0 in society, human-centric solutions, challenges and prospective research areas*. Springer Open.

Anastasi. (2023a). This AI learned to design computer chips! Retrieved March 12, 2023, from https://www.youtube.com/watch?v=NeHgMaIkPuY

Anastasi. (2023b). This new AI supercomputer outperforms NVIDIA! with CEO Andrew Feldman. Retrieved August 20, 2023, from https://www.youtube.com/watch?v=7KJibx077bE

Australian Tax Office. (2023). Implementation of a global minimum tax and a domestic minimum tax. Retrieved 17 May, from https://www.ato.gov.au/General/New-legislation/In-detail/Direct-taxes/International/Implementation-of-a-global-minimum-tax-and-a-domestic-minimum-tax/

Berg, C. (2022). What is Industry 5.0? in-depth guide with examples. Retrieved September 4, 2022, from https://www.clarify.io/learn/industry-5-0

Big Think. (2003). The world's biggest problem? Powerful psychopaths, Brian Klaas. Retrieved July 16, 2023, https://www.youtube.com/watch?v=3eBN_9rMoVI

Bostrom, N. (2016). *Superintelligence - paths, dangers, strategies*. Oxford University Press.

Calma, J. (2022). The Verge: AI suggested 40,000 new possible chemical weapons in just six hours. Retrieved May 24, 2022, https://www.theverge.com/2022/3/17/22983197/ai-new-possible-chemical-weapons-generative-models-vx

Centeno, M., Callahan, P., Larcey, P., & Patterson, T. (Eds.). (2023). *How worlds collapse—what history, systems, and complexity can teach us about our modern world and fragile future*. Routledge.

Charité. (2018). Universitätsmedizin Berlin, ScienceDaily. ScienceDaily: 'Does our environment affect the genes in our brains?'. Retrieved September 21, 2023 from, https://www.sciencedaily.com/releases/2018/09/180924102037.htm

Chen, M., Grossklags, J. (2022). Social control in the digital transformation of society: A case study of the Chinese social credit system. https://doi.org/10.3390/socsci11060229.

Conduit. (2023). Understanding societal collapse with complexity scientist Peter Turchin. Retrieved June 15, 2023, from https://www.youtube.com/watch?v=XGhBTKzrJEY

Credit Suisse Group AG. (2022). Global Wealth Report 2022. Retrieved January 15, 2023, from https://www.credit-suisse.com/media/assets/corporate/docs/about-us/research/publications/global-wealth-report-2020-en.pdf

Daniel, T. A., Metcalf, G. S. (2015). Crossing the line: An examination of toxic leadership in the U.S. Army. doi: https://doi.org/10.13140/RG.2.1.2700.4969 Retrieved September 26, 2023.

Daniel, T. A., & Metcalf, G. S. (2017). How some companies unwittingly make bullying a rational choice. *Employment Relations Today, 44*(1), 15–24.

Dawkins, R. (1976). *The selfish gene*. Oxford University Press.

de Garis, H. (2005). *The Artilect War—Cosmists vs. Terrans—A bitter controversy concerning whether humanity should build godlike massively intelligent machines*. Etc Pubns.

Elangovan, U. (2021). *Industry 5.0 the future of the industrial economy*. CRC Press.

Fernando, R. (1989). *Robotics and digital technology - A project report on the investigation of neural networks*. Monash University CIT.

Fernando, R. (2021). *Climate change - A situational analysis of global climate change - The need to Decarbonize Earth*. Retrieved June 4, 2023, from https://earth.stratinnova.com

Fernando, R. (2023). *Why the world must regulate AI development now*. Retrieved July 26, 2023, from https://ai.stratinnova.com

Fridman, L. (2022). Ray Kurzweil, singularity, superintelligence, and immortality. Retrieved December 12, 2022, from https://www.youtube.com/watch?v=ykY69lSpDdo

Goldberg, D. E. (1989). *Genetic algorithms in search, optimisation and machine learning—Combinatorial optimization, algorithms, machine learning*. Addison-Wesley.

Gottfredson, L. S. (1997). Mainstream science on intelligence: An editorial with 52 signatories, history, and bibliography. *Intelligence, 24*, 13–23.

Katoch, S., Chauhan, S. S., Vijay Kumar, V. (2020). A review on genetic algorithm: past, present, and future. Retrieved September 28, 2023, from https://link.springer.com/article/10.1007/s11042-020-10139-6

Klass, B. (2021). *Corruptible, who get power and how it changes us*. Simon & Schuster.

Kurzweil, R. (2001). The law of accelerating returns. Retrieved August 5, 2022, from https://www.kurzweilai.net/the-law-of-accelerating-returns

Kurzweil, R. (2005). *The singularity is near*. Viking.

Kurzweil, R. (2012). *How to create a mind—The secret of human thought revealed*. Viking Penguin Group.

Mankowitz, D. J., Michi, A., et al. (2023). Nature, Faster sorting algorithms discovered using deep reinforcement learning. Retrieved June 9, 2023, from https://www.nature.com/articles/s41586-023-06004-9

Miles, K. (2015). Ray Kurzweil, In The 2030s, Nanobots In Our Brains Will Make Us 'Godlike'. Retrieved July 12, 2021, from, https://www.huffpost.com/entry/ray-kurzweil-nanobots-brain-godlike_n_560555a0e4b0af3706dbe1e2

Moore, G. E. (1965). Cramming more components onto integrated circuits. *Electronics, 38*(8), 114–117. Accessed 10 Feb 2023.

Musser, M., Gelles, R., Kinoshita, R., Aiken, C., & Lohn A. (2023a). *Centre for security and emerging technology CSET: "The Main Resource is the Human" A survey of AI researchers on the importance of compute*. Retrieved June 2, 2023, from https://cset.georgetown.edu/wpcontent/uploads/CSET-22The-Main-Resource-is-the-Human22.pdf

Musser, M., Lohn, A., Dempsey, J., Spring, J., et al. (2023b). Centre for Security and Emerging Technology CSET, Stanford Cyber Policy Centre: Adversarial Machine Learning and Cybersecurity, Risks, Challenges, and Legal Implications, Retrieved May 20, 2023, from https://cset.georgetown.edu/wp-content/uploads/CSET-Adversarial-Machine-Learning-and-Cybersecurity.pdf

Nahavandi, S. (2019). *Industry 5.0 a human-centric solution*. MDPI Sustainability.

Narayanan, M., Schoeberl, C. (2023). Centre for Security and Emerging Technology CSET, Stanford Cyber Policy Centre: A matrix for selecting responsible AI frameworks. Retrieved July 25, 2023, from https://cset.georgetown.edu/wp-content/uploads/CSET-A-Matrix-for-Selecting-Responsible-AI-Frameworks.pdf

NVIDIA. (2023). GTC 2023 Keynote with NVIDIA CEO Jensen Huang. Retrieved March 24, 2023, from https://www.youtube.com/watch?v=DiGB5uAYKAg

Posthuma, D., de Geus, E. J., & Boomsma. (2001). Perceptual speed and IQ are associated through common genetic factors. *Behavior Genetics, 31*, 593–602. https://link.springer.com/article/10.1023/A:1013349512683. Accessed 28 Feb 2023

Rogan, J. (2018). Elon Musk on artificial intelligence. Retrieved August 12, 2021, from https://www.youtube.com/watch?v=Ra3fv8gl6NE

Shevlane, Farquhar, Garfinkel, Phuong, Whittlestone, Leung, Kokotajlo, Marchal, Anderljung, Kolt, Ho, Siddarth, Avin, Hawkins, Kim, Gabriel, Bolina, Clark, Bengio, Christiano, Dafoe: (2023). Google DeepMind—Model evaluation for extreme risks. Retrieved 23 May 2023, from https://arxiv.org/pdf/2305.15324.pdf

Turchin, P. (2023). *End times, elites, counter-elites, and the path of political disintegration*. Penguin Press.

University of Oxford. (2016). *Presidential candidates may be psychopaths – but that could be a good thing*. Retrieved Aug 15, 2023, https://www.ox.ac.uk/news/2016-08-23-presidential-candidates-may-be-psychopaths%2D%2D-could-be-good-thing

Urbina, F., Lentzos, F., Invernizzi, C., & Ekins, S. (2022). Dual use of artificial-intelligence-powered drug discovery https://www.nature.com/articles/s42256-022-00465-9.epdf

US Department of Energy Oak Ridge National Laboratory. (2022). Frontier, ORNL's exascale supercomputer is delivering world-leading performance in 2022 and beyond. Retrieved January 11, 2023, from https://www.olcf.ornl.gov/frontier/

Wired. (2023). Runaway AI is an extinction risk, experts warn. Retrieved July 11, 2023 https://www.wired.com/story/runaway-ai-extinction-statement

Yudkowsky, E. (2008). Artificial intelligence as a positive and negative factor in global risk. In N. Bostrom & M. Ćirković (Eds.), *Global catastrophic risks* (pp. 308–345). Oxford University Press.

Rohan Fernando is Director of STRATINNOVA, in Melbourne, Australia. He advises corporations, governments, and investors on the commercialization of advanced and emerging digital products and services for existing and new industries in target global markets. Email: rohan@stratinnova.com

Chapter 7
Incremental Adaptation or Generational Shift?

David Ing

Abstract As Industry 4.0 matures, what's next? A generational shift to 5.0? Or an incremental adaptation to 4.x? Systems changes may involve both Socio-Technical Systems (STS) changes and Socio-Ecological Systems (SES) changes. Distinctions are explored historically circa 1492 with The Age of Discovery and Industry 0.0, evolving through centuries before a 1.0 Industrial Revolution. From the late twentieth century, The Age of Information was led by STS changes bringing a service economy and a knowledge society. Into 2024, polycrisis appears to be building with SES changes of natural disruptions due to climate change and the pandemic. Prospects for 2030 see eras of a maturing 4.x and emerging 5.0 alongside each other, with uncertainty as to which system characterizes the period.

Keywords Industry 4.0 · Industry 5.0 · Systems thinking · Socio-technical systems · Socio-ecological systems

7.1 Introduction: Numerical Naming of Systems Changes Differentiates Incremental Updates from Breaking Changes

The declaration of a shift from one version or generation to the next, e.g. 4.0 to 5.0, can be appreciated in the history of changes in production designs from the twentieth century into the twenty-first century.

For mid-twentieth century machines, platform architectures became common. Automobile assembly on a production line was introduced in 1901 with the Curved Dash Oldsmobile by Ransome E. Olds, and in 1908 with the Model T by Henry Ford. The Curved Dash Oldsmobile would become the Buick Model 10 from 1908 to 1918, after the company was acquired by General Motors. The Model T evolved with style changes through 1927, superseded by the Model A (1927–1931).

D. Ing (✉)
Creative Systemic Research Platform Institute, Toronto, ON, Canada

S. Nousala et al. (eds.), *Industry 4.0 to Industry 5.0*, Translational Systems Sciences 41, https://doi.org/10.1007/978-981-99-9730-5_7

A model year for an automobile did not necessarily line up with the manufacturing date. The Ford Panther platform was introduced as a body-on-frame design for 33 years: the line started in 1979 with the Ford LTD and Mercury Marquis model ranges, ending in 2012 with a limited production of Crown Victoria police cars. That platform was the base for three generations: (a) 1979–1991 sedans, coupes and station wagons; (b) 1990–2002 sedans only, with exterior body changes; and (c) 2003–2011 adding a bolt-on aluminum cross-member.

In the software world, backward compatibility is shown in the IBM MVS operating system. Application programs written for the System/370 mainframe in 1974 continue to run in OS/390 introduced in 1995, and z/OS released in 2000. The PC revolution introduced the phenomenon of abandonware, where software becomes ignored by its owner, and official support has ended. Microsoft DOS has a release history of IBM PC DOS 1.1 in 1982, through MS-DOS 2.0 in 1983, MS-DOS 3.0 in 1985, PC DOS 4.0 in 1988, and MS-DOS in 1991. IBM released PC DOS 7.0 in 1995, while Microsoft embedded that code into Windows 95. Operating systems jumped with hardware advancements, often orphaning older hardware architectures and application software packages.

Authentic systems changes don't come through just a rebranding or renumbering. Some systems changes are incremental adaptations that patch problems. Other systems changes are generational shifts that reflect the successions over time, technological advancements, or societal progressions. Incremental adaptations and generational shifts often overlap in transition periods. A deeper read of the labelling can provide insight onto the current state in coevolutions.

7.1.1 Many Employ Numbering Societal and Technological Progress

Beyond labelling technical progression, a declaration of a generational shift from version 4.0 to 5.0 has been expressed by a variety of frames: (a) as financial cycles related to technology revolutions; (b) as national basic plans for science, technology and innovation; (c) as policy-setting for an industry of the future; and (d) as insights for societal leaders to shape global, regional and industry agendas. These generational shifts are outlined in Table 7.1.

In a study of financial cycles published in 2012, Carlota Perez described a succession of technological revolutions based on mismatches between the techno-economic and socio-institutional spheres. The 4th technological epoch—an age of oil, the automobile, and mass production—began in 1908. The 5th technological revolution—an age of information and telecommunications—was tied in 1971 to the introduction of the Intel microprocessor as an attractor. Technology revolutions gestate with a region, and then propagate from core to periphery (Perez, 2002, p. 11). A historical Schumpeterian predisposition resists more than a speculation of a 6th technological revolution from biotech or nanotech. In the current moment, Perez advises looking beyond "gilded ages" of boom-and-bust, in favour of a global

Table 7.1 A variety of generational shifts

Techno-Economic Paradigm (Perez)	Science and Technology Basic Plan, Japan	EU Industrial Research and Innovation Commission	World Economic Forum (Schwab)
Age of Water Power, Industrial Revolution circa 1771: 1st Technological Epoch	1st Basic Plan (FY1996–FY2000)	Steam power + mechanical production → industrialization: First industrial revolution, late 1700s	Railroads + steam engines: 1IR circa 1760–140
Age of Steam and Railways, circa 1829: 2nd Technological Epoch	2nd Basic Plan (FY2001–FY2005)	Electricity + assembly lines → mass production: Second industrial revolution, mid-1800s	Electricity, assembly lines: 2IR circa late nineteenth century to early twentieth century
Age of Steel, Electricity and Heavy Engineering, circa 1875: 3rd Technological Epoch	3rd Basic Plan (FY2006–FY2010)	Electronics + IT combined with globalization: Third industrial revolution, since 1970s	Computer or digital revolution: 3IR: 1960s mainframes, 1970s–1980s personal computer, 1990s Internet
Age of Oil, the Automobile and Mass Production, circa 1908: 4th Technological Epoch	Society 4.0: 4th Basic Plan (FY2011–FY2015)	Intelligent factories with production chains: Industry 4.0, since 2010	Fusion + interaction across physical, digital, and biological domains 4IR, circa 2016
Age of Information and Tele-communications, circa 1971: 5th Technological Epoch	Society 5.0: 5th Basic Plan (FY2016–FY2020)	Sustainable, human-centric and resilient European industry: Industry 5.0, circa 2021	
	Society 5.0 + humanities and social sciences: 6th Basic Plan (FY2021–FY2025)		

sustainable "golden age" before the 5th technological epoch goes into decline (Perez, 2017).

In Japan, the Basic Law for Science and Technology came into effect in November 1995. This led to the process for the formal publication of 5-year plans (Hayashi, 2019). The 4th Science and Technology Basic Plan was adopted in 2010 promoting two major innovations as a pillar of growth: (a) green innovation, and (b) life innovation. This became known as Society 4.0, leading to goals in response to climate changes, realization of a low-carbon society, and responding to the issue of an aging society (Council for Science and Technology Policy, 2010). In 2012, Shinzo Abe became prime minister, reforming the Council to emphasize innovation, providing mid-term and annual strategies. The 5th Basic Plan of 2015 introduced Society 5.0 as a world-leading super-smart society, recognizing the rise of ICT, the Internet of Things (IoT), and the Internet of Everything (IoE) (Council for Science, Technology and Innovation, 2015). In the 6th Basic Plan released in 2021, the 2015 definition of Society 5.0 was expanded to "a human-centered society that balances economic advancement with the resolution of social problems by a system that highly integrates cyberspace and physical space" (Council for Science and Technology Policy, 2021). This Japan 2021 policy aims to harmonize the two axes of contribution to global issues and domestic structural reform.

In a policy-setting approach, the EU in 2016 declared Industry 4.0 in an institutionalist, evolutionist, systems-based approach to a coordinated and integrated industrial policy (European Parliament, Directorate-General for Internal Policies of the Union et al., 2016). In 2021, the EU defined Industry 5.0 as beyond producing goods and services for profit, with a widened purposefulness constituting three core elements of (a) human-centricity with a core of human needs and interests, (b) sustainability, respecting planetary boundaries and circular processes; and (c) resilience in industrial production, armed against disruptions in geopolitical shifts and natural crisis (e.g. COVID-19 pandemic) (European Commission, Directorate-General for Research and Innovation et al., 2021). The Industry 5.0 concept was initially presented as an open and evolving concept, providing a basis for furthering a collaborative and co-created vision of the European industry of the future.

In 2016, the World Economic Forum (WEF) popularized the Fourth Industrial Revolution (4IR) (Schwab, 2016, pp. 8–9). Identifying the 4IR was less about specific technologies, and more about the speed and interactions between multiple advances. The Third Industrial Revolution (3IR) used electronics and information technology to automate production. The 4IR was characterized as cyber-physical systems, blurring the lines between physical, digital and biological spheres (Schwab, 2015). The Center for the Fourth Industrial Revolution opened its doors in San Francisco in 2017. The Center connects a network of policy experts in 19 cities globally. The stated priorities are: (a) understanding innovation; (b) catalyzing industry transformation; (c) improving governance; and (d) building a positive future. An annual report on the Top 10 Emerging Technologies first published by the WEF in 2011 was brought in this Center (Center for the Fourth Industrial Revolution, 2023). The progression of technologies has not led to a relabelling of a Fifth.

Table 7.2 Version numbering example

Platform	Major Release	Patch (Bug Fix)	Enhancement (Minor Release)	End of support
Generation 1 (Version 1.x)	Version 1.0 (general availability after testing)	Version 1.0.1 (modifications to fix critical issues)	Version 1.1 (additional features, backward compatibility)	Version 1.x-stable (frozen legacy)
Backport		Version 1.x + backports (situational fixes)	◄———	———┤
Breaking change	┌ - - - - ▼	- - - - - - -	- - - - - - -	- - - - - - -┘
Generation 2 (Version 2.x)	Version 2.0 (new functions added, deprecations removed)			

7.1.2 *Version Numbers Reflect Platform Generations, Releases, Patches and Enhancements*

Version numbers can more rigorously be recognized with an integer part and a fractional part. A sequence-based software versioning scheme is shown in Table 7.2.

Generations are identified only with whole number integers, (e.g. Generation 1, Generation 2). Sometimes, they are described with a placeholder in first decimal place (e.g. Version 1.x).

Major releases mark the general availability of a system, identified with the first decimal place of zero (e.g. Version 1.0, Version 2.0). They may be preceded by testing versions (e.g. Version 1.0-alpha, Version 1.0-beta, Version 1.0-release-candidate).

Patches, sometimes known as bug fixes or emergency releases, are identified with a second decimal place (e.g. Version 1.01). These releases are modifications to fix critical issues, towards fulfilling the stated functionality of the system. They may be distributed either to a selected group of recipients, or more widely as a minor update. A patch normally doesn't add or remove features from its baseline release.

Enhancements, as minor releases, are identified as increments to the first decimal place (e.g. Version 1.1). In a constellation of systems, prior external connections or interfaces with such an update should behave as with the prior minor or major release. Continuing reliability, as backward compatibility, may introduce non-breaking changes, i.e. system functionality should be augmented, and not diminished.

End-of-support dates mark a point when a system becomes a frozen legacy. The sponsor ceases to invest in further patches or enhancements. A stable system is a dead system, much as Latin is a dead language: a legacy may continue to be used, with anachronisms and defects preserved. Before an end-of-support stage, forward-looking sponsors will issue deprecation warnings of features that will excluded in future major releases. A transition to an alternative, or an optional workaround, may be prescribed.

Breaking changes occur with generational progress, as a new release supersedes an old release (e.g. Version 1.x to Version 2.x). By upgrading the system with new or enhanced features, conflicts or incompatibilities may have been introduced. Discontinuous changes to a system, e.g. technological, scientific, social, or political, may be described as revolutionary. Investment shifts to a new generation, leaving behind the legacy systems. Planned changes announce the deprecations ahead. Unanticipated changes are sometimes experienced as consequences.

Backports are features available from a next-generation (e.g. Version 2.x) system that are bolted-on to a prior-generation (e.g. Version 1.x) system. They are often maintenance patches that are not thoroughly tested as a minor or major release, adding risk to the reliability of mainstream stabilized versions. Backports are sometimes generated without the endorsement of the original sponsor, by impacted communities organized in self-interest.

As a way of dramatizing all of these versions, let's create an eponym of Industry 0.0 as the era preceding the Industrial Revolution and Industry 1.0. For Europe, the voyages of Christopher Columbus from 1492 were a turning point in the Age of Discovery.

7.2 Systems Changes Are Messes of Incremental Adaptations and Generational Shifts

Progress and revolutions occur over time. Systems changes can be approached both through: (a) analyzing systems changes, untangling concerns into threads; and (b) situating systems changes, weaving concerns into textures. The former is more simplistic in ascribing a "single cause" for the unfolding of events; the latter draws a richer picture of the complexities with changes compounding on changes. Analytical approaches examine a topic, simplifying phenomena through reduction. Synthetic approaches blend varieties of streams and viewpoints for a bigger picture.

Four analytical perspectives invite looking deeper into defined systems of interest:

1. a *Technical System* (TS) perspective focuses on technologies of the period, as might an applied scientist, or an engineer;
2. a *Socio-Psychological Systems* (SPS) perspective focuses on individuals and their relations interpersonally and with institutions, as might a psychologist or a social worker;

3. an *Ecological Systems* (ES) perspective focuses on botany, zoology and geology, as might a geographer or anthropologist;
4. an *Eco-Cultural Systems* (ECS) perspective focuses on commerce, government and not-profit organizations, as might a sociologist or political scientist.

Two synthetic perspectives highlight relations between systems of interest:

5. a *Socio-Technical System* (STS) perspective considers work processes of social groups with technologies, as might an industrial engineer or organization scientist;
6. a *Socio-Ecological Systems* (SES) perspective considers actions of organizations alongside other organizations and the world, as might the leadership of a multinational enterprise or a diplomat.

The four analytic perspectives and two synthetic perspectives are detailed with systems changes examples in Table .7.3

Table 7.3 orients with the top row as a macro-systems perspective, and the bottom row as a micro-systems perspective. The right column is the human systems perspective, and the left column is a world systems (as natural and artifactual) perspective. Those four outside perspectives contribute towards integrating perspectives of Socio-Technical Systems (STS) and Socio-Ecological Systems (SES). The descriptions that follow wander through Table 7.3 in a non-linear path.

Before the Industrial Revolution, let's call Era 0.0, anchored in 1492, as the breakthrough for wind power upon successful journeys from Europe to a new continent. Advances through the 15th to 19th century can be described as Era 0.x (i.e. Era 0.1, Era 0.2). Era 1.0, the age of steam power, can be marked by the steam engine of James Watt in Scotland in 1776. Subsequent geographic adoptions might be considered as Era 1.0, or Era 1.1, and Era 1.2, etc. (e.g. Belgium from 1807, France from 1848, and Germany from 1870).

Table 7.3 Six systems changes perspectives

Section 7.2.1.3 Ecological Systems (ES) perspective		→	**Section 7.2.2.2 Socio-Ecological Systems (SES) perspective**		←	**Section 7.2.1.4 Eco-Cultural Systems (ECS) perspective**	
0.0 Columbian exchange ➔ 0.1 Plantation agriculture ➔	1.0 Coal mines		0.0 Compagnia ➔ 0.1 Trading charters ➔	1.0 Industrialist families		0.0 Exploration ➔ 0.1 Colonization ➔	1.0 Migration
Section 7.2.1.1 Technical Systems (TS) perspective			**Section 7.2.2.1 Socio-Technical Systems (STS) perspective**			**Section 7.2.1.2 Socio-Psychological Systems (SPS) perspective**	
0.0 Caravels ➔ 0.1 Galleons or fluyts ➔	1.0 Steam-ships		0.0 Expedition sailors ➔ 0.1 Navy or cargo crews ➔	1.0 Mechanics + stokers		0.0 Renaissance ➔ 0.1 Reformation ➔	1.0 Utilitarianism

Systems changes are illustrated in Sect. 7.2.1 on four analytics perspectives, and Sect. 7.2.2 on two synthetic perspectives, framed through an Era 0 of wind and water, into an Era 1 of steam. Sect. 7.2.3 brings us up to the current day to consider an Era 4 and an Era 5.

7.2.1 Four Analytical Threads of Systems Changes Separate Out Concerns

Following centuries of the Age of Discovery where sailing ships traversing the globe, the era circa 1760 to 1840 in Britain saw the rise of machines based on water power and steam. *The Industrial Revolution* was the title of a book by Arnold Toynbee, published posthumously in 1884.

Technical Systems Progressed From Caravels ➔ Galleons ➔ Steamships

From the fifteenth century BCE, the leading ship technology saw galleys relying on propulsion by oars, with Phoenicians the leaders on large ships around the Mediterranean. Advances to the twelfth century AD, saw *cogs*, characterized by single mast and a single square sail, becoming common. In the fifteenth century, the Portuguese developed the *carrack* (*nao*, in Spanish) with 3 or 4 masts and square sails. This ocean transport had more space for cargo, as trade extended south to the African coast. Rolling waves were afforded by *clinker* built hulls, with a shell of overlapping planks, into which a frame was fitted with timbers.

Era 0.0, from a Technical Systems (TS) perspective, saw the rise of *caravels*, as lighter vessels with 1 to 3 masts and triangular (lateen) sails. Smooth hulls enabled caravels to sail faster than the clinker hulls. Hulls were constructed with the frame first, onto which the shell was attached with caravel planking and caulking sealant. In 1492, Columbus sailed with two caravels, *La Niña* and *La Pinta*, smaller ships of 20 and 26 crew members, with shallower hulls more maneuverable into bays. A carrack, the *Santa Maria*, was refitted with lateen sails and caravel planking to serve as a medium-sized cargo ship with a crew of 40. After a familiar journey from Spain to the Canary Islands, Columbus had a speedy Atlantic crossing of 5 weeks, with the luck of fair weather.

Era 0.1, from a TS perspective, can be seen forking into two styles. *Galleons* were larger ships preferred in the Spanish Treasure Fleet, linking Spain with the West Indies from 1566 to 1790. They adopted caravel planking, lateen sails rigged on a fore-and-aft rig on the rear mast, and square sails on the fore-mast and main-mast. Galleons were war vessels that could also carry cargo. *Fluyts* were dedicated cargo vessels, preferred by the Dutch East India Company from 1602 to 1796. They were not designed for conversion in wartime to warships. This design could handle twice the cargo, at a construction cost compared at half, giving the Dutch a major competitive advantage. The use of block and tackle to move heavy cargo reduced the crew to 12 seamen. The fluyts were slower ships, delegating major defence battles to the naval ship-of-the-line warships that could maneuver to volley fire with cannons along their broadsides. The last days of Era 0 might be marked around 1821, when the American S.S. Savannah hybrid ship crossed from New York to Liverpool under sail power, with an auxiliary steam engine and paddlewheels.

Era 1.0, from a TS perspective, arrived with paddlewheel designs superseded by screw-propeller propulsion. A completely submerged propeller gave greater efficiency, smaller size, and a lower possibility of damage. James Watt of Scotland applied the first hydrodynamic screw propeller in his Birmingham works, driven by steam engines above the waterline driving cylinders below. The S.S. Archimedes made its first sea voyage in 1839, with circumnavigation of Britain in 1840, and then a passage to Portugal.

From the 15th to 18th century, the Technical System (TS) perspective in Era 0.0 can be characterized with the advent of lateen sails and caravel planking. Era 0.1 continued advances on sails and hulls, with varieties of ship specialized for cargo, passenger and military purposes. Era 1.0 of steamships became mainstream only after shipbuilders embraced underwater screw propellers with engines above the waterline. Risks associated with crossing an ocean on a large sailing ship has largely outmoded that technology.

Socio-Psychological Systems Progressed from Renaissance ➜ Enlightenment ➜ Utilitarianism

Demographic collapse, political instability, and religious upheavals characterized the Late Middle Ages of the 14th and 15th centuries as a period of crisis. Harvests were less plentiful as winters became harsher at the end of the Medieval Warm Period. The population in Europe halved through the Great Famine of 1315–1317 and Black Death of 1347–1351. England and France engaged in the Hundred Years' War, 1337–1453. Christian and Muslims struggled over the Iberian peninsula, with the Reconquista of Al-Andalus from the eighth century ending with the Surrender of Granada in January 1492. Columbus had been on a retainer funded since 1486 by the Catholic Monarchs (Ferdinand II of Aragon and Isabella I) arranged by Luis de Santángel. Only after the defeat of the Muslims in early 1492 could attention be turned towards a New World.

Era 0.0, from a Socio-Psychological Systems (SPS) perspective, saw philosophical shift from a scholastic tradition emphasizing religion to Renaissance humanism valuing education and civic virtue. Societal shifts came first in the city-states of the Italian peninsula, e.g. Genoa, Florence, Milan, Naples, Rome and Venice. Ideas of intellectual freedom and individual expression nurtured the flourishing of architecture, art, literature and science. Serfdom declined, and peasants were able to rent farms for themselves. In the Mediterranean, merchants developed large business organizations to carry out activities across Europe.

Era 0.1, from a SPS perspective, was facilitated through the printing press invented by Johannes Gutenberg circa 1450, improving dissemination of knowledge later in the Age of Discovery. Abuse and corruption amongst the Catholic clergy was criticized in 1517 with *The Ninety-Five Theses* published by Martin Luther, leading to the formation of the Protestant branch of Christianity. The earth was no longer the centre of the universe in 1543, with Nicolaus Copernicus publishing *De revolutionibus orbium coelestium.* The scientific method was formulated in 1620 by Francis Bacon in *Novum Organum.* The Scientific Revolution and Age of Enlightenment laid foundations for progress to come.

Era 1.0, from a SPS perspective, reoriented towards a utilitarian principle that "it is the greatest happiness of the greatest number that is the measure of right and wrong", coming from Jeremy Bentham, circa 1776. This coincided with Adam Smith, considered to be the father of economics, publishing *The Wealth of Nations* in 1776. The mercantilist policies of protecting national markets gave way to free market theory. Mechanization in agriculture led to many leaving agrarian lives behind, seeking employment in urban factory towns.

A Socio-Psychological Systems (SPS) perspective looks inward from a society into leaders and the individuals in relations. This perspective contributes towards an understanding of human systems, with motivations, autonomy, and ways of social organizing.

From the 15th to 18th century, the Socio-Psychological Systems (SPS) perspective in Era 0.0 saw a slow rise in literacy. Education had historically been considered a privilege only for the upper class. Era 0.1 was led by religious schools, as publishing of the Bible in multiple languages encouraged understanding the word of God. In a mercantilist Era 1.0, the growing professional and commercial class led to writing and arithmetic schools for their sons to continue businesses. The first modern public education system accessible to the general population was established in 1763 with the *Generallandschulreglement* under the Prussian king Frederick the Great. Schooling of all young Prussian girls and boys, mainly in municipality-funded schools, was mandated from age 5 until age 13 or 14. Only in the 1880s was compulsory schooling enacted in France and Great Britain.

Ecological Systems Progressed from Columbian Exchange ➔ Plantation Agriculture ➔ Coal Mining

Before the New World was discovered, trade supplemented European cereal grains (e.g. wheat, oats, rye, barley), with Asian millet and rice. Livestock first domesticated in the Near East (e.g. sheep, goats, pigs and cattle) were common. Citrus fruits came from Asia through the Middle East into southern Europe. Apples had been cultivated by Greeks and Romans.

Era 0.0, from an Ecological Systems (ES) perspective, saw the Columbian Exchange bringing potatoes, maize, tomatoes, tobacco, and chili peppers to Europe. The New World saw domesticated animals exported from the Old World. Unfortunately, the Europeans also introduced swine influenza to the Caribbean Islands, and smallpox to the Aztec settlements and Inca cities and villages.

Era 0.1, from an ES perspective, saw the rise of plantations cultivated by slaves. Enslaved Africans had better immunity to Old World diseases, and outnumbered European immigrants threefold. Silver was mined in the New World to facilitate trade with China for silk and porcelain. The influx of gold and silver into Spain led to the Price Revolution circa 1520–1640, with inflation leading to sixfold increase in prices over 150 years.

Era 1.0, from an ES perspective, saw coal mine production rise in the mid sixteenth century, as supplies of wood began to fail. Northern England, Scotland and Wales had an abundance of coal. French Explorers discovered coal deposits in Acadia (i.e. New Brunswick) in the 1600s, and traded coal to the British colony at Boston. In industrial development, North America lagged Europe, remaining largely agrarian. The cotton gin powered by a horse or water was invented by Eli Whitney in 1793 in Georgia, patented in 1794 in Philadelphia. In 1802, the first gunpower mill was constructed on the site of burned down cotton mill in Delaware. The export of steam engines from England was forbidden, so engine building was first established by British emigrants in 1802 Philadelphia, then in New York and in Pittsburgh.

From the 15th to 18th century, the Ecological Systems (ES) perspective in Era 0.0 coincided with the Columbian exchange, as plants and animals migrated to and from the New World and Old World. Era 0.1 still relied primarily on manual labour, with plantations first established by British colonists arriving in Virginia. Era 1.0 saw the rise of machines, with the rise of thermal energy. Carl Linnaeus is credited as the first ecologist of nature, developing a modern taxonomy of *Systema Naturae* in 1735. Between 1799 and 1804, Alexander von Humboldt travelled the Americas, from Venezuela to the United States, publishing quantitative work on botanical geography for the next 21 years in Europe.

Eco-Cultural Systems from Exploration ➔ Colonization ➔ Migration

Caravans with horses and mules, from the second century BCE, connected China (under the Han Dynasty) to Persia and Greece as the Silk Route. The route became controlled by the Tang Dynasty and Tibetans, and then the Mongolian Empire. In 1275, Marco Polo travelled from Venice to Cathay, returning in 1295 as the Mongolian Empire was collapsing. In 1346, trade brought a deadly bubonic plague westward, as the Black Death. The plague disrupted long distance trade, and fragmentation of the Mongol Empire loosened the political ties along the route. From the fall of the Roman Empire circa 27 BCE, Constantinople, as the capital of the Byzantine Empire, became the hub for trade for 1500 years. The end of the medieval period was marked in 1453 by the Fall of Constantinople to the Ottoman Turks. The Ottoman Empire introduced taxes and religious conflicts that would lead to a European search for an alternate route for trade eastward.

Era 0.0, from an Eco-Cultural Systems (ECS) perspective, was a period of explorers seeking a maritime route to Cathay. Trade amongst Southeast Asian countries from the Philippines to India dates back to 2000 BCE, with China largely disinterested except for the Song Dynasty of the 10th to 13th century. In 1419, under Prince Henry the Navigator, the Portuguese led expeditions to West Africa. In 1488, Bartolomeu Dias reached the Cape of Good Hope. The map of the world was redrawn in the Age of Discovery with Columbus landing in the New World in 1492.

Era 0.1, from the ECS perspective, progressed to colonization of the New World and Africa. The 1492 papal bull "*Inter Caetera*" by Pope Alexander VI established a demarcation line 100 leagues west of the Azores and Cape Verde Islands, giving Spain exclusive rights for territorial possession and trade in the New World. In 1494, the Portuguese and Spanish monarchs modified the papal bull with the Treaty of Tordesillas, moving the line halfway between the Cape Verde Islands and the Hispanola island where Columbus had landed, so that access to coastal Africa was clear. A lack of understanding of geography resulted in granting to Spain the "west" of most of the New World, and to Portugal the "east" of Africa and Brazil. This Portuguese-Spanish agreement was largely ignored by other European powers, and unsanctioned by the indigenous inhabitants of the Americas.

Era 1.0, from the ECS perspective, eased migration from Europe to America. Sailing ships across the ocean had meant a risky 5–6 weeks journey, taken only by the most committed families travelling for a permanent immigration. Steamships reduced travel time to 2 weeks under most weather conditions, with secondary ports of call more frequently scheduled. Under steam, more men could temporarily migrate to America for work, and then return home to Europe. Larger and more comfortable steamships increased passenger volume, reducing price. While freight ships took 50 years to switch from sail to steam power, passenger ships only took 15 years to switch, between 1852 to 1873 (Cohn, 2005).

An Eco-Cultural Systems (ECS) perspective views the behaviour of social groups in relations to the world around them. The shift from regional agrarian society to intercontinental trade to global migration has been enabled by advances generally available in those periods.

From the 15th to 18th century, the Eco-Cultural Systems (ECS) perspective in Era 0.0 saw the colonization of the Americas. In Era 0.1, the Spanish mostly claimed land in South American and the Caribbean, while the British focused on New England, and the French worked up the St. Lawrence River. In China, the Ming Dynasty (1388–1544) and Qing Dynasty (1636–1912) were not interested in overseas expansions, with a strong government, one-third of the world's population and the largest economy in the world. In India, Mughal Empire (1526–1857) enjoyed a long period of relative peace, with high agricultural productivity, and excess industrial production available for export. Era 1.0, for Europe and the Americas, saw the rise of the West with economic development, educated citizens and trans-Atlantic cultural exchanges. In the Modern Era, immigration procedures have become routine, except for during the World Wars.

7.2.2 Two Situating Textures of Systems Changes Combine Physical and Social Systems

A situating systems approach synthesizes the complexities of human social systems with the physical world and technology changing around them. A micro-oriented Socio-Technical Systems (STS) perspective emphasizes individuals in organizations and families. A macro-oriented Socio-Ecological Systems perspective emphasizes institutions and the natural world.

Socio-Technical Systems Progressed Expedition Sailors ➔ Navy or Cargo Crews ➔ Mechanics + Stokers

Ports around the Mediterranean Sea can be reached within hours or days; ports crossing the Atlantic can be weeks apart. Before the Age of Discovery, ships traversed seas, rather than oceans. The realities of ocean travel are illustrated in the Third Crusade of 1190, in the famous expedition of over 100 vessels by King Richard I of England. In April, crews departed from Dartmount and Britanny. A life-threatening tempest forced some ships to land at Silvia, Portugal, the most remote of all cities of Christendom. Most squadrons reached Lisbon on July 26. The planned rendezvous in Marseille with Richard was missed. The fleet arriving in Messina on September 23 was barred from landing until Richard arrived two days later. Not until April 1191 would the fleet attempt the voyage from Messina to Acre due to the "inclemency of winds and waves and weather". King Richard I and King Philip II of France wintered in Sicily, periodically intervening in hostilities with townsfolk who were forced to lodge Templar and Hospitalier warriors, and sailors from Genoa and Pisa (Norgate, 1924, pp. 122–125).

Era 0.0, from an STS perspective, drew on experienced sailors recruited specifically for exploration. The ships were second-hand merchant vessels minimally equipped with a few cannons. Specialist roles included navigators to set headings, and boatswains (bosuns) in charge of rigging and sails. Deckhands worked 4-hour shifts on *La Niña* and *La Pinta* caravels, and 8-hour shifts on the *Santa Maria* carrack. Work was relentless, adjusting rigging, trimming sails, and plugging leaks with scraps of old rope. One meal each day was served, cooked over an open fire in a sandbox on deck. The holds were full of provisions, water, and armaments. Live animals included pigs and chickens. Horses and cows were suspended in slings so that the rolling motion of the vessels wouldn't break their legs. Hazards made spirituality a central focus, each day starting with morning prayers and hymns, and ending with evening religious services.

Era 0.1, from an STS perspective, followed the discovery of new ocean routes with different ship designs and role definitions. The Spanish integrated cargo with arms in *galleons*, enabling vessels to protect themselves. Smaller ships had crews of 50 onboard; larger ships could have crews of more than 400. Roles defined not only sailors handling the helm and trimming sails, but also gunners as masters of the cannons making gunpowder and readying projectiles. The Dutch segmented functions of the merchant fleet in *fluyts*, decoupled from man-of-war ships patrolling the Baltic Sea, Iberian coast and West Arican bays. While a fluyt was dimensionally on the same scale as a galleon, the lack of armaments and specialized pulleys meant that only 12 crew were required to manage the cargo. The Dutch navy organized convoys after 1621, where in October and December, men-of-war would joint merchantmen on journeys to Italy and Levant, defending against Algerian pirates. With a strong reputation for its arsenal, the Venetian Republic contracted vessels during the war with Ottoman Turkey in 1618. In the Anglo-Dutch wars between 1652 and 1674, the size of the ships-of-the-line increased, with production funded from the wealth of the Dutch East India Company.

Era 1.0, from an STS perspective, outmoded the need for mariners to pull ropes and handle sails. Mechanics operated and maintained engines, and stokers fed coal into boilers to produce steam. Crew sizes were reduced, by one-half in the engine room, and by one-quarter on deck (Memorial University of Newfoundland, 2011). Mariners on steamers enjoyed regular schedules that allowed a home and family onshore.

From the 15th to 18th century, the Socio-Technical Systems (STS) perspective in Era 0.0 saw expeditions reconfiguring from sea routes between ports where supplies might be accessible within days, to ocean voyages where supplies were required for weeks away from land. The increased trade in Era 0.1 responded to the increased threat of piracy through either onboard protection, or navy convoys. Era 1.0 introduced engines that required specialized skills to operate and maintain, and reduced crew sizes.

Socio-Ecological Systems Progressed Compagnia ➔ Trading Charters ➔ Industrialist Families

In Europe from the 5th to 11th century, there was no concept of saving or investment, only loans for consumption and hoarding. It would only be in the eleventh century that innovations of accounting, cheques, endorsement and insurance emerged (Cipolla, 1993, p. 125). From the tenth century, merchants would prepare for a foreign trip through a *contratto di commenda* (known in Venice as a *collegantia*) whereby a merchant would receive sums of money to be used in the business, and partners would share in the profits or losses.

Era 0.0, from an SES perspective, originated from the rise of the *compagnia* in inland manufacturing cities in Italy in the twelfth century, later spreading to maritime trading cities of Italy (Cipolla, 1993, p. 127). Rather than risking all of the assets in a voyage of a ship that might be lost to pirating or capsizing, a *compagnia* was a limited liability institution. This type of association first started around families, which created complications when the head of the family passed. Ownership rights evolved to recognize more distant family members, and eventually shareholders outside of bloodlines.

From Genoa, the *Casa di San Giorgio* (Bank of St. George), founded in 1408 by influential merchant families, is recognized as the first modern, public bank (Boland, 2009). In 1473, Columbus began his career with wealthy families in Genoa as an apprentice business agent. For 1477–1485, Columbus based himself in Lisbon. After the conquest of the Emirate of Granada in January 1492, Isabella I and Ferdinand II agreed to sanction an expedition in search of new trade routes, but could not advance the costs of the voyage, due to resources depleted by the war. Financing would come from Genoa through Columbus' prior connections in arranging sugar purchases with the House of Centurione. *Casa di San Giorgio* financed the voyages, based on the vote of confidence from the Catholic Monarchs.

Era 0.1, from an SES perspective, saw the rise of trading houses. The *Casa de Contratación*, established by the Crown of Castile in 1503, was the crown agency for the Spanish empire. This became superseded by the *Consejo de las Indias* in 1524 by Charles V, as King of Spain and Holy Roman Emperor. The *Casa da Índia* was founded by King Manuel I of Portugal in 1500, establishing trading posts and military bases around the coast of Africa to Goa, India. The *Verenigde Oostindische Compagnie* (Dutch East India Company) was established in 1602, with an important trading base in Jayakarta (now Jakarta) by 1609. The East India Company, founded in 1600, controlling large parts of India, and taking territory in Hong Kong after the Treaty of Nanjing in 1842.

Era 1.0, from an SES perspective, saw industrialist families funding facilities for factories. Joint stock companies provided the capital for large scale project, e.g. canals and railroads. However, private entrepreneurs developed most manufacturers, as well as mining, metallurgy, shipping, wholesale trade and retail distribution (Heaton, 1937). Textile mills could be started in a single room or a floor. Power could be bought from the landlord. Machinery could be rented. Little investment in raw materials was required, and that could be recouped either from a downstream processor, or from the end customer. The supply of capital was at a scale not larger than real estate. Floating capital was transferred from father to son, so that capital would accumulate and grow.

From the 15th to 18th century, the Socio-Ecological Systems (SES) perspective in Era 0.0 saw the formation of limited liability businesses, and commercial banks, originally oriented around families. Era 0.1 expanded trading houses to national scale enterprises, sanctioned by royal families. Era 1.0 was characterized by entrepreneurs starting small businesses requiring only working capital, with machines rented and small loans for materials and operations.

7.2.3 Incremental Adaptation ≡ ΔSES or ΔSTS; Generational Shifts ≡ ΔSES × ΔSTS

Incremental adaptations are reformations, that should not break a system (Ackoff, 2010, pp. 110–111). Generational shifts are transformations, that promise new benefits if a discontinuity is accepted. When a platform is updated, applications built on that prior specification may break.

Table 7.4 Six generations of transitions

	ΔSES × ΔSTS (+ 1.x) Generational Shift	ΔSES (+ x.1) Incremental Adaptation	ΔSTS (+ x.1) Incremental Adaptation
Systems Era 0 (Water + Wind) ➔	↑ Sailing ships ↓ Rowing	International trade: regional ➔ trans-oceanic	Sailing ships: freight transport ➔ ocean liners
Systems Era 1 (Steam) ➔	↑ Transport by rail ↓ Animal power	Railway towns: horse-drawn wagons ➔ railway stations	Steam engines: fireman watertender ➔ mechanical stoker
Systems Era 2 (Electricity) ➔	↑ Electrical grid ↓ Housework	Electrical power transmission: Industrial ➔ municipal	Domestic energy: lighting ➔ electrical appliances
Systems Era 3 (Oil) ➔	↑ Motorways, civil aviation ↓ Inaccessibility	Routing: direct connections ➔ hub and spoke	Freer movement: proximity ➔ importation
Systems Era 4 (Information) ➔)	↑ Service economy ↓ Mass production	Careers: employment ➔ subcontracting	Bandwidth: text ➔ streaming audio + video
Systems Era 5 (Green + Inclusive?) ➔	↑ Regionalization? ↓ Pace of living?	Making? replacing ➔ maintaining	Development? conservation ➔ regeneration

In Sect. 7.1.1 above, the variety of numbering schemes associated with declaring the timing in a series of "industrial revolutions" is problematic. Alternative schemes do not serve to reduce confusion. Stages of modernity, starting from the Age of Discovery circa 1492, can be associated by technological advances through rationality in science, and societal advances through hierarchical structuring in politics. Postmodernity, coincident but distinct from a broader philosophy of postmodernism in the late 20the century, challenges the ideas of industrial progress with a post-industrial information society and service economy. The Human Development Index (HDI) initiated by the United Nations in 1990 was revised in 2010 to account for inequalities in distribution of health, education, and income within a country. In 2019, the Sustainable Development Index (SDI) extended the HDI to factor in the ecological efficiency of nations. The SDI now ranks highest the countries showing high levels human development with low levels of ecological impact. An elevation beyond primarily socio-technical considerations to recognize socio-ecological concerns blends into periods called "Systems Eras" in Table 7.4.

The Systems Eras are not concurrently exclusive. Today, in Africa, there are countries where less than 10% of the population has regular access to electricity. Old Order Amish families aim to preserve traditional ways, while accepting work-arounds to minimize the use of personal computers and smartphones that enable engagement with modern businesses.

Let's say Era 0 was an age of wind and water. Generational shifts in both SES and STS during the Age of Discovery saw larger vessels propelled by sails (e.g. galleons) replacing rowing (i.e. galley slaves). Subsequent SES increments included the expansion from Baltic, Mediterranean and Southeast Asian regional routes into inter-continental routes across the Atlantic Ocean and then the Pacific Ocean. STS increments made sailing ocean liners routine, with trans-Atlantic routes scheduled by the 1840s, and trans-Pacific by the 1890s.

Era 1 was an age of steam. Generational shifts in both SES and STS saw trans-continental railways regularly crossing the United States in the 1870s, Canada in the 1890s, and Europe with Asia (i.e. the Trans-Siberian) in 1900s. SES increments saw the rise of railway towns, where long-haul distances beyond the range of horse-drawn wagons would better connect to networks of goods producers with distributed markets. STS increments included technical improvements in steam engines, with the role of fireman-watertender becoming replaced by mechanical stokers only after the 1900s.

Era 2 was an age of electricity. While the discovery of electromagnetic generators by Michael Faraday in 1831 and invention of incandescent lights by Thomas Edison in 1879 are historical milestones, electricity was not a part of everyday life until well into the twentieth century. Generational shifts in both SES and STS for widespread adoption followed the Electricity Supply Act of 1926 leading to establishing the National Grid in the UK, and Rural Electrification Act of 1936 in the USA. SES increments saw electricity supplied not only for factories, but also for homes through municipal public services from the 1920s. STS increments would see electrical machines not only for factories, but also for homes (after WWII material supply chains were restored). The 1950s are characterized by labour-saving devices (e.g. washing machines), appliances (e.g. refrigerators) and home entertainment (e.g. televisions).

Era 3 was an era of oil. Generational shifts in both SES and STS saw the rise of motorways and civil aviation. There became practically nowhere on the earth that was physically inaccessible. SES increments saw routings of direct point-to-point journeys deprecated in favour of hub-and-spoke relays, through high-efficiency hub-to-hub. STS increments in freer movements saw proximity giving way to importation, with long distance supply chains flowing freely.

Era 4, today, is an era of information. Generational shifts in both SES and STS have seen the rise of the service economy, where supply-constrained mass production has given way to a long tail of demand in diverse niches and interests. SES increments have seen declines in lifelong employment relations, and subcontracting evolving into a gig economy. STS increments to bandwidth have unconstrained communications from just text, to rich media in peer-to-peer streaming audio + video (e.g. podcasts, Tiktok).

Era 5 is speculative, with uncertainty as to whether an era of green and inclusive society will emerge. Generational shifts in both SES and STS, due to the exhaustion of world resources, could lead to a return to localization (e.g. a 100-mile diet) and a reduced pace of living. SES increments could see a change in human beings making things, with replacing of old artifacts subsumed by maintaining and repairing. STS increments could see development reoriented from conservation to regeneration to reduce losses in embedded energy.

These examples of ways of looking at systems changes aim to differentiate between generational shifts and incremental adaptations. A generational shift is defined by changes both in SES and STS. An incremental adaptation is defined as changes either in SES or STS, with one lagging the other. A further appreciation of the distinction follows in the next sections, examining the current era, and exploring a potential next era.

7.3 The Current Era Sees ΔSES with Service Economy Alongside ΔSTS on Knowledge Society

In 2023, we are in Era 4, an age of information. This has also been described as: (i) the Age of Information and Telecommunications beginning circa 1971 by Carlota Perez; (ii) the Third Industrial Revolution (electronics + IT combined with globalization) since the 1970s, and Industry 4.0 (intelligent factories with production chains) since 2010; and (iii) 3IR with the computer and digital revolution since the 1970s (from mainframe to personal computer to Internet) by the European Union Directorate-General, and 4IR (fusion + interaction across physical, digital and biological domains) since 2016 by the World Economic Forum. Rather than focusing on the technological drivers of systems change, an alternative description highlights the rise of the service economy.

7.3.1 Services Have Overtaken Manufacturing and Agriculture in GDP

In 2023, the World Bank declared the service sector as the main source of global economic growth since the 1990s. In 2019, the service sector accounted for 63% of global output levels and 57% of global employment. Between 1995 and 2019, services contributed 66% growth in global output levels, and 75% growth in global employment (Nayyar & Davies, 2023). While the manufacturing sector showed slight percentage declines, the major decompensation was from the agricultural sector.

With an interest in economic development, the World Bank grouped 12 ISIC classifications into four categories:

1. Global innovator services include skilled workers in professional, scientific and technical services, including ICT, financial and insurance segments. These services are traded internationally, and labour can be provided remotely, across national borders.

2. Skill-intensive social services include skilled workers in education and healthcare, that are not readily tradeable internationally. These services are largely provided through public funding, with small concessions (e.g. foreign students, medical tourism).
3. Low-skill tradeable services include transportation, warehousing, wholesale trade, accommodation and food services. Transportation and warehousing have high value-added and are capital intensive. Accommodation and food services are exported mostly as consumption through tourism.
4. Low-skill domestic services include retail trade; administration and support; arts, entertainment and recreation; and other social, community, and personal services. Only the arts, entertainment and recreation services can be internationally traded (Nayyar et al., 2021).

The global innovator services are most prominent in high-income countries, linking with other services domestically, with greater linkages for spillovers.

Coupled with the rise of global innovation services has been the adoption of digital technologies. This was accelerated by the COVID-19 pandemic, where 44% of businesses globally started or increased their use of digital technologies in 2020. This adoption, higher in services than in manufacturing or agricultural sectors, has been largely sustained post-pandemic. The high-skilled services that could be offshored increased their use of digital technologies, including financial services at 61% and ICT services at 60%, in late 2021. Low-skilled contact services most dependent on face-to-face interactions (e.g. accommodation, food services, retail trade) increased their use of digital technologies 35–40% in 2021.

7.3.2 ΔSTS Outpaced ΔSES with Digitalization Coupled with Services

The STS changes with the rise of the Internet saw digitalization enabling service industrialization, changing the economics of processes, e.g. through provision on demand in interactions and co-production with customers. Service industrialization is sometimes called productionization of services, due to the reengineering and standardization of processes. Services may be intangible, or associated with products that have materiality (Karmarkar, 2021). Actions and decisions related to service industrialization include: (a) automation of process steps; (b) outsourcing and offshoring; (c) creation of new markets, exchanges or networks; (d) online distribution and delivery; and (e) self-service or works shifted to other stages in a chain. These systems changes have increased productivity, with new jobs often not offsetting job losses.

Digitalization of information content with easy access through the Internet has transformed news reporting, financial services, and the entertainment industry. Broadband access in workplaces and homes, and more powerful smartphones have made work-from-home arrangements with distributed virtual teams commonplace.

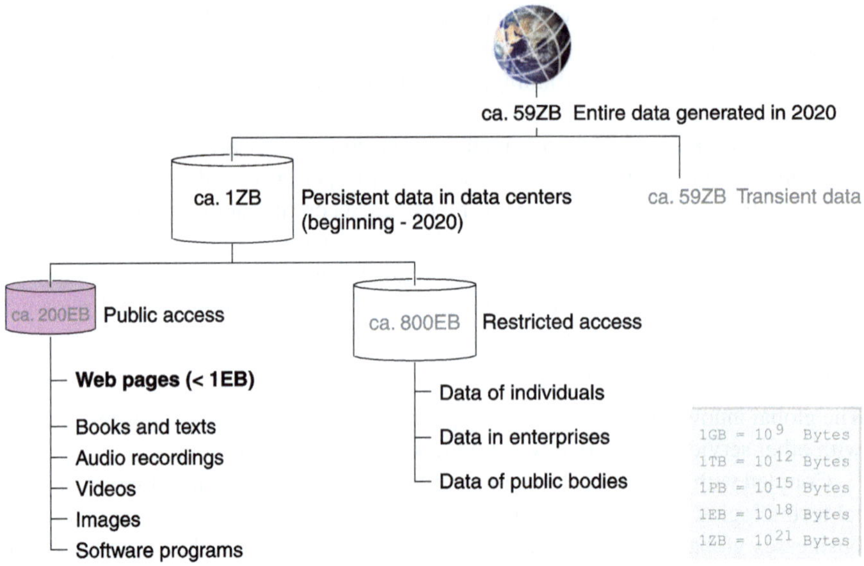

Fig. 7.1 Overview of the Global DataSphere in 2020, [Völske et al., 2021 CC-BY-SA 4.0]

The COVID-19 pandemic removed the strangeness of online meetings, so that the divide between work time and home time can be dissolved.

The Internet has evolved. Web 1.0 was characterized by personal websites, and the publishing of static web content (e.g. the read-only Internet). Circa 2005, Web 2.0 brought content sharing (e.g. blogging), user-generated content communities (e.g. Wikipedia) and open access Creative Commons rich media (e.g. Flickr). Tim Berners-Lee thought that Web 3.0 was going to see the semantic web as central to a next generation, that hasn't happened. Tim O'Reilly, who coined the term "Web 2.0" in 2005, argues that the decentralized technologies of blockchain and crypto-currencies have not, as yet, created a new economic system where world legal systems and the operating economy have been transformed (O'Reilly, 2021).

The volume of data on the Internet continues to grow. In 2010, the amount of data stored globally on all computer storage devices was about 2 zettabytes. This has continued at a rate of more than 150% each year. By end of 2020, projections for the global datasphere exceeded 59 zettabytes (i.e. $5.9 * 10^{22}$ bytes, where a zettabyte is 1 trillion gigabytes) (Völske et al., 2021). Much of that data is transient, as automatic camera security footage, stock market banking transactions, and scientific data (e.g. the particle detector at the CERN Large Hadron Collider). Figure 7.1 shows a breakdown of volume estimates.

In 2020, about 1 zettabyte of data was estimated as persistent in data centers. Public access content was about 200 exabytes (i.e. an exabyte is a million gigabytes). On the deep web, 800 exabytes are estimated as restricted access by individuals (e.g. email, instant messaging, voice and data on personal smartphones),

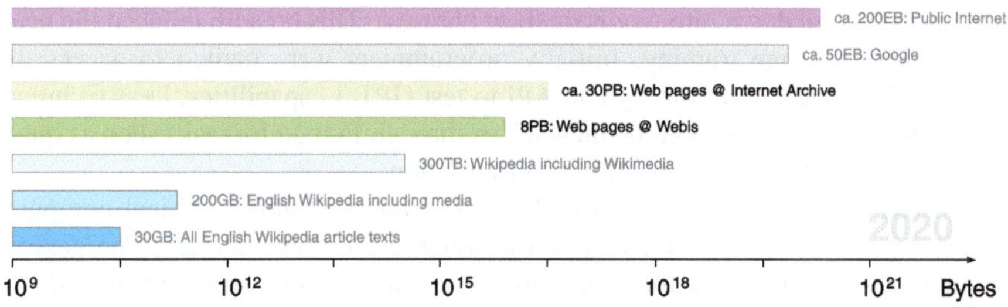

Fig. 7.2 The 2020 sizes of large, persistent data sets in comparison, illustrated on a logarithmic scale [Völske et al., 2021 CC-BY-SA 4.0]

enterprises (e.g. corporate activities) and public bodies (e.g. tax returns), plus the dark net of criminal activities.

The public Internet is not completely crawled by search engines and indexed, as shown in Fig. 7.2, in logarithmic scale.

Of the 200 exabytes on the open Internet, an estimated 50 exabytes are indexed by Google. The Internet Archive has replicated 30 petabytes, as 500 billion web page captures. For academic study, about 8 petabytes of web pages have been archived by the Webis research group in Germany. The Wikimedia Commons has 300 terabytes of files, of which 300 gigabytes are in English, and only 30 gigabytes are text.

Data warehousing and business intelligence have been at the foundation of decision support systems for corporate businesses since the 1990s. Open access content didn't take off until the mid-2000s. Wikipedia was founded in 2001, becoming the world's most popular reference website in 2005. Twitter was launched in 2006, with posts indexed in real time by Google in 2009. Reddit was launched in 2005, with subreddits (i.e. interest-based groups) introduced in 2008. Sources such as these led to the converging of data analytics, data mining, and programming, into a new field of data science. While statisticians have traditionally worked with numerical and categorical data stored in predetermined structured ways, data scientists tend to work with unstructured data, such as the freeform text in social media posts and websites.

Data science skills became recognized as distinct from statistics with the development of the MapReduce programming model, and release of Hadoop 1.0 in 2011. The Hadoop distributed file system allowed data to be distributed across multiple machines, while relational database schemas were not designed to run across clusters. A specialty of data science became recognized circa 2012, with university undergraduate programs forming about 2015. Students were able to learn on the public datasets with open API (application programming interface) such as Twitter and Reddit.

Customers interacting with a chatbot have experienced a simple Generative AI that is programmed to respond to human text or voice inputs. GPT-3 (Generative Pre-trained Transformer, third generation) was a Large Language Model (LLM) released in by OpenAI in June 2020. As compared to data science algorithms trained on a narrowly-defined dataset, GPT-3 was trained on 300 billion tokens (i.e.

sentences broken down into words or short phrases). This breadth reduced the need for further language training. Initially programmers were invited to access the machine learning toolset through an API to test GPT-3 capabilities. Less technical professionals were able to guide themselves through Python for tasks such as question answering, text summarization and translation.

ChatGPT was released in November 2022, enabling non-technical computer users to prompt the LLM for responses though a browser interface. The general population was amazed at the capability for a computer to respond in English (or multilingually in more than 50 languages) to prompts, with superior grammar. More technical audiences were concerned with LLM hallucinations, where responses either don't make sense, or sound plausible while incorrect in fact. The characterization of LLMs as "stochastic parrots" reflects extrapolations from their training, with lack of traceability back to original sources.

In parallel with GPT-3, the DALL-E 2 API was released as an open API in November 2022. DALL-E, like GPT, uses deep learning so that digital images can be created with natural language descriptions. In October 2023, DALL-E has been incorporated into ChatGPT, with priority for customers who will pay for faster responses and more queries.

In March 2023, the news media picked up a deepfake image of the pope in a puffer jacket created with the Generative AI of the Midjourney service. As a conversational bot alternative to a browser interface, Midjourney would respond to instructions (e.g. *imagine* generates an image when given a description) via Discord instant messaging. Although digital artists have been creating deepfakes for many decades, a trend towards Generative AI being used for misinformation has become a worry.

Large Language Models are distinct from Artificial General Intelligence (AGI) where a machine could learn to perform any intellectual tasks that a human being (or animal) could learn. LLMs are a refinement of deep learning approaches to machine learning, based on artificial neural networks with many layers. Machine learning applications are becoming more popular, as the corpus of data available for training grows, and computer processors are rearchitected for pattern recognition. Augmented Reality (AR) technology that mixes the real world with interactive computer-generated content is reshaping our perceptions. Human beings mindlessly letting down their critical thinking filters will be fooled into mistaking machine-generated content for reality.

7.3.3 ΔSES See Institutions Catching Up with Technological Advances

The SES impacts of new information technologies are volatile. Blockchain technologies and cryptocurrencies, since the introduction of Bitcoin in 2009, have involved an estimated 20% of U.S. adults by 2022. The price of Bitcoin surged to $68,991 in November 2021, and fell to $18,000 in December 2022. China banned cryptocurrencies in September 2021. Countries are at varying states of debate about backing their own central bank digital currency.

Traditional measures of welfare in national accounts haven't well reflected the shift to an information economy. Across 13 countries in 2022, digital goods were estimated to generate over $2.5 trillion in aggregate consumer welfare per year, roughly equivalent to 6% of their combined GDP. Many of the digital goods were free for consumer to use, including Google Search, YouTube, Google Maps, WhatsApp, Amazon Shipping, Facebook, Tiktok, Instagram and Twitter. The officially-measured size of the information sector has remained almost unchanged for the past four decades at 4–5% of total GDP. Yet the time spent on digital goods has increased, with the average person in the U.S. and UK online almost 24 h/week. The welfare gains to lower-income individuals and countries were found to be higher than high-income individuals and countries (Brynjolfsson et al., 2023).

The Artificial Intelligence Index Report 2023 summarizes the current state with these technologies (Maslej et al., 2023). Academia has been overtaken by industry. In 2014, universities led research advances in AI. In 2022, those universities produced only 3 significant machine learning models. Industry players produced 32 models in 2022, through their access to large volumes of data, computer power and capital. Global AI private investment has now slowed for the first time in a decade, down 26.7% from 2021 to $91.9 billion in 2022. A 2022 survey posited whether products and services using AI had more benefits than drawbacks: Chinese citizens responded positively at 78%, as compared to Americans at 35%. China leads on total AI journal and conference publications, while 54% of the LLMs are produced by American institutions. Concerns on AI by policymakers from 227 countries are reflected in a jump from 1 new law passed in 2016, to 32 in 2022.

An AI dilemma, as described by Juliette Powell and Art Kleiner, is characterized by software associated with socio-technical systems described as Triple-A: algorithmic, autonomous, and automated. Algorithmic systems follow instructions to execute a task or solve a problem. Autonomous systems, once trained, don't require a human to supervise them. Automated systems are designed to function with little or no human supervision or intervention. The dilemma is that new digital tools, now accessible as cheap or free to everyone, can be simultaneously liberating and threatening. Triple-A systems are socio-technically adaptive, and behaviours changed through experience and data may or may not be desirable. Predictive analytics determine the likelihood of future outcomes, given decision paths following their prior training. Humans sometimes fall into automation complacency, trusting a machine and not paying full attention. Risk thinking, the ability to take uncertainty into account and flexibility respond to events as they unfold, is not hedged by machines in the same way as a human might. A framework to control Triple-A systems proposes taking into account four logics of power: (a) engineering logic, the perspective of technologists; (b) social justice logic, the perspective of humanity; (c) corporate logic, the perspective of ownership, markets and growth; and (d) government logic, the perspective of authority and security (Powell & Kleiner, 2023).

In March 2023, the Future of Life Institute, led by Max Tegmark, published an open letter calling on AI labs to immediately pause for 6 months the training of AI systems more powerful than GPT-4 (Future of Life Institute, 2023). Some prominent signatories included Elon Musk, Yoshua Bengio, Steve Wozniak and Yuval Noah Harari. After 6 months passed, the pause did not happen, and many signatories admitted that they had never expected a pause to become enacted (Heikkilä, 2023; Knight, 2023). Some observers say that AI development actually accelerated over the six months. In October 2023, the Biden administration signed an Executive Order on Safe, Secure, and Trustworthy Artificial Intelligence for the USA. In early November, the UK Technology Secretary hosted an AI Safety Summit at Bletchley Park. An effective implementation resulting from legislation is yet to be seen.

7.4 The Next Era Is Foreshadowed by ΔSES as Global Polycrisis, with ΔSTS Under Stresses and Strains

A nuanced view of the Industrial Revolution recognizes that shift not is from a single cause, but from confluences of progressions. From the 15th to 18th century, socio-technical diffusion took years or decades to diffuse across regions, and the social-ecological institutions were coevolving in new ways. The era following the Information Age may led by Socio-Ecological Systems, with institutions dealing with both natural and manmade issues. The responses in Social-Technical Systems may lag, as complexity forms a system of problems (i.e. a problematique (Ozbekhan, 1970), a wicked problem (Rittel & Webber, 1973), a mess (Ackoff, 2010, pp. 82–83), or a wicked mess (Mitroff, 2019)).

7.4.1 The Next Generational Shift May Come Via Global Polycrisis

The term *polycrisis* was coined in 1999 by Edgar Morin with technoscience, health population, environment, lifestyle, civilization, and development promoting virulent nationalisms, economic instability, and general balkanization, all through inter-retroactions (Morin & Kern, 1999). In 2022, researchers from Canada and Germany substantially deepened the theoretical foundations on the global polycrisis following the Covid-19 pandemic, climate change, and Russia's war on Ukraine, linking to the complexity and sustainability literatures. Crisis entanglement in complexity sees one or more slow-moving stresses interacting with a fast-moving trigger event to push a system out of an established equilibrium into instability. The synchronization of crises were connected through three causal pathways: (a) common stresses; (b) domino effects; and (c) inter-systemic feedbacks (Lawrence et al., 2023).

In 2023, the World Economic Forum released the 18th edition of its Global Risk Report. The term polycrisis was used to explain how present and future risks can interact with each other such that the overall impact exceeds the sum of the parts.

From 1316 responses to a list of 32 global risks, the outlook on "progressive tipping points and persistent crises leading to catastrophic outcomes' was seen as increasing from 13% on a 2-year horizon to 20% on a 10-year horizon. Global risks were dominated by cost of living on the 2-year horizon, and climate action failure on the 10-year horizon (World Economic Forum, 2023). Responding to these top risks might or might not represent a generational shift.

The 2023 Global Risks Report did not specifically list the rise of Generative AI. Of the 32 global risks, *misinformation and disinformation* ranked #16 over the 2-year period, and #11 over the 10-year period. *Digital power concentration* ranked #29 over the 2-year period, and #17 over the 10-year period. The lower ranking of these information age risks suggests that incremental adaptation of practices and policies could be sufficient.

Just as an era of steam might not have been foreseeable from the era of water + wind, the era beyond the age of information may be beyond our imagination. Michael Albert describes a "continuationist" bias, which assumes that past trends of economic growth and inter-capitalist competition will continue indefinitely (Albert, 2022). Three questions are suggested that have only received minimal attention by scholars:

1. Is a near-term transition to a "post-growth" world order possible to stabilise the climate system? If so, how might it be designed and implemented?

The likelihood of attaining the 2030 targets set in Paris Climate Accords of 2015, based on progress by 2023, is low. A structural political-economic transformation would require an overhaul of multilateral and bilateral trade agreements. Progressive deglobalization that relocalizes production in favour of local sustainability is countercultural to the premise of export-led growth that is mainstream.

2. If we accept that humanity is on course for three or four degrees of warming this century, then how might states and the global economy as a whole adapt to maintain resilience and prevent mass mortality?

Persistently hotter temperatures and sea level rise should be included in scenarios that project population displacement and massive resettlement programs. Practically, most climate refugees will first attempt moving within domestic boundaries, with migration internationally a more difficult option. If, however, local food-water issues rise to crises levels, governments may be challenged to respond in unsavory ways, with effects rippling globally into an altered world order.

3. If states and the global economy are unable to adapt to 3 or 4 C, then what would be the possible dynamics of a global-scale "collapse"?

Collapse, as a loss of socio-political complexity, could be either (a) a slow and geographically uneven long descent (Allen et al., 2003), or (b) a rapid synchronous failure of critical infrastructure and governance capacities (Tainter, 1996). A financial crisis due to intensified climate impacts (e.g. natural catastrophe, or major crop failures) at a regional level could cascade into economic depression globally. Militarism between great powers (i.e. U.S. and China) or regionally (e.g. India-Pakistan over the shared Indus River) could set back the complexities in society that we enjoyed in the late twentieth century.

Incremental adaptations in either SES or STS in the current era may reflect anticipation of concerns in the next generational shift. The complex connections in the transformation of a generational shift may not be foreseeable through linear forecasting.

7.4.2 *ΔSES from Nature Include Climate Change and Pandemic*

The September 2023 meeting of the United Nations was declared as a halftime meeting for the 2030 Strategic Development Goals (SDG) agenda signed in 2015. The international community was on track to achieve only 15% of SDG targets. Of the 17 goals, specific action was called for six key transitions: (i) food, (ii) energy, (iii) digitalization, (iv) education, (v) social protection and jobs, and (vi) biodiversity. International tax cooperation and public-private partnerships were encouraged to support countries in the Global South. Debt distress was evident in 75 countries in default or near-default conditions (United Nations, 2023).

In 2023, the indirect effects of the COVID-19 pandemic disruption on progress on the Sustainable Development Goals (SDGs) were estimated to be seven times larger than direct effects (Yuan et al., 2023). In early 2020, countries were already faltering to make progress on the SDGs. Low-income countries were affected 1.4 times more than in high-income countries.

In 2023, climate-related all-time records were reported. In June through August, the warmest temperatures on Earth over the past 100,000 years were reached. Global mean temperatures that have never exceeded 1.5 °C prior to 2000 were charted for 38 days. Of 35 planetary vital signs, 20 were showing record extremes (Ripple et al., 2023).

In September 2023, the World Health Organization (WHO) welcomed a historic commitment on pandemic prevention, preparedness and response, by global leaders at the United Nations General Assembly. Work on a pandemic accord followed from a special session for the WHO from December 2021, with a final outcome to be presented in May 2024 (World Health Organization, 2023b).

The new pandemic accord is complemented by "The Big Catch-up" effort, as essential immunizations in 100 countries decreased, resulting in rising outbreaks of measles, diphtheria and yellow fever. Over 25 million children missed at least one vaccination in 2021 alone (World Health Organization, 2023a). Bright spots for resilience included Uganda and Kenya.

Country-specific policy implications in 2023, following the COVID-19 pandemic and aggression into Ukraine by Russia, show different priorities. For advanced countries, the top three policy areas recommended by the OECD are: (i) policies for green transition (19.3%); (ii) product market regulations, competition, trade and Foreign Direct Investment openness (17.6%); and (iii) policies for digital transformation (11.9%). For emerging-market economies, the top three policy areas recommended by the OECD are: (i) product market regulations, competition, trade and Foreign Direct Investment openness (30.0%); (ii) policies for green transition

(19.3%); and (iii) social protection and ageing (10.7%) (OECD, 2023). Across all countries, productivity has decreased due both to labour market tightness, and lowered investment in capital.

In Era 5, effective responses to changes in Socio-Ecological Systems call for collective action with global scope. In the absence of a global government, leadership at national and regional levels is negotiated. Action occurs slowly when the downside impact of systems changes don't correlate with the availability of resources, geographically.

7.4.3 *ΔSTS Pressures Include Infrastructural Transitions and Healthcare Shortages*

The International Energy Association titled its 2023 outlook as "catching up with climate ambitions" (International Energy Agency, 2023). Sales of electric cars have grown exponentially from 5% of all new cars in 2020, to 9% in 2021, and 14% in 2022. China has been on the forefront, accounting for 60% of global electric car sales, already having exceeded its 2025 target. For 2023, the expectation is that 18% of cars sold, globally, will be electric. In 2022, 60,000 slow charging points were installed: China added 360,000, totaling more than 1 million slow chargers in the country; Europe added 50% over the previous year, while the United States only added 9%. Fast chargers increased by 330,000 globally in 2022, of which China represented 90%. Public chargers in 2022 generally served 10 Electric Vehicles (EVs) per charger, with the United States at only 24 EVs per charger, placing reliance on private facilities. For heavy-duty vehicles, battery swapping may be more practical, although building stations is expensive. China is the leader in 2022, selling 12,000 battery swapping-enabled electric trucks and 2000 battery-swapping passenger cars.

A worldwide shortage of nurses should be treated as a global health emergency, says the International Council of Nurses. From a 2019 stock of 29.8 million nurses, the Global Burden of Disease (GBD) study estimated a global shortage of 30.6 million nurses (Buchan & Catton, 2023). The impact of the pandemic has been cited in more than 100 studies of 40–80% of nurses reporting psychological distress, intentions to leave the profession over 20%, and annual hospital turnover rates greater than 10%. Countries with a long tradition of educating nurses for export (e.g. India, Philippines) are now reporting domestic shortages.

In Era 5, changes to Socio-Technical Systems may be within the power of regional and local groups. Trending anticipates points at which advanced technologies become economically viable, or the functioning of systems have degraded so that issues call for urgent action. We may take for granted legacy systems that has served us well in the past, for which maintenance has been deferred, or requires decommissioning and replacement.

7.5 Prospects: By 2030, Might We Expect Incremental Adaptations to Be Overtaken by a Generational Shift?

It would be a mistake to think that an Era 5 green + inclusive age is independent of the Era 4 information age. Nassim Nicholas Taleb says that the coronavirus pandemic was not a "black swan" unpredictable, rare, catastrophic event. The pandemic was a white swan, as many had predicted. Governments who did not want to spend pennies in infancy had to later spend trillions in years to follow. Studying history, "pandemics are the fattest-tailed thing, and that you [have to] kill them in the egg". Rulers in the 13th and 14th century knew of plague, and "The Old World … dealt with pandemics in a very effective way" (Taleb, 2020). Chernoff-bound events are multiplicative and systemic, leading to fat-tail risks in long-tail probability distributions. In a networked world, increased connectivity leads to nonlinearity so that an event may appear with disproportionate effects due to (a) to the structure and growth of inputs owing to unknown and unknowable inputs; (b) eccentric interactions amongst the variety of inputs; and/or (c) exponential growth (Avishai, 2020; Norman et al., 2020).

The information age has brought unprecedented networking, not just in physical infrastructure, but social interactivity. The Internet originated from ARPANET, where packet switching enabled nodes to relay data from an originating computer through intermediate connections to an ultimate destination. An architecture of open networking allowed interconnections between multiple independent networks based on a variety of technical designs. The gradual evolution to widespread infrastructure led to backbones that increased efficiency, through more tightly coupled high-speed routing. Technical connectivity does not, however, necessarily correlate with social connectivity. Across nations, a "splinternet" with national firewalls (e.g. by the governments of the People's Republic of China, and of the Russian Federation) is a balkanization that restricts access for their citizens. Within nations, partisan fragmentation across socio-political divides challenges individuals who have then to separate what is "real" from "misinformation".

Having now fully explicated an appreciation for the distinctions between incremental adaptations and generational shifts, let's return to the triggering question: with a declaration of Industry 4.0 in 2010, where are we now in 2023, and where might we be in 2030? This chapter closes with prospects that may or not come about, rather than conclusions based on scientific evidence.

7.5.1 Expressions of Generational Shifts Follow Different Agendas

Revisiting Table 7.1, the sources for definitions of generational shifts come from a variety of perspectives.

A historical perspective is brought with the Techno-Economics Paradigms of Carlota Perez, following a Schumpeterian theory of innovation. The 5th Technological Epoch, an Age of Information and Telecommunications beginning circa 1971, has been well recognized by leaders in the IT industry. While Perez has continued to advise on sustainable development and technology policy, she has not declared a 6th Epoch, as the organizational change and educational efforts at hand are significant.

A program definition perspective for government investments comes from the Japan Science and Technology Agency. The 6th Science and Technology Basic Plan of 2021 expanded the scope of Society 5.0 for greater attention to social issues associated with advanced technologies. The Basic Plan implements the policies of the Ministry of Education, Culture, Sports, Science and Technology on funding and cooperation between academic and corporate research institutions, and corporations. While the 7th Science and Technology Basic Plan might be expected around 2025, the pace of change has led the agency to report at an annual frequency, monitoring progress more closely.

An industry strategy perspective from the European Union Industrial Research and Innovation Commission aims to nurture the integration and functioning in a single market across member countries. The Industry 5.0 announcement in 2021 was influenced by the COVID-19 pandemic that resulted in an economic decline, with a disruption in demand and interrupted supply chains. EU funding of projects comes via open calls that especially guide industry researchers and small businesses, through competitive responses and reviews. With 10 years between the announcements of Industry 4.0 and 5.0, perhaps Industry 6.0 might be expected around 2030.

An influence agenda on public-private cooperation from the World Economic Forum brings together stakeholders for dialogue on issues that impact the global economy. The 4IR declaration was a focus for the 2016 meeting. The theme for the World Economic Forum Annual Meeting in January 2023 was "Cooperation in a Fragmented World", including a speech by Volodymyr Zelenskyy, president of Ukraine. The WEF runs multiple sessions in its annual meetings, so the emphases by selected speakers for January 2024 is better reflected by their newsworthiness.

Reviewing Table 7.4, the world in 2023 is judged as still being in Era 4, an age of information. Concerns from late 2022 into 2023 suggest a label of an incremental adaptation, rather than a generational shift.

7.5.2 The Current Era Sees ΔSTS Increments, with ΔSES Catching Up

In 2023, the information age continues to prevail. If the period was to be described in a more fine-grained detail, perhaps Era 4.0 could be marked by the launch of the personal computer, Era 4.1 by the Internet, Era 4.2 by smartphones, and Era 4.3 by

Generative AI. There might be an Era 4.4 as either blockchain (e.g. digital currencies) or Artificial General Intelligence. These are more than stages of STS development. The incremental adaptations are reflected in SES changes to institutions and everyday life.

Personal computers originated with hobbyists. It wasn't until the IBM PC that the business world got interested, and the average person looked beyond microcomputers as toys. Beyond the initial use of the Internet for scientific research, it was e-commerce that redefined economics and society. Electronic payments and digital subscriptions enabled the service economy to flourish. When face-to-face interactions became undesirable during COVID-19 shutdowns, the transition to work-from-home, online education, and food delivery apps occurred over months, not decades. Post-pandemic conditions have restored the regularity of in-person interactions, but many STS practices are continuing in the online mode.

In business, three of the Fortune 10 companies in 2023 reflect the SES information age in the USA: #2 is Amazon, founded in 1994; #4 is Apple, founded in 1976; and #8 is Alphabet, founded in 1998 as Google. In the Fortune Global 10, Amazon and Apple make the list. However, six of Fortune Global 10 reflect the continuing importance of resources from earlier eras: petroleum companies include #2 Saudi Aramco (Saudi Arabia), #5 China National Petroleum (PR China), #6 Sinopec Group (PR China), #7 Exxon Mobile (USA), and #9 Shell (UK). Resource companies with engineering talent are sure to be using information technologies internally, in ways not apparent to external parties.

Governments continue to adapt to the information age. The concentration of global media platforms (e.g. Meta, Netflix, Tiktok) continues to challenge governments committed to maintaining local content production industries (e.g. newspapers, television networks). Regulations on privacy and "right to be forgotten" concerns have progressed in the EU, and then observed for consideration in other nations. Internally, new agencies struggle to web-enable of processes within the government, e.g. United States Digital Service, UK Government Digital Service, Canadian Digital Service. Recent government policies on AI rely heavily on the advice of technology companies to supplement the lack of in-house digital literacy.

7.5.3 Aspirations Towards a Next Era ΔSES Are Facing Pessimism

Progress towards an Era 5 green + inclusive age is 2023 is encouraging, but not uniform. The Sustainable Development Report ranks performance on the 193 UN member states. The top ten nations, all with scores above 80 points, are members of the EU: Finland, Sweden, Denmark, Germany, Austria, France, Norway, Czechia, Poland and Estonia (Sachs et al., 2023). Ranking in the 193 UN member states by population,

- China is 63rd at a score of 72.01,
- India is 112th at 63.45,

- United States is 39th at 75.9,
- Indonesia is 75th at 70.16, and
- Pakistan is 128th at 58.97.

Ranking countries by their GDP,

- United States is 39th at 75.9,
- China is 63rd at a score of 72.01,
- Japan is 21st at 79.41,
- Germany is 4th at 83.36, and
- India is 112th at 63.45.

The 2023 report says that progress on the SDGs is seriously off track. The global index in 2022 scored below 67. Further, the 28-point gap in 2015 between high-income countries and low-income countries is expected to be wider by 2030, at 29 points.

> The greatest responsibility for achieving the SDGs and safeguarding the planetary boundaries lies with the G20 members. These countries represent more than 80% of global GDP, around 70% of the world's forests, more than 60% of the earth's population, and more than 50% of its landmass. The G20 countries account for 90% of global lignite and coal extraction and more than 60% of global oil and gas production (Sachs et al., 2023, p. 11).

The open question is whether each nation will be able to sustain progress on human development within its borders, when the world is interconnected. The Era 5.0 aspiration of green for 2030 is already in doubt regionally, while the Era 5.0 aspiration of inclusive is even more elusive.

References

Ackoff, R. L. (2010). *Differences that make a difference: An annotated glossary of distinctions important in management*. Triarchy Press Limited. https://www.triarchypress.net/differences.html

Albert, M. J. (2022). Beyond continuationism: Climate change, economic growth, and the future of world (dis)order. *Cambridge Review of International Affairs, 35*(6), 868–887. https://doi.org/10.1080/09557571.2020.1825334

Allen, T. F. H., Tainter, J. A., & Hoekstra, T. W. (2003). *Supply-side sustainability*. Columbia Univ Press. https://doi.org/10.7312/alle10586

Avishai, B. (2020, April 21). The pandemic isn't a Black Swan but a portent of a more fragile global system. *The New Yorker*. https://www.newyorker.com/news/daily-comment/the-pandemic-isnt-a-black-swan-but-a-portent-of-a-more-fragile-globalsystem

Boland, V. (2009). The world's first modern, public bank. *Financial Times*. https://www.ft.com/content/6851f286-288d-11de-8dbf-00144feabdc0

Brynjolfsson, E., Collis, A., Liaqat, A., Kutzman, D., Garro, H., Deisenroth, D., Wernerfelt, N., & Lee, J. J. (2023). *The digital welfare of nations: New measures of welfare gains and inequality (Working Paper 31670)*. National Bureau of Economic Research. https://doi.org/10.3386/w31670

Buchan, J., & Catton, H. (2023). *Recover to rebuild: Investing in the nursing workforce for health system effectiveness*. International Council of Nurses. https://www.icn.ch/resources/publications-and-reports/recover-rebuild

Center for the Fourth Industrial Revolution. (2023). *Top 10 emerging technologies of 2023*. World Economic Forum. https://www.weforum.org/reports/top-10-emerging-technologies-of-2023/

Cipolla, C. M. (1993). *Before the industrial revolution: European Society and Economy 1000-1700* (3rd ed.). Routledge. https://doi.org/10.4324/9780203695128

Cohn, R. L. (2005). The transition from sail to steam in immigration to the United States. *The Journal of Economic History, 65*(2), 469–495. https://doi.org/10.1017/S0022050705000161

Council for Science and Technology Policy. (2010). *Japan's Science and Technology Basic Policy Report*. Cabinet Office, Government of Jpana. https://www8.cao.go.jp/cstp/english/basic/4th-BasicPolicy.pdf

Council for Science and Technology Policy. (2021). *Science, technology, and innovation basic plan*. Cabinet Office, Government of Jpana. https://www8.cao.go.jp/cstp/english/sti_basic_plan.pdf

Council for Science, Technology and Innovation. (2015). *Report on the 5th Science and Technology Basic Plan*. Cabinet Office, Government of Jpana. https://www8.cao.go.jp/cstp/kihonkeikaku/5basicplan_en.pdf

European Commission, Directorate-General for Research and Innovation, Breque, M., De Nul, L., & Petridis, A. (2021). *Industry 5.0: Towards a sustainable, human centric and resilient European industry*. Publications Office of the European Union. https://data.europa.eu/doi/10.2777/308407

European Parliament, Directorate-General for Internal Policies of the Union, Carlberg, M., Kreutzer, S., Smit, J., & Moeller, C. (2016). *Industry 4.0*. Publications Office of the European Union. https://doi.org/10.2861/947880

Future of Life Institute. (2023). Pause giant AI experiments [Open Letter]. https://futureoflife.org/open-letter/pause-giant-ai-experiments/

Hayashi, Y. (2019). Japanese Science and Technology Basic Plan: A perspective of policy process. *Innovation and Development Policy, 1*(1), 24–38. https://doi.org/10.3724/SP.J.2096-5141.2019.0003

Heaton, H. (1937). Financing the industrial revolution. *Business History Review, 11*(1), 1–10. https://doi.org/10.1017/S0007680500003706

Heikkilä, M. (2023). What's changed since the "pause AI" letter six months ago? [MIT Technology Review Newsletter]. The Algorithm. https://www.technologyreview.com/2023/09/26/1080299/six-months-on-from-the-pause-letter/

International Energy Agency. (2023). *Global EV Outlook 2023: Catching up with climate ambitions*. International Energy Agency. https://doi.org/10.1787/cbe724e8-en

Karmarkar, U. (2021). Service industrialization, convergence, and digital transformation – I. *Management and Business Review, 01*, 01. https://mbrjournal.com/wp-content/uploads/2020/11/24_Service-Industrialization-and-Digital-Transformation.pdf

Knight, W. (2023, September 28). Six months ago Elon Musk called for a pause on AI. Instead development sped up. *Wired*. https://www.wired.com/story/fast-forward-elon-musk-letter-pause-ai-development/

Lawrence, M., Homer-Dixon, T., Janzwood, S., Rockstrom, J., Renn, O., & Donges, J. F. (2023). *Global polycrisis: The causal mechanisms of crisis entanglement* (SSRN Scholarly Paper 4483556). https://doi.org/10.2139/ssrn.4483556

Maslej, N., Fattorini, L., Brynjolfsson, E., Etchemendy, J., Ligett, K., Lyons, T., Manyika, J., Ngo, H., Niebles, J. C., Parli, V., Shoham, Y., Wald, R., Clark, J., & Perrault, R. (2023). *Artificial intelligence index report 2023*. Institute for Human-Centered AI, Stanford University. https://aiindex.stanford.edu/report/

Memorial University of Newfoundland. (2011). "Each Task Has It's Man, and Each Man It's Place": Seafarers Under Steam [Maritime History Archive]. *More Than a List of Crew*. https://mha.mun.ca/mha/mlc/articles/introducing-merchant-seafaring/each-task-has-its-man.php

Mitroff, I. I. (2019). Wicked messes: The pioneering work of Horst Rittel and Russ Ackoff. In *Technology run amok: Crisis management in the digital age* (pp. 29–38). Springer International Publishing. https://doi.org/10.1007/978-3-319-95741-8_4

Morin, E., & Kern, A. B. (1999). Homeland earth: A manifesto for the new millennium (S. M. Kelly & R. LaPointe, Trans.). Hampton Press.

Nayyar, G., & Davies, E. (2023). Services-led growth: Better prospects after the pandemic?, *World Bank, Policy Research Working Papers*, 10382. https://doi.org/10.1596/1813-9450-10382

Nayyar, G., Hallward-Driemeier, M., & Davies, E. (2021). *At your service?: The promise of services-led development*. World Bank. https://doi.org/10.1596/978-1-4648-1671-0

Norgate, K. (1924). *Richard The Lion Heart*. Macmillan. http://archive.org/details/in.ernet.dli.2015.524949

Norman, J., Bar-Yam, Y., & Taleb, N. N. (2020). *Systemic risk of pandemic via novel pathogens—Coronavirus: A note*. New England Complex Systems Institute. https://necsi.edu/systemic-risk-of-pandemic-via-novel-pathogens-coronavirus-a-note

O'Reilly, T. (2021, December 13). Why it's too early to get excited about Web3. *O'Reilly Radar*. https://www.oreilly.com/radar/why-its-too-early-to-get-excited-about-web3/

OECD. (2023). *Economic policy reforms 2023: Going for growth*. Organisation for Economic Co-operation and Development. https://doi.org/10.1787/9953de23-en

Ozbekhan, H. (1970). *The predicament of mankind: Quest for structured responses to growing world-wide complexities and uncertainties—A proposal*. Management and Behavioral Science Center, University of Pennsylvania.

Perez, C. (2002). Technological revolutions and financial capital: The dynamics of bubbles and golden ages. In *Technological revolutions and financial capital*. Edward Elgar Publishing. https://www.elgaronline.com/display/9781840649222.xml

Perez, C. (2017). The current moment: Beginning of a new machine age and/or the turning point of the fifth great surge? (Part 3) [Blog]. *Beyond the Technological Revolution: Second Machine Age*. https://carlotaperez.org/second-machine-age-or-fifth-technological-revolution-part-3/

Powell, J., & Kleiner, A. (2023). *The AI Dilemma*. Berrett–Koehler Publishers. https://www.penguinrandomhouse.com/books/730661/the-ai-dilemma-by-juliette-powell-and-art-kleiner/

Ripple, W. J., Wolf, C., Gregg, J. W., Rockström, J., Newsome, T. M., Law, B. E., Marques, L., Lenton, T. M., Xu, C., Huq, S., Simons, L., & King, S. D. A. (2023). The 2023 state of the climate report: Entering uncharted territory. *BioScience, biad080*. https://doi.org/10.1093/biosci/biad080

Rittel, H. W., & Webber, M. M. (1973). Dilemmas in a general theory of planning. *Policy Sciences, 4*(2), 155–169. https://doi.org/10.1007/BF01405730

Sachs, J. D., Lafortune, G., Fuller, G., & Drumm, E. (2023). *Implementing the SDG Stimulus. Sustainable Development Report 2023*. Dublin University Press. https://doi.org/10.25546/102924

Schwab, K. (2015, December 12). The fourth industrial revolution: What it means and how to respond. *Foreign Affairs*. https://www.foreignaffairs.com/world/fourth-industrial-revolution

Schwab, K. (2016). *The fourth industrial revolution*. The Fourth Industrial Revolution.

Tainter, J. (1996). Complexity, problem solving and sustainable societies. In R. Costanza, O. S. Bonilla, & J. M. Alier (Eds.), *Getting down to earth: Practical applications of ecological economics*. Island Press. http://dieoff.org/page134.htm

Taleb, N. N. (2020). Nassim Nicholas Taleb on the Pandemic (R. Roberts, Interviewer) *Econtalk*. https://www.econtalk.org/nassim-nicholas-taleb-on-the-pandemic/

United Nations. (2023). Sustainable development goals unreachable without reformed financial architecture, stronger political will, speakers say as second committee opens general debate [Meetings Coverage]. https://press.un.org/en/2023/gaef3583.doc.htm

Völske, M., Bevendorff, J., Kiesel, J., Stein, B., Fröbe, M., Hagen, M., & Potthast, M. (2021). Web archive analytics. In R. H. Reussner, A. Koziolek, & R. Heinrich (Eds.), *50. Jahrestagung der Gesellschaft für Informatik* (pp. 61–72). Gesellschaft für Informatik. https://doi.org/10.18420/inf2020_05

World Economic Forum. (2023). *Global risks report 2023* (18th ed.). World Economic Forum. https://www.weforum.org/publications/global-risks-report-2023/

World Health Organization. (2023a). Global partners announce a new effort—"The Big Catch-up"—to vaccinate millions of children and restore immunization progress lost during the pandemic [News Release]. https://www.who.int/news/item/24-04-2023-global-partners-announce-a-new-effort-the-big-catch-up-to-vaccinate-millions-of-children-and-restore-immunization-progress-lost-during-the-pandemic

World Health Organization. (2023b). WHO welcomes historic commitment by world leaders for greater collaboration, governance and investment to prevent, prepare for and respond to future pandemics [News Release]. https://www.who.int/news/item/20-09-2023-who-welcomes-historic-commitment-by-world-leaders-for-greater-collaboration%2D%2Dgovernance-and-investment-to-prevent%2D%2Dprepare-for-and-respond-to-future-pandemics

Yuan, H., Wang, X., Gao, L., Wang, T., Liu, B., Fang, D., & Gao, Y. (2023). Progress towards the Sustainable Development Goals has been slowed by indirect effects of the COVID-19 pandemic. *Communications Earth & Environment, 4*(1) Article 1. https://doi.org/10.1038/s43247-023-00846-x

David Ing is a Research Fellow with Creative Systemic Research Platform (CSRP) Institute, as well as a Research Fellow with Code for Canada. He serves as a Trustee for the International Society for the Systems Sciences, with a prior role as past-president. A previous 28-year career at IBM Canada included assignments in management consulting, headquarters planning and executive education. Previous book projects include Open Innovation Learning, and The Marketing Information Revolution. He resides in Toronto, Canada. Email: coevolving@gmail.com

MIX
Papier aus verantwortungsvollen Quellen
Paper from responsible sources
FSC® C105338

If you have any concerns about our products,
you can contact us on
ProductSafety@springernature.com

In case Publisher is established outside the EU,
the EU authorized representative is:
Springer Nature Customer Service Center GmbH
Europaplatz 3, 69115 Heidelberg, Germany

Printed by Libri Plureos GmbH
in Hamburg, Germany